CRIMINAL SENTENCING
THE NEW LAW

CRIMINAL SENTENCING
THE NEW LAW

Richard Ward LLB, Solicitor
Professor of Public Law and Head of the
Department of Law
De Montfort University, Leicester

JORDANS

1997

Published by
Jordan Publishing Limited
21 St Thomas Street
Bristol BS1 6JS

© Jordan Publishing Limited 1997

British Library Cataloguing-in-Publication Data
A catalogue record for this book is available from the British Library.

ISBN 0 85308 422 X

Typeset by Mendip Communications Ltd, Frome, Somerset
Printed by Bookcraft (Bath) Ltd, Midsomer Norton

PREFACE

The Crime (Sentences) Act 1997 and the Sex Offenders Act 1997 were the final legislative offerings of the last Conservative government in the field of criminal justice. Aspects of this legislation remain controversial, especially the provisions relating to mandatory and minimum sentences, and attracted significant judicial and legal opposition although they were not opposed in principle (as opposed to detail) by the then Labour opposition. It remains to be seen what the impact of the change of government following the general election on 1 May will be. Certainly, despite the fact that this legislation was not opposed 'root and branch', it by no means follows that all of these provisions will be implemented, at any rate in the current form. In particular, indications exist that the minimum sentence provisions in respect of repeat drug trafficking and domestic burglary offences may not be implemented.

It is not the purpose of this book to debate the merits of the provisions of this legislation, but rather to provide a guide and an analysis to what are extremely complex issues, for the benefit of practitioners and others who have to work with the new legislation. In writing this book, I have received much assistance, direct and indirect, from others. In particular, the opportunity to draw on the professional expertise of Sarah Ward, manager of the NSPCC DOVE project, Derby, in relation to matters appertaining to the regulation and treatment of sex offenders, has been of considerable value. However, responsibility for the text is mine alone. There is also the need to gratefully acknowledge the great help and support of the team at Jordans.

The law is stated as at 14 August 1997.

Richard Ward
Leicester
August 1997

CONTENTS

TABLE OF CASES

References are to paragraph numbers except where they are in *italics* which are references to page numbers.

TABLE OF STATUTES

References are to paragraph numbers except where they are in *italics* which are references to page numbers.

TABLE OF STATUTORY INSTRUMENTS

References are to paragraph numbers except where they are in *italics* which are references to page numbers.

Chapter 1

INTRODUCTION

1.1 This book is mainly concerned with the provisions of the Crime (Sentences) Act 1997 which apply to England and Wales.[1] It is divided into two parts: the narrative, followed by the full text of the new Act, with annotations. The narrative and text serve different purposes. The narrative is intended to set out, explain and comment on the provisions of the new Act, to give reasons for them and to set them in the context of the pre-existing law. Generally, it eschews detailed definitions in the Act which are not essential to a basic understanding of the Act and its operation. The purpose of the annotations is to deal with those matters of definition excluded from the narrative and, where appropriate, to provide some explanation of the various concepts and rules that underpin the provisions of the new Act.

In both the narrative and the annotations, references to other statutory provisions are to those provisions as amended by other legislation other than the new Act. For the sake of simplicity the amending legislation has not been referred to unless this has proved essential for the purposes of explanation.

---

1 Section 57 prescribes the extent of the Act.

1.2 This book also deals with those provisions of the Sex Offenders Act 1997 which apply to England and Wales.[1] Where appropriate, that Act is referred to by its name, or as 'the 1997 Act' or by the abbreviation 'SOA 1997'. References to 'the new Act' do not refer to that Act, but to the Crime (Sentences) Act 1997. It will invariably be clear from the context which piece of legislation is being referred to.

References are made occasionally to the date on which this book went to press. That date is 14 August 1997.

---

1 For its extent, see Sex Offenders Act 1997, s 10, and para **5.18**.

1.3 In both parts of this book, references are made to the Parliamentary debate on the Crime (Sentences) Bill. The Parliamentary progress of that Bill was as follows.

HOUSE OF COMMONS
First Reading: 24 October 1996
Second Reading: HC Deb, vol 284, no 9, col 911, (4 November 1996).

Committee:	Standing Committee A, cols 1–381.
Report:	HC Deb, vol 288, cols 26–114, 343–422 (13 and 15 January 1997).
Third Reading:	HC Deb, vol 288, cols 422–429 (15 January 1997).

HOUSE OF LORDS

Second Reading:	HL Deb, vol 577, cols 967–1074 (27 January 1997).
Standing Committee:	HL vol 578, cols 332–446, 555–678, 817–894, 1295–1408.
Report:	vol 579, cols 788–884 (18 March 1997).
Third Reading:	vol 579, cols 884–891 (18 March 1997).

Commons' consideration
of Lords' amendments: cols 981–994 (19 March 1997).

ROYAL ASSENT
21 March 1997.

1.4 Reference to the Parliamentary history of the Sex Offenders Act 1997 is made, where appropriate, at the relevant part of the text. That Act received Royal Assent on 21 March 1997.

Commencement

1.5 The new Act will come into force on such day or days as are appointed by statutory instrument (s 57(2)). Different days may be appointed for different provisions or purposes. At the date of going to press of this book, only one such commencement order had been made, namely the Crime (Sentences) Act 1997 (Commencement) (No 1) Order 1997,[1] which brought into effect paras 14 and 19 of Sch 1 to the Act on 15 June 1997, and parts of the Act may not operate in their totality for some time. In particular, the provisions in s 4 relating to minimum sentences for domestic burglary are unlikely to be brought into effect before October 1999.[2]

By virtue of the Sex Offenders Act 1997 (Commencement) Order 1997,[3] the Sex Offenders Act 1997 comes into force on 1 October 1997.

This book is written on the basis that the whole of each Act is in force. The applicability of different provisions of the legislation to offences committed prior to the commencement of each Act is dealt with at the appropriate parts of the text.

---

1 SI 1997/1581.
2 *Protecting the Public* (HMSO, 1996) Cm 3190, para 13.7; Mr David Maclean, MP, Minister of State, Home Office, HC Committee, col 149.
3 SI 1997/1920.

Outline of the new act

1.6 The main provisions of the Crime (Sentences) Act 1997 are based on proposals contained in a White Paper entitled *Protecting the Public*, published in 1996.[1] That White Paper, was based on a belief that 'prison works':[2]

> 'First, by taking offenders out of circulation it prevents them from committing yet more crime. The majority of crimes are committed by a relatively small number of criminals. Research has suggested that between three and 13 offences could be prevented for each convicted burglar imprisoned for a year. Second, prison protects the public from dangerous criminals. Third, prison – and the threat of prison – acts as a deterrent to would-be criminals. Finally, time spent in prison can be used to rehabilitate offenders, for example by improving their training or education. The most recent reconviction rates show that criminals sent to prison are no more likely to reoffend than those given community sentences – a recent survey based on a sample of 192 cases showed reconviction rates within two years of 51% for those released from prison, 55% for those who received a community sentence and 58% for those who received a probation order.'[3]

The White Paper contained, or identified, wide-ranging initiatives or policy proposals in the areas of policing, crime prevention and the disposition of offenders after conviction and sentence.

The philosophy that prison works has led to record numbers of persons being held in prison, the figure reaching 61,571 in June 1997.[4] It is not the purpose of this book to comment on the efficacy of that policy. However, it was in response to these proposals, especially those relating to minimum and mandatory sentences, that the then Lord Chief Justice, Lord Taylor of Gosforth, was moved to observe:

> 'I venture to suggest that never in the history of our criminal law have such far-reaching proposals been put forward on the strength of such flimsy and dubious evidence.'[5]

The new Act, nevertheless, seeks to give effect to the main thrust of those White Paper proposals. It contains provisions 'designed to improve the protection of the public against serious, dangerous and persistent offenders, and to increase public confidence in the sentencing process'.[6]

---

1 *Protecting the Public* (HMSO, 1996) Cm 3190.
2 Ibid, para 1.12.
3 Ibid, para 1.12.
4 Rutherford 'Labour and the Prison Numbers Crisis' (1997) 147 NLJ 1004.
5 HL Deb, col 1025 (23 May 1996).
6 Mr Michael Howard, QC, MP, Home Secretary, HC Second Reading, 4 November 1996.

1.7 The new Act seeks to achieve these aims through provisions relating to the sentence that should be imposed in a case of serious violent or sexual offence, in a case involving a drug trafficking offence or in certain cases of domestic burglary.[1] Other provisions seek to reform the rules governing the length of time that a prisoner serving a term of imprisonment should serve. It also introduces a series of other measures, or changes, designed to overcome obstacles in the way of the courts dealing with offenders in an effective or appropriate way.[1]

---

1 See s 4(5) and annotations to s 4.

1.8   At the heart of the new Act are the provisions, in Pt I, which deal with mandatory and minimum custodial sentences. These prescribe that a mandatory life sentence is to be imposed on an offender found guilty of the commission of a second serious violent or sexual offence, and require the imposition of minimum terms of imprisonment of seven years for a third class A drug trafficking offence, and a minimum of three years in respect of a third domestic burglary. The provisions have been roundly condemned by some as unnecessary, and as amounting to an unwarranted interference with the discretion of the judges to impose the sentence appropriate in all the circumstances of the individual case.[1] In so arguing, critics are adopting the basic principle that it is both wrong and undesirable for Parliament to tie the hands of the courts. The principle has been explained as follows:

> 'Attempts by the executive arm of government to influence sentencing are unconstitutional, attempts by the legislature to interfere with the sentencing discretion of the courts are, even if not strictly unconstitutional, bound to result in both potential confusion and injustice to defendants, the sentencing powers of the courts should therefore be left to the wisdom of the courts under the guidance of the Court of Appeal.'[2]

The extent of that Court of Appeal guidance has been patchy, with guideline judgments being given on an ad hoc basis. However, whatever the arguments of principle, it is clear that these proposals will, if fully implemented, lead to a significant increase in the prison population by some 11,000 additional prisoners.[3]

---

1 See, eg, Lord Woolf CJ, HL Second Reading, cols 996–999.
2 Ashworth, *Sentencing and Penal Policy* (Wiedenfeld and Nicholson, 1983) at p 54.
3 See Cavadino and Dignan, *The Penal System*, 2nd edn (Sage Publications, 1997) at pp 198–201, and the sources therein cited. Similar figures are cited by Lord MacIntosh, HL Second Reading, col 982.

1.9   The new Act also contains new provisions governing the time to be served by a prisoner. It introduces a scheme for early release and for the determination of sentence length. This marks a significant departure from the pre-existing scheme which has subsisted only since 1993, when the provisions of the Criminal Justice Act 1991 came into effect. This new scheme contains detailed provisions relating to the length of a term of imprisonment to be imposed by a court, as to the credit to be given for periods on remand or for good behaviour, relating to the calculation of the date of early release and in relation to the supervision arrangements which apply after release. Further, the provisions introduced by the Criminal Justice Act 1991 are, in their re-enactment, modified to give effect to obligations that arise under the European

Convention on Human Rights in respect of the arrangements for the release of persons detained during Her Majesty's pleasure.

Apart from the central provisions of the new Act relating to sentence length, and the periods of time to be served, it confers additional sentencing powers on the courts. These include new provisions in respect of fine defaulters, persistent petty offenders and mentally disordered offenders. It also makes other miscellaneous sentencing and procedural changes.

1.10 The Sex Offenders Act 1997 makes two important changes in respect of sex offenders. First, it introduces a scheme whereby sex offenders are required, on an on-going basis, to inform the police of their names, addresses and of any changes to those names or addresses. This duty of notification will subsist in respect of any individual to whom the requirement applies during prescribed notification periods. The length of that notification period is calculated in accordance with criteria set out in that Act, and which are based on the length of the custodial sentence imposed by the court for that offence. This notification procedure is intended to assist in the monitoring of the where-abouts and conduct of such offenders, and must be viewed as complementary to the supervision requirements contained in the Crime (Sentences) Act 1997.[1] The second part of the Sex Offenders Act 1997 extends the jurisdiction of the courts of England and Wales in respect of sexual offences committed outside the jurisdiction, and is intended to deal with the problem more colloquially known as 'sex tourism'.[2]

---

1 See para **3.38**.
2 See para **5.53**.

1.11 It has already been noted[1] that one purpose of the new Act was to increase protection for the public. It is far from clear that, in reality, the new Act will necessarily have that effect. Nor is it self-evident that these provisions were necessary to achieve that purpose. Debate has for some years focused on the question as to the role imprisonment should play in penal policy.

Another objective was to secure a measure of clarity in areas of sentencing bedevilled by confusion, technicality and obscurity. In *Governor of Brockhill Prison, ex parte Evans*,[2] Lord Bingham CJ, dealing with the rules governing release dates, uttered the following cri-de-coeur:

> 'The principle that a prisoner's release date should be beyond dispute, and that the provisions governing it should be easy to apply, is of great importance, for reasons both of fairness and good administration. It is not, on any showing, a test which the present provisions meet. They are not clear to the courts, or the legal profession, or prisoners or (it would seem) the prison authorities. They are certainly not simple. It appears that defendants are remaining in prison when the sentencing court did not intend that they should. The Law Commission has described it as an important feature of any criminal justice system that sentencing provisions should be accessible and comprehensible and has recommended the enactment of a comprehensive statutory consolidation of sentencing provisions . . . We hope that this may be seen as a task commanding a high degree of priority.'

1 See para **1.6**.
2 [1997] 1 All ER 439, at 454.

1.12 The new Act contains some useful changes and new provisions relating to sentences, and the sentencing process. It also contains some provisions which clearly are controversial, a fact evidenced by the strong opposition voiced by senior members of the judiciary to key aspects of the new Act. What it does not do is provide the comprehensive consolidation statute urged on the previous Government by the Lord Chief Justice. Still less does it address the wider concerns as to consistency in sentencing, or the lack of a comprehensive range of guideline judgments. It does nothing, for example, to deal with the 'veritable wasteland in terms of guidance' that exists in respect of sentence for offences of domestic burglary.[1] The case for the most controversial aspects of the new Act, the mandatory and minimum sentence provisions in Pt I, was based on a perceived lack of judicial willingness to impose sentences at appropriate levels of severity.[2] One way to overcome that problem would be the adoption of proposals, mooted for some years, for the creation of a Sentencing Council. Such proposals have in the past been rejected by the then Government.[3] Nothing in the new Act removes such ideas and proposals from the agenda. The new Act thus leaves fundamental issues of sentencing consistency and levels unresolved.

1 See Ashworth, *Sentencing and Criminal Justice*, 2nd edn (Butterworths, 1996). See, now, *Brewster, Thorpe, Ishmael, Blanchard, Woodhouse, H(R)* (1977) *The Times*, 4 July (CA).
2 See, eg, Coad 'Mandatory Sentences: Putting the Record Straight' (1997) 161 JP 159.
3 *Crime, Justice and Protecting the Public: The Government's Proposals for Legislation* (HMSO, 1990) Cm 965, para 2.20.

Chapter 2

MANDATORY AND MINIMUM CUSTODIAL SENTENCES

Mandatory life sentence for second serious offence – minimum of seven years for second Class A drug trafficking offence – minimum of three years for third Class A drug trafficking offence – minimum of three years for third domestic burglary

INTRODUCTION

2.1 Part I of the Act contains provisions which require, subject to limited exceptions, a sentencing court to impose a mandatory life sentence on an offender convicted for a second time of a serious offence (s 2(2)). The offences defined as 'serious offences' by s 2(5) basically comprise the more serious violent or sexual offences. The reason for the introduction of this provision is that the Government believed it to be wrong that, under pre-existing provisions relating to such offences, an offender had to be released at the conclusion of a determinate sentence irrespective of whether he posed a continuous danger to the community.[1]

Secondly, Pt I requires a sentencing court, again subject to limited exceptions, to impose a minimum term of imprisonment of seven years for a third Class A drug trafficking offence[2] (s 3(2)). The Government believed that this would provide a 'real' deterrent for those who deal in 'hard drugs'.[3]

Thirdly, Pt I requires a sentencing court, subject to limited exceptions, to impose a minimum custodial sentence of three years on an offender who is convicted of a third domestic burglary (s 4(2)).[4] Once again, the rationale is that such a sentence will amount to a more effective deterrent than pre-existing levels of sentence. As Baroness Blatch, Minister of State, put it:[3]

> 'persistent burglars and dealers in hard drugs are a menace to society, and they must know that if they continue offending they will go to prison for a long time.'

---

1 The Butler Committee in 1977 had recommended the adoption of reviewable sentences, which would have involved the obtaining of medical evidence to establish whether the offender was a danger, and, every two years, consideration of the offender's position. If the offender was discharged from prison, he could be subject to a lifelong licence. Such a scheme was rejected by the Government as 'adding nothing to discretionary life sentences' and that 'no part of the proposals [of the Butler Committee] for punishment and deterrence': Baroness Blatch, Minister of State, Home Office, HL Report, col 814. See, further, para **6.3**.
2 See s 3(5) and annotations to s 3.
3 Baroness Blatch, col 970.

4 See annotations to s 4.

MANDATORY LIFE SENTENCES FOR SERIOUS OFFENCES

The mandatory sentence

2.2 Where the pre-conditions contained in s 2(1) are satisfied, a court must impose on the offender a sentence of imprisonment for life (or, in the case of an offender under the age of 21 at the date of sentence, custody for life)[1] unless the court is of the opinion that exceptional circumstances exist which justify the non-imposition of such an offence. What amount to exceptional circumstances is discussed at para **2.25**. 'Exceptional circumstances' do not include an early indication of an intention to plead guilty.[2]

---

1 Pursuant to the Criminal Justice Act 1982, s 8(2).
2 See para **2.32**.

The reason for change

2.3 A wide range of serious violent and sexual offences attract a maximum term of life imprisonment. In such cases, the question as to whether a discretionary life sentence should be imposed is governed by the principles set out in *Hodgson*.[1] The White Paper identified that 'very little use' was made of this power.[2]

Offences carry a maximum term of imprisonment of considerable length.[3] The Government's White Paper set out the sentencing pattern during 1994 for the major violent or sexual offences which attract a discretionary life sentence.[4]

Violent offences	*Convictions*	*Life*	*Average Sentence*
Attempted murder	65	3	8.3
Threat or conspiracy to murder	18	2	4.9
Manslaughter	197	5	4.9
Wounding with intent to do GBH	1159	8	3.2
Robbery involving use of firearm	576	0	6.0
Possession of firearm with intent	207	0	3.1
Sexual offences			
Rape and attempted rape	434	12	6.6
USI with girl under 13	65	0	3.4

The Government accepted[5] that that did not mean that sentences were too lenient, but concentrated on the determinate nature of the sentence. Although s 2(2)(b) of the Criminal Justice Act 1991 entitles a court to impose a sentence that is longer than is commensurate with the seriousness of the offence, if the offences are violent or sexual offences,[6] and such longer term is necessary to protect the public from serious harm from the offender, that term of imprisonment must be within the maximum term of imprisonment for that offence. Further, the sentence imposed must be proportionate to the offence, ie, bear a 'reasonable relationship' to the offence for which it was imposed.[7] It does not permit the imposition of a disproportionate term for the purposes of the protection of the public. In addition, a judge is required to reach a judgment on risk and the needs of public protection, on the evidence before him, and might even reach a conclusion which contradicts expert psychological evidence.[8]

1 (1968) 52 Cr App R 113 (CA). See para **2.8** and annotations to s 2.
2 White Paper, op cit, Ch 10, para 10.4.
3 See annotations to s 2.
4 White Paper, op cit, p 47.
5 Ibid, para 10.5.
6 See annotations to s 2.
7 *Mansell* (1994) 15 Cr App R (S) 771 (CA); *Crow, Pennington* (1994) 16 Cr App R (S) 409 (CA); *Carpenter* [1996] Crim LR 603 (CA); *Rickhart* [1995] Crim LR 574 (CA).
8 See *Smith* (1997) *The Times*, 26 June (CA).

2.4   The purpose of this new mandatory life sentence provision was explained[1] as follows:

'[It] is twofold. First, it will ensure that offenders who are convicted of a serious violent or sexual offence are not released from prison if they continue to prove a real danger to the public. Secondly, offenders who are released will remain under supervision and subject to recall for the rest of their lives. These two safeguards will provide real protection for the public against some of the most dangerous criminals in our society.'

The White Paper made it clear that the thrust of the Government's justification for the new provisions was not that existing sentencing practice is wrong, but rather that mechanisms need to be in place to ensure that before potentially dangerous offenders are released, an assessment of the risk they pose should be carried out.[2]

1 Baroness Blatch, Minister of State, Home Office, HL Second Reading, cols 968–969 (27 January 1997).
2 White Paper, op cit, para 10.6.

2.5   The advantage created by the imposition of a life sentence is that the offender will not be released if it is considered that he or she poses a risk to society sufficient to justify his or her continued detention. Recent reports in relation to sex offenders[1] illustrate the problem: there is no power to detain further an individual who has served the appropriate part of a determinate sentence.[2] This is so irrespective of the levels of risk considered to exist. By contrast, a life sentence permits the offender to be detained for such further period as is necessary, and until the level of risk has reduced to such level as to justify release. Because the mandatory life sentence imposed under s 2(2) is not to be regarded as a sentence fixed by law (s 1(4)), the procedures and powers applicable to discretionary life sentences apply. The trial judge will set the tariff for the part of the sentence to be served for the purposes of punishment and deterrence.[3] The sentence will then be subject to the early release provisions of Pt II, Ch II of the new Act.[4] Because of this, the offender will be released only on the recommendation of the Parole Board,[5] and such a recommendation will be made only when the Board is satisfied that it is no longer necessary for the protection of the public that the prisoner should be confined (s 28(5)).

---

1 See, eg, the furore over a case of a Liverpool man, Graham Seddon, in respect of whom no powers of detention existed despite his threats to assault children: (1997) *The Times*, 5 July.
2 Unless detention under the Mental Health Act 1983, s 38, is justified. For the proposals of the Butler Committee, see fn 1 to para **2.1**, and see para **6.3**.
3 Currently under the Criminal Justice Act 1991, s 34, and, under the new Act, s 28(2).
4 See paras **4.9–4.16**.
5 See s 28(6). An exception to this is where release is exceptionally made, on compassionate grounds: see para **4.16**, and annotations to s 10.

2.6   Some research provides support for the principle inherent in s 2. One research study has concluded that 'a single variable – previous known violence – can be used to separate adult men into different probability groups in relation to future violence'.[1] The same is true in respect of sex offenders: a previous sexual offence is a significant factor in assessing the risk of re-offending.[2]

---

1 Walker, *Sentencing Theory, Law and Practice* (Butterworths, 1985). See also Walker (ed), 'Ethical and Other Problems', in *Dangerous People* (Blackstone Press, 1996).
2 McGrath, *Sex Offender Risk Assessment and Disposition Planning: A Review of Clinical and Empirical Findings* (1994) International Journal of Offender Therapy and Comparative Criminology.

The objections to the new law

2.7   Strong objections of principle to the new provisions were raised during the passage of the Act through Parliament. In summary, these objections concentrated on the principle that it is undesirable to tie the hands of the judiciary by imposing mandatory sentence requirements.[1] Until the new Act, such requirements, with the exception of the mandatory life sentence for murder, have been confined to certain non-custodial disqualifications.[2] Lord Woolf CJ was of the opinion that, by implementing the wishes of Parliament expressed in the Act, the judiciary would be surrendering its traditional role of giving effect to what the interests of justice demand, thus amounting to a 'departure from our traditions', with 'the legislative taking over what always has been accepted to be the proper role of the judiciary'.[3] The provisions in s 2 will have the effect, for the offences to which s 2 applies, of overturning the guidelines which have been developed by the Court of Appeal for the imposition of life sentences in cases other than murder.[4] On the other hand, some commentators doubt that there is in fact any improper interference with judicial discretion, arguing that 'there is no constitutional principle which forbids or even discourages Parliament from limiting the discretion of sentencers if it can be persuaded ... that this has advantages ...'.[5]

However, the fact that Parliament has the right to limit judicial discretion does not mean that it should do so. Whether it should arguably depends on the nature of those changes.

The objections to the mandatory sentence provisions were cogently stated by Lord Bingham CJ:[6]

> 'It is a cardinal principle of just sentencing that the penalty should be fashioned to match the gravity of the offence and to take account of the circumstances in which it was committed. Any blanket or scatter-gun approach inevitably leads to injustice in individual cases. Such a result is, I suggest, obvious.'

In the view of critics of the mandatory sentence provisions, the evidence relating to the mandatory life sentence provision was not such as to demonstrate a clear need for such provision. Nor does s 2 really address cases which are not within the terms of s 2 but where significant risk to the public exists. The number of Attorney-General's references, made pursuant to the Criminal Justice Act 1988, does not suggest the commission by the courts of widespread errors of sentencing principle in cases which, in the future, would be likely to fall within the terms of s 2. During 1995 and 1996, the Court of Appeal reviewed the cases of some 86 offenders in whose cases a life sentence could have been imposed for a second serious offence. Only in four of such cases did the Attorney-General ask the court to impose a life sentence, and such a sentence was imposed in two out of four of those cases. In one further case, the Court of Appeal imposed a life sentence without being requested to do so.[7]

---

1 See also para **1.8**.
2 See, eg, disqualification for holding or obtaining a driving licence for certain driving offences: see, generally, the Road Traffic Act 1988.
3 HL Second Reading, col 997.
4 See para **2.8**.
5 Walker and Padfield, *Sentencing: Theory, Law and Practice* (Butterworths, 1996) at p 380.
6 HL Second Reading, op cit, at cols 997–998.
7 Lord Bingham, MR, HL Second Reading, col 987.

2.8 Quite apart from objections of principle, the practical contribution which the mandatory life sentence provision in s 2 will make to the fulfilment of the stated objectives of the Government is uncertain. Each of the offences which, if committed in England and Wales, would amount to a serious offence[1] and thus potentially attract a mandatory sentence if the pre-conditions in s 2(1)[2] are satisfied, carry a maximum punishment of life imprisonment.

The criteria justifying the imposition of a discretionary life sentence were set out in *Hodgson*.[3] These are as follows:

(a) the offence or offences are in themselves grave enough to require a very long sentence;
(b) it appears from the nature of the offences or from the defendant's history that he is a person of unstable character likely to commit such offences in the future;
(c) if such offences are committed, the consequences to others may be specially injurious. Such a sentence is to be regarded as exceptional, and imposed in circumstances where it is important to monitor the prisoner's progress in prison so that release from custody will only occur when public safety will not be jeopardised by release of the prisoner.[4] Such a

sentence may be imposed even where, in the absence of continued dangerousness, the offence would not justify a long, determinate sentence.[5]

In order to justify the imposition of a discretionary life sentence, it is not required that the offender suffers from mental instability. What is required is that there be a 'serious' danger to the public.[6] The grounds which would found such a belief might often be based on the offender's mental state,[7] but that is not inevitably so. For example, a persistent paedophile may be the subject of a discretionary life term.[8]

A sentence of life imprisonment should not be imposed when a determinate sentence proportionate to the gravity of the offence would provide a sufficient level of protection.[9] Nor is a discretionary life term available in respect of offences which are not violent or sexual offences within the meaning of s 31 of the Criminal Justice Act 1991.[10]

Despite the potentiality for the imposition of a life sentence under pre-existing law, it is striking that such sentences are, in fact, infrequently imposed. Of 217 offenders convicted during 1994 of a second serious violent or sexual offence, only 10 were sentenced to life imprisonment.[11] It can be argued that these figures demonstrate the new mandatory sentence provision to be unnecessary, and that it will require the imposition of a sentence which, hitherto, has been considered unnecessary in the vast majority of cases. On the other hand, supporters of the new provision argue that such statistics merely show the inadequacies of pre-existing sentencing policy, and of the *Hodgson* criteria.[12]

---

1 Defined by s 2(5). See para **2.16**.
2 See para **2.10**.
3 (1968) 52 Cr App R 113 (CA).
4 *Wilkinson* (1983) 5 Cr App R (S) 105 (CA).
5 *Blogg* (1981) 3 Cr App R (S) 114 (CA); *Allen* (1987) Cr App R (S) 169 (CA).
6 *A-G Reference No 32 of 1996 (Steven Alan Whitaker)* [1996] Crim LR 917 (CA).
7 *Wilkinson* (1983) 5 Cr App R 105 (CA); *Pither* (1979) 1 Cr App R (S) 209 (CA).
8 *Hatch* [1996] Crim LR 679 (CA), cf *J* (1992) 14 Cr App R (S) 500 (CA); *Roche* (1995) 16 Cr App R (S) 849 (CA).
9 *Hercules* (1980) 2 Cr App R (S) 156 (CA); *Lundberg* [1995] Crim LR 577.
10 See annotations to ss 21 and 27; see, eg, *Robinson* [1997] Crim LR 365 (CA).
11 Mr Michael Howard, QC, MP, Home Secretary, HC Second Reading, cols 912–913.
12 See, eg, Coad, *Mandatory Sentences: Putting the Record Straight* (1997) JP 159.

2.9 In some cases, courts have in fact imposed discretionary life sentences where the conditions for the making of a hospital order existed. In *Moore*[1] the offender was convicted of rape and of possessing an imitation firearm whilst committing a scheduled offence. He suffered from schizophrenia and was also mentally impaired. This was a case, the Court of Appeal concluded, where a hospital order was appropriate, in preference to a sentence of life imprisonment.[2] However, the facts of this case would not bring it within the new mandatory sentence provisions in s 2. In *Mitchell*[3] the appellant was convicted of three counts of manslaughter by reason of diminished responsibility. In

1990, he had been convicted of possessing an offensive weapon and common assault. Again, this was a case where, because of schizophrenia, a hospital order with a restriction order[4] was appropriate, but where s 2 would not, if the facts were repeated, apply. It should be noted that if s 2 did apply, the choice hitherto open to the court in these cases to make a hospital order would not be open to it.[5]

---

1 [1996] Crim LR 604 (CA).
2 See *Howell* (1985) 7 Cr App R (S) 360 (CA); *McBatha* (1985) 7 Cr App R (S) 373 (CA).
3 [1996] Crim LR 604 (CA).
4 See para **6.3**.
5 See para **2.31**.

The pre-conditions

2.10 The pre-conditions for the requirement to impose a life sentence under s 2(2) are to be found in s 2(1). By s 2(1), the mandatory sentence requirement applies where:

(a)   a person is convicted of a serious offence committed after the commencement of s 2;[1] and

(b)   at the time when that offence was committed, he was 18[2] or over and had been convicted in any part of the UK[2] of another serious offence.

---

1 As to commencement, see s 57(2).
2 See general annotations.

2.11 Several points should be noted. First, the conviction for the offence for which the offender is now being sentenced (hereafter referred to as 'the current offence') must be by a court in England and Wales,[1] because Pt I of the new Act applies only to England and Wales (s 57(4)).

Secondly, the offence must be a 'serious offence', as defined by s 2(5)–(7). It is not enough that an offence which amounts to an associated offence within the meaning of s 31(2) of the Criminal Justice Act 1991[2] is a serious offence, if the offence for which the offender is being sentenced is not such an offence.

Thirdly, the current offence must have been committed after the date of commencement of s 2. Section 2(2) does not apply where an offender is being sentenced, after commencement, for an offence which was committed prior to commencement. Thus, sentencers will require evidence which establishes the date of commission of the offence.[3]

Fourthly, the offender must have been 18[1] or over at the date of commission of the second offence. However, this age restriction does not apply in respect of the earlier offence. The age of the offender at the date of commission of, or sentencing for, the earlier offence is irrelevant save to the extent that it might, in an appropriate case, provide a basis for arguing that exceptional circumstances exist which justify the non-imposition of the otherwise mandatory sentence.[4]

Finally, the offender must, at the time of the commission of the second offence, have been the subject of a previous conviction for another serious offence. That conviction can be by a court anywhere in the UK,[1] and is not limited to a conviction in England and Wales. The wording of s 2(1)(b) makes it clear that it is the date of *conviction* for that earlier offence that matters for the purposes of s 2(1)(b). That conviction must be prior to the commission of the current offence, because the whole of s 2(1)(b) is qualified by the expression 'at the time when that offence was committed' to be found at the commencement of s 2(1)(b). It is not sufficient that the offender has been convicted of a serious offence after the commission of, but before sentencing for, the current offence.

---

1 See general annotations.
2 Section 31(2) states that an offence is associated with another for the purposes of Pt I of the 1991 Act if:

(a)   the offender is convicted of it in the proceedings in which he is convicted of the other offence, or (although convicted of it in earlier proceedings) is sentenced for it at the same time as he is sentenced for that offence; or
(b)   the offender admits the commission of it in the proceedings in which he is sentenced for the other offence and requests the court to take it into consideration in sentencing him for that offence.
3 See para **2.24**.
4 See para **2.25**.

2.12   There are no time-limits as to when the previous conviction for a serious offence must have occurred. It has already been noted[1] that that conviction must pre-date the commission of the offence for which the offender is being sentenced, but that previous offence may pre-date the commencement of s 2, and, indeed, be many years old. Nothing in the Rehabilitation of Offenders Act 1974 prevents that earlier conviction from being taken into account. The 1974 Act provides that a conviction can become spent, if it attracted a sentence of less than 30 months, and provided the offender has kept out of trouble for the period specified in the 1974 Act.[2] Attempts were made during the passage of the new Act to prevent spent convictions from counting for the purposes of the operation of the mandatory sentence provision of s 2.[3] These attempts were successfully resisted by the Government. The result is that the previous conviction could have occurred many years prior to the commission of the offence for which the offender is now being sentenced, and at a time when the offender was young. There are no provisions in s 2 stipulating what age the offender must have been when he is convicted of the offence which amounts to the earlier offence for the purposes of s 2.

---

1 See para **2.11**.
2 A conviction never becomes spent under the 1974 Act if it attracted a sentence of 30 months imprisonment or more. If a sentence is imposed of a term between six and 30 months, the conviction becomes spent after 10 years. If the term of imprisonment is less than six months, the conviction becomes spent after seven years. Shorter rehabilitation periods apply where a person is the subject of a fine, conditional discharge or probation order.
3 See Lord Carlisle of Bucklow, HL Report, cols 788–792.

2.13 As noted above, the date of conviction for the earlier offence does not have to be after the date of commencement of s 2. At first sight, the wording of the new Act might appear to point to a contrary conclusion. This is because the new means of proof of such convictions, contained in s 6, apply only to convictions which occur after commencement of s 6. However, it would be wrong to conclude from this that the earlier conviction must also be after the date of commencement. Comparison between the wording of s 2(1) and that of s 4(1) shows clearly that the parliamentary intent was that s 2 should apply irrespective of whether the convictions occurred prior to, or after, the commencement of Pt I of the new Act. Section 4(1)(c) confined the operation of *that* section (ie s 4) to cases where the previous offences were committed after commencement. Section 2(1)(b) is not so confined.

The obligation under s 2(2) does not apply to cases where a person is convicted of two serious offences at the same time, or committed two or more such offences in series but had not been convicted until the proceedings currently before the court in which the court will be sentencing that offender. It does arise where a person has been convicted, but not sentenced, for one serious offence at the time of commission of another.

2.14 It is the second, current, offence which, if the pre-conditions in s 2(1) are satisfied, attracts the mandatory sentence, not the first. This is so, irrespective of the fact that the second offence may be less serious than the first. Nothing in the pre-existing law prevented a sentencer from imposing a discretionary life term for that earlier offence when the offender was originally sentenced for that offence, provided the maximum punishment permitted was, potentially, a term of life imprisonment and the *Hodgson* principles[1] relating to the imposition of discretionary life sentences were satisfied. It is the *repetition* of a serious offence that provides the justification for the mandatory sentence under s 2, not the offence seriousness per se, although clearly the level of seriousness of the offences to which s 2 applies is high. In imposing a s 2 mandatory sentence, a court does not have to assess the level of offence seriousness for the purposes of ss 1 and 2 of the Criminal Justice Act 1991.[2] This is because s 55(1) of, and Sch 4 to, the new Act amend those provisions. Schedule 4, para 15 inserts the words 'or falling to be imposed under section 2(2) ...' into s 1(1) of the 1991 Act, and a similar amendment is made to s 2(1) by para 15(3).

---

1 See para **2.8**.
2 As amended by the new Act, Sch 4, para 15, ss 1 and 2 to the 1991 Act provide as follows:

'1(1) This section applies where a person is convicted of an offence punishable with a custodial sentence other than one fixed by law or falling to be imposed under section 2(2), 3(2) or 4(2) of the Crime (Sentences) Act 1997.

(2) Subject to subsection (3) below, the court shall not pass a custodial sentence on the offender unless it is of the opinion—
   (a) that the offence, or the combination of the offence and one or more offences associated with it, was so serious that only such a sentence can be justified for the offence; or
   (b) where the offence is a violent or sexual offence, that only such a sentence would be adequate to protect the public from serious harm from him.

(3) Nothing in subsection (2) above shall prevent the court from passing a custodial sentence on the offender if he fails to express his willingness to comply with a requirement which is proposed by the

court to be included in a probation order or supervision order and which requires an expression of such willingness.

(4) Where a court passes a custodial sentence, it shall be its duty—
    (a) in a case not falling within subsection (3) above, to state in open court that it is of the opinion that either or both of paragraphs (a) and (b) of subsection (2) above apply, and why it is of that opinion; and
    (b) in any case, to explain to the offender in open court and in ordinary language why it is passing a custodial sentence on him.

(5) A magistrates' court shall cause a reason stated by it under subsection (4) above to be specified in the warrant of commitment and to be entered in the register.

2(1) This section applies where a court passes a custodial sentence other than one fixed by law or falling to be imposed under section 2(2), 3(2) or 4(2) of the Crime (Sentences) Act 1997.

(2) Subject to sections 3(2) and 4(2) of that Act, the custodial sentence shall be—
    (a) for such term (not exceeding the permitted maximum) as in the opinion of the court is commensurate with the seriousness of the offence, or the combination of then offence and one or more offences associated with it; or
    (b) where the offence is a violent or sexual offence, for such longer term (not exceeding that maximum) as in the opinion of the court is necessary to protect the public from serious harm from the offender.

(3) When the court passes a custodial sentence for a term longer than is commensurate with the seriousness of the offence, or the combination of the offence and one or more offences associated with it, the court shall—
    (a) state in open court that it is of the opinion that subsection 2(b) above applies and why it is of that opinion; and
    (b) explain to the offender in open court and in ordinary language why the sentence is for such a term.

(4) A custodial sentence for an indeterminate period shall be regarded for the purposes of subsections (2) and (3) above as a custodial sentence for a term longer than any actual term.

(5) Section (3) above shall not apply in any case where the court passes a custodial sentence falling to be imposed under subsection (2) of section 3 or (4) of the Crime (Sentences) Act 1997 which is for the minimum period specified in that subsection.'

2.15 As already noted at para 2.10, a conviction for two separate serious offences is a pre-condition for the operation of s 2(2). If the conviction for the earlier offence is quashed, then the basis for the imposition of a mandatory life sentence disappears. If that earlier conviction for a serious offence is, in fact, quashed, notice of appeal against the mandatory sentence imposed under s 2 may be given within 28 days from the date of that quashing (s 5(2)).

Serious offence

2.16 What amounts to a 'serious' offence is dealt with by s 2(5)–(7).

By s 2(5), the following offences[1] committed in England and Wales[2] each amount to a serious offence:

(a) attempted murder, conspiracy to murder or incitement to murder;
(b) an offence under the Offences Against the Person Act 1861, s 4, (soliciting murder);
(c) manslaughter;
(d) an offence under the Offences Against the Person Act 1861, s 18 (wounding, or causing grievous bodily harm, with intent);
(e) rape, or attempted rape;
(f) an offence under the Sexual Offences Act 1956, s 5 (intercourse with a girl under 13);

(g) an offence under the Firearms Act 1968, s 16 (possession of a firearm with intent to injure), s 17 (use of a firearm to resist arrest) or s 18 (carrying a firearm with criminal intent);

(h) robbery where at some time during the commission of the offence, the offender had in his possession a firearm or imitation firearm[3] within the meaning of the Firearms Act 1968.

These offences overlap in scope. For example, a robbery committed by a person who is armed with a firearm may involve charges both under (g) and (h), as well as, perhaps, manslaughter under (c). For the purposes of s 2, this overlap is unimportant, because the fact that two or more 'serious offences' are charged in the same indictment is irrelevant. Conviction for two or more serious offences at the same time does not trigger the mandatory sentence requirement. That requires convictions for two or more serious offences on separate occasions although, of course, those convictions do not have to be consecutive. Thus, for example, convictions for offences that are not 'serious' within the meaning of s 2(5) may occur after the conviction for the earlier serious offence and before the commission of the second serious offence, but do not interfere with the operation of s 2. In such a case, s 2(2) requires a mandatory sentence to be imposed.

---

1 By s 7(1), equivalent offences under service law amount to 'serious offences'.

2 See general annotations.

3 The problem that was identified in *Touriq Khan* (1994) 16 Cr App R(S) 180 (CA) (offence with imitation or unloaded firearm not a 'violent offence') is avoided. See also *Palin* (1995) 16 Cr App R (S) 888 (CA).

2.17 Certain offences committed in Scotland are to be regarded as 'serious offences'. By s 2(6), an offence[1] committed in Scotland is a serious offence for the purposes of s 2 if the conviction for it was obtained on indictment in the High Court of Justiciary and it amounts to any of the following offences:

(a) culpable homicide;

(b) attempted murder, incitement to murder or conspiracy to murder;

(c) rape or attempted rape;

(d) clandestine injury to women or an attempt to cause such injury;

(e) sodomy, or an attempt to commit sodomy, where the complainer, that is to say, the person against whom the offence was committed, did not consent;

(f) assault, where the assault:
   (i) is aggravated because it was carried out to the victim's severe injury or the danger of the victim's life; or
   (ii) was carried out with an intention to rape or to ravish the victim;

(g) robbery where, at some time during the commission of the offence, the offender had in his possession a firearm or imitation firearm within the meaning of the Firearms Act 1968;

(h) an offence under s 16 (possession of a firearm with intent to injure) s 17 (use of a firearm with intent to resist arrest) or s 18 (carrying a firearm with criminal intent) of that Act;

(i) lewd, libidinous or indecent behaviour or practices; and

(j)   an offence under s 5(1) of the Criminal Law (Consolidation) (Scotland) Act 1995 (unlawful intercourse with a girl under 13).

These differ from the offences set out in s 2(5), and are, in some respects, wider. For example, the offence of 'lewd, libidinous or indecent behaviour or practices'[2] is wider than the offences that constitute a serious offence if the conviction occurs in England and Wales.[3]

The offences specified in s 2(6) relate to offences that potentially can constitute the earlier, serious offence. Clearly, the second, *subsequent*, offence will have been committed in England and Wales. This is because s 2 does not apply to Scotland, and an offence committed in Scotland will be tried there, and be governed by s 1 of the Crime and Punishment (Scotland) Act 1997.[4]

---

1 The provision in s 7 relating to offences under service law does not apply in the context of s 2(6).
2 See annotations to s 2. For an example of such a conviction being relevant under pre-existing law, see *Carpenter* [1996] Crim LR 603 (CA).
3 See general annotations.
4 This contains a list of offences equivalent to that in s 2(6) of the new Act. Similar considerations apply to convictions in Northern Ireland, which fall within s 2(7).

2.18   By s 2(7), an offence[1] committed in Northern Ireland is a serious offence for the purposes of s 2 if it is any of the following, namely:

(a)   an offence falling within paras (a)–(e) of s 2(5);
(b)   an offence under s 4 of the Criminal Law Amendment Act 1885 (intercourse with a girl under 14);
(c)   an offence under art 17 (possession of a firearm with intent to injure), art 18(1) (use of a firearm to resist arrest) or art 19 (carrying a firearm with criminal intent) of the Firearms (Northern Ireland) Order 1981, SI 1981/155; and
(d)   robbery where, at some time during the commission of the offence, the offender had in his possession a firearm or imitation firearm within the meaning of that Order.

---

1 The provision in s 7 relating to offences under service law does not apply in the context of s 2(6).

2.19   Clearly, s 2 is designed to deal with offenders who, because of their repeated commission of serious offences, are considered to constitute a continued risk to the public. However, the serious offence for which the offender is being sentenced does not have to be of the same type as the earlier offence or offences. Thus, a man who is convicted of an offence of manslaughter is subject to a mandatory sentence if, many years before, he was convicted, as a 16-year-old, of an offence of sexual intercourse with a girl under 13, contrary to s 5 of the Sexual Offences Act 1956. Again, a mandatory life sentence falls to be imposed on an elderly man who is convicted of raping his wife, he having returned home drunk and forced her to have intercourse, if he had been found guilty, aged 18, of robbery. A third example is a case of a middle-aged woman who strikes out at her husband in rage and after suffering considerable abuse. Following his unexpected death following that blow, she is found guilty of manslaughter. She will be subject to a mandatory life sentence if, many years earlier, she acted as a look-out for a gang of teenage robbers, and was convicted of robbery as an accessory. In each case, the mandatory sentence is imposed, irrespective of the levels of actual risk to the public that the offender might pose. Only if exceptional circumstances are found to exist will the offender escape the effects of s 2.

2.20 Nor does the Act address all categories of case where risk to the public genuinely exists. It is, inevitably, arbitrary, and, for this reason, is open to significant criticism. It limits judicial discretion and does so in a way that creates anomalies. This can be demonstrated by a few examples:

(a) a man who is convicted, at age 16, of sexual intercourse with a 12-year-old girl will automatically be sentenced to life imprisonment if, in middle age, he intentionally causes serious injury in the course of a public house brawl;

(b) a young man convicted of wounding with intent to cause serious injury will automatically sentenced to life imprisonment if, later in life aged 50, he returns home drunk and attempts to have intercourse with his wife against her wishes;

(c) a man with no previous convictions is apprehended after many years, having committed a series of rapes. He is convicted of those offences at one trial. The evidence in the case shows a consistent pattern of violent attacks on women. No mandatory life sentence is required by s 2, although, of course, an indeterminate sentence is a possible option for the court to consider;

(d) a woman is convicted of manslaughter, having, whilst acting as a child-minder, caused the death of an eight-month-old child by shaking the child.[1] The offender may claim lack of intent to kill, and be convicted on the basis of gross negligence.[2] If that offender had been convicted some years earlier for manslaughter by gross negligence (eg in a motoring incident) a mandatory life sentence requirement would apply;

(e) a man who repeatedly robs at knifepoint[3] does not fall within the terms of s 2, no matter how many convictions for that type of offence he has, and irrespective of the danger to the public;

(f) a man who repeatedly threatens to kill likewise does not fall within s 2. In *Rickhart*[4] the appellant threatened to kill the victim, and sent a bullet, in an envelope, through the post. Reports on the offender suggested that he fantasised about mass killing, and was possibly suffering from mental illness. Despite the clear risk, such a person does not attract a mandatory sentence.

---

1 See the facts of *Cawthorne* [1996] Crim LR 526 (CA).
2 As was claimed (unsuccessfully) to be the position in *Cawthorne*.
3 *Bibby* (1994) 16 Cr App R 127 (CA).
4 [1995] Crim LR 534.

2.21 The scope of the offences that amount to 'serious offences' is wide. In particular, the position in respect of offences under s 18 of the Offences Against the Person Act 1861 gave rise to considerable debate during the passage of the new Act. Although by definition 'grievous bodily harm' with intent is a serious offence (in a non-technical sense), the s 18 offence encompasses a broad range of conduct and, at the bottom end of the range of seriousness, overlaps with the offence of occasioning actual bodily harm under s 20 of the 1861 Act. Section 18 of the 1861 Act involves 'really serious bodily harm',[1] with intent to cause such harm, or with intent to resist arrest. This formulation covers a wide range of conduct all of which may be regarded, in a non-technical sense, as serious, but not all of which would appropriately carry a life sentence if a court had any choice in the matter. The conduct may have been impulsive, may have occurred within a situation of considerable provocation or where significant mitigation existed. For example, the offender may have attacked another man with whom the offender's wife was having an affair whilst he (the offender) was recovering in hospital from a car crash.[2] Such a course of events may, on their own, justify a short term of imprisonment, but will attract a mandatory life sentence if the offender happens to have a previous conviction for one of the offences in s 2(5)–(7).

'Grievous bodily harm' may also go beyond purely physical violence. Case-law makes it clear that psychiatric injury is capable of constituting actual bodily harm for the purpose of s 20 of the 1861 Act.[3] It follows that serious psychiatric injury can amount to grievous bodily harm for the purposes of s 18, and, therefore, a s 18 offence is committed if the requisite intent is present although it will not often be the case that such a person intends to cause serious psychiatric injury. In the rare 'stalking' case where such intent can be proved, then, the offence amounts to a 'serious offence' within the meaning of s 2(5).[4]

These problems relating to the different levels of seriousness of different examples of the same offence are, under the new scheme, to be dealt with through regulating the life sentence imposed. As Mr David Maclean, Minister of State, put it:

> 'In future, where there are variations in section 18 and a person is convicted of grievous bodily harm, it will be entirely up to the judge to set up an appropriate tariff within the automatic life sentence, taking into account the seriousness of the assault for which the person had been found guilty ....'[5]

In reality, the distinctions between s 18 and s 20 offences are often fine. There may be a temptation on the Crown Prosecution Service to downcharge, and proceed on a s 20 rather than a s 18 charge.[6] There may also be a willingness on the part of defendants to plead guilty to a s 20 offence, but to plead not guilty to a s 18 charge, leading to plea bargaining. Attempts during the passage of the new Act to limit the operation of s 2 by restricting the types of s 18 offence that should fall within it were strongly resisted by the Government, and failed.

---

1 *DPP v Smith* [1961] 2 AC 190 (HL); *Cunningham* [1982] AC 566 (HL); *Brown* [1994] 1 AC 212 (HL).
2 These are the facts of *Haley* (1983), unreported. The sentence imposed was 18 months' imprisonment, nine of which were suspended. See Mr Alun Michael, MP, HC Committee, col 61.

3 *Chan-Fook* (1994) 99 Cr App R 147 (CA); *Mandair* [1995] 1 AC 208 (HL); *Burstow* [1997] Crim LR 452 (CA). Such conduct does not constitute a violent offence for the purposes of the Criminal Justice Act 1991, s 31; see *Rickhart* [1995] Crim LR 574 (CA).

4 For other provisions relating to stalking, see the Protection from Harassment Act 1997.

5 HC Committee, col 66. This tariff, announced in court, may in reality be low: for the concept of 'honesty in sentencing' see para **3.5**.

6 See Sir Ivor Lawrence, QC, MP, HC Committee, cols 63–66.

2.22 The position in respect of sexual offences is also open to criticism. An offence under s 5 of the Sexual Offences Act 1956 (intercourse with a girl under 13) is to be regarded as 'serious', despite the fact that only 55 per cent of such offences result in the imposition of a custodial sentence. Indeed, the girl may have consented. Conversely, the offences under s 6 (intercourse with a girl under 16) or s 12 (buggery committed on a boy under 13) are not to be regarded as serious offences for the purpose of s 2. Nor is a sexual relationship, involving indecent assaults and penetrations, between a woman and a girl aged under 13 a serious offence under s 2, although an equivalent relationship between a man and a girl under 13 would be.[1] Further, although rape, and attempted rape, are serious offences, burglary with intent to rape is not. Thus, a man with a previous conviction for rape who burgles with intent to rape, but does not rape, because he is disturbed by occupants of the dwelling, will not fall within the scope of the Act, even though he may be a clear and continuing danger to society. By contrast, a 16-year-old who has consensual intercourse with a precocious 12-year-old is within the scope of s 2.

Indecent assaults are not included in the list of offences that trigger the mandatory sentence, even if such conduct may evidence a high risk of sexual offending. In *Webb*[2] the appellant pleaded guilty to indecent assault on a female. He had eight previous court appearances for sexual offences, including attempted rape, indecent assault, gross indecency with a child and indecent exposure. He was described in a psychiatric report as an inadequate, immature person who lost his inhibitions and sought sexual gratification when under the influence of alcohol. His sentence was raised to six years, and imposed as a longer than commensurate sentence under s 2(2)(b) of the 1991 Act.[3] It is far from clear that if such an offence were to reoccur then the offender would fall within the mandatory life sentence provisions, despite the clear risk such an offender poses to the public. Again, in *Carpenter*,[4] the Court of Appeal considered a three-year term, imposed under s 2(2)(b) of the 1991 Act, to be appropriate in respect of an offender who (having convictions in Scotland for sodomy and lewd and libidinous practices with a boy aged 10)[5] pleaded guilty to an indecent assault on a boy aged 12 whom he had befriended. Again, such a case would fall outside s 2, despite the clear risk that this sexual offence, committed in a context of breach of trust, demonstrates.

---

1 See *Allen* [1996] Crim LR 208 (CA) (appellant sentenced to 18 months).

2 [1995] Crim LR 965 (CA).

3 See para **2.3**.

4 [1996] Crim LR 603 (CA).

5 See para **2.17**, and annotations to s 2.

2.23   Such inconsistencies are inevitable once an approach based on named offences is adopted: by definition, any list will be arbitrary, and not focus on the degree of risk the offender is likely to pose. The approach taken by the new Act is not based simply upon the seriousness of that particular offence. Thus, offences under ss 16, 17 or 18 of the Firearms Act 1968 can be punished by a fine alone, but are, nevertheless, serious offences within the meaning of s 2(5). Arson is not on the list of offences within s 2(5), but, arguably, is an offence where the risks to the public posed by a repeat offender are extremely high.

Proof of the earlier conviction

2.24   The burden of proving the fact of the previous conviction, or convictions, and the date of that conviction, lies on the prosecutor. That burden can be discharged by proving those matters in the normal way, by certificate of conviction under s 73(1) of PACE.[1] That is so irrespective of the age of the offender at the time of the conviction. Section 16(2) of the Children and Young Persons Act 1963 provides for offences committed by children under 14 to be disregarded for the purpose of evidence relating to previous convictions. However, a new subsection, s 16(3), is inserted into the 1963 Act by s 55(1) and Sch 4, para 4 of the new Act: nothing in s 16(2) of the 1963 Act prevents the adducing of evidence of previous convictions for the purposes of Pt I of the new Act.

The means of proof contained in s 73(1) is in addition to, and not to the exclusion of, any other authorised means of proof.[2] The new Act creates another means of proof of the fact that the offender has been convicted of a serious offence. By s 6(1) where:

(a)   on any date after the commencement of s 6 a person is convicted in England and Wales[3] of, inter alia, a serious offence; and

(b)   the court by or before which he is so convicted states in open court that he has been convicted of such an offence on that date; and

(c)   that court subsequently certifies that fact,

the certificate shall be evidence, for the purposes of s 2, that he was convicted of such an offence on that date.

Section 6 does not state that such a certificate is conclusive proof of the fact of conviction, nor does it, on its face, create a presumption in favour of such a conclusion, unlike s 73(2) of PACE.[4] However, once such a certificate is accepted as a valid certificate of conviction, it is inconceivable that a court would not accept its accuracy, save in the face of compelling evidence although, of course, the burden of proof remains on the prosecutor. Section 6 does not create a presumption that the certificate is valid.

Further, and unlike s 73(4) of PACE, no specific statement is contained in s 6 that the stated method of proving the conviction is in addition to, and not to the exclusion of, any other method of proof. Arguably, this is the case, and the failure to so state explicitly does not matter. There are three reasons for that conclusion. First, the wording of s 6(1) is 'shall be evidence' and not 'shall be proved by' or some other similar form of words. Secondly, s 6 only applies in respect of offences in respect of which a person is convicted after the commencement of s 6, despite the fact that s 2 is not so confined. The key fact to be proved for the purposes of s 2 is that the offender has a previous conviction. That conviction does not have to be on a date after commencement of s 2 or, for that matter, of s 6.[5] Such convictions will have to be proved by other means. Thirdly, s 6 only applies to convictions in England and Wales.[6] Convictions in Scotland or Northern Ireland will also have to be proved by other means.

---

1 Section 73(1) provides:

> 'Where in any proceedings the fact that a person has in the United Kingdom been convicted or acquitted of an offence otherwise than by a Service court is admissible in evidence, it may be proved by producing a certificate of conviction or, as the case may be, of acquittal relating to that offence, and proving that the person named in the certificate as having been convicted or acquitted of the offence is the person whose conviction or acquittal of the offence is to be proved.'

Section 73(3) provides that '... a document purporting to be a duly signed certificate or acquittal under this section shall be taken to be such a certificate unless the contrary is proved'.

2 PACE, s 73(4).
3 See general annotations.
4 In respect of Scotland and Northern Ireland, s 73 only applies to the extent permitted by s 120 of PACE.
5 See para **2.13**.
6 See general annotations.

Exceptional circumstances

2.25 As noted at para **2.2**, s 2(2) creates an exception to the general duty imposed on a court by s 2 to impose a life sentence. A court need not impose such a sentence if it is of the opinion that there are exceptional circumstances relating to either of the offences or to the offender which justify its not doing so. If it is of that opinion, it shall state so in open court, and state what the exceptional circumstances are (s 2(3)). In determining whether it would be appropriate not to impose a life sentence the court shall have regard to the circumstances relating to either of the offences or to the offender (s 1(2)). Section 1(2) must be read in the light of s 2(3). Those circumstances must be such as to amount to 'exceptional circumstances' within the meaning of s 2(3). The words 'relating to either of the offences or to the offender' were added to the Act during its passage through Parliament, and are intended to put beyond doubt the fact that there are no potential limits as to what matters can be taken into account. This fact, of itself, was not a matter of serious dispute, the Government accepting that any circumstances could be such as to be relevant for this purpose.[1] However, the words of s 1(2) and s 2(2) should be contrasted with those in s 1(3), s 3(2) and s 4(2), in respect of minimum sentences, and which refer to 'specific' circumstances. In the House of Lords, Baroness Blatch, Minister of State, struggled to ascribe a meaning, or any significance, to the word 'specific', and it may be that it has no significance at all. It is difficult to think of any relevant circumstances that are not specific. No doubt the words are intended to emphasise the fact that there must be identifiable matters justifying the application of the exception to s 3 or s 4, the exception not being activated simply because of the nature of the case. On this basis, the absence of the word 'specific' from s 2 is unimportant.

---

1 HC Committee, col 41. See para **2.29**.

2.26 Exceptional circumstances must be shown. It is not enough that such a sentence would be unjust, a conclusion confirmed not only by the parliamentary debates but also by comparison between the wording of s 2(2) ('exceptional circumstances ... which justify its not doing so') and that of the equivalent provisions in s 3(2) and s 4(2) ('specific circumstances which ... would make the prescribed custodial sentence unjust in all the circumstances'). During the passage of the Act through Parliament an amendment was tabled, which, if it had been accepted, would have conferred discretion on a sentencing court not impose a life sentence where to do so would be unjust. In particular, Lord Bingham CJ asked, powerfully:[1]

> 'How can it be contrary to good government or the administration of justice that those draconian sentences should not be imposed mandatorily where it is not in the interests of justice to impose them or where it is contrary to justice to do so?'

There would be, he argued, enough cases where the interests of justice were not served by the mandatory and minimum sentence provisions[2] to bring the test into disrepute. However, the amendment was strongly resisted by the Government, on the basis that to permit such a discretion would frustrate the very purpose of s 2.[3] Unlike the minimum sentence provisions in s 3 and s 4, the 'exceptional circumstances' test therefore remains the basis of operation of the exception.

---

1 Lord Bingham CJ, HL Report, cols 803–805. See also Sir Peter Lloyd, MP, HC Report, col 378; Sir Ivor Lawrence, QC, MP, HC Report, cols 385–386.
2 The comments, although applicable to both the mandatory and minimum sentence provisions, were made in the context of an amendment relating to s 2.
3 Baroness Blatch, Minister of State, ibid, cols 810–815.

2.27 What amount to 'exceptional circumstances' is a matter for the sentencer. In order for a court to be able to determine whether 'exceptional circumstances' exist which justify the imposition of a sentence other than that required by s 2, a sentencing court will need to be in full possession of the information relating to that offence and in respect of the offender. In respect of an earlier offence, a judge will need to have details not only of the fact of conviction, but also details of the offence in respect of which the earlier sentence was passed. If issues in respect of 'exceptional circumstances' arise, a certificate of conviction[1] may not suffice. Arguably, an obligation is imposed on the legal representatives for the accused to inform a prosecutor that an argument based on exceptional circumstances relating to an earlier offence is to be put to the court, in order that the necessary information can be made available by the prosecutor to the court.

In a case where a guilty plea has been entered, a *Newton* hearing may be required to determine the factual basis on which an offender should be sentenced. In cases where a not guilty plea was entered, and the verdict of the jury is consistent with two, alternative, views of the facts (such as a case of murder where a verdict of manslaughter is delivered) the trial judge is entitled to deal with the matter himself, sentencing on his view of the facts as they appeared from the evidence.[2] In respect of matters relating to the offender, it will clearly be necessary to establish these by evidence whether contained in reports, other documentary evidence or, if appropriate, oral evidence. In particular, the pre-sentence report may be of considerable importance. It will therefore be necessary to ensure that in a case where exceptional circumstances issues arise a court does not dispense with the need for a PSR under s 3(5) of the Criminal Justice Act 1991.

---

1 See para **2.24**.
2 *Cawthorne, Boyer,* (1981) 3 Cr App R(S) 35 (CA); *Soloman* and *Triumph* (1984) 6 Cr App R (S) 120 (CA).

2.28 The meaning of 'exceptional circumstances' caused considerable debate during the passage of the Act. In the White Paper, it was stated:[1]

'... the court will also have discretion not to pass the automatic life sentence in genuinely exceptional cases. This is intended to allow for occasional quite unforeseeable circumstances where it would plainly be unjust and unnecessary to impose the life sentence. But it should be emphasised that this provision will be designed to cover only genuinely exceptional cases.'

Some guidance can be gained from caseload dealing with 'exceptional circumstances' in the context of suspended sentences, under s 22(2) of the Powers of Criminal Courts Act 1973, although there may be a considerable difference between the concept of 'exceptional circumstances' for the purposes of suspended sentences, and 'exceptional circumstances' for the purposes of preventing an individual from being sentenced to imprisonment for life. It cannot be assumed that the judiciary will be as restrictive in interpreting s 2(2) as it has been in interpreting s 22 of the 1973 Act.[2] However, the case-law in respect of s 22 is instructive, if not entirely consistent. Matters such as good character, youth and an early plea of guilty have been held not to constitute 'exceptional circumstances'.[3] Nor have arguments based on provocation generally been accepted as amounting to exceptional circumstances.[4] Other matters which have been held not to constitute 'exceptional circumstances' are financial difficulties,[5] and depressive illness, although the authorities are, on these matters, not wholly confined to this narrow approach.[6]

---

1 Op cit, para 10.10.
2 See Sir Ivan Lawrence QC, MP, HC Committee, col 24.
3 *Okinikan* [1993] 1 WLR 173 (CA).
4 *Sanderson* (1993) 14 Cr App R (S) 361 (CA); cf *Huntley* (1993) 14 Cr App R (S) 795 (CA).
5 *Lowry* (1993) 14 Cr App R (S) 485 (CA); cf *French* (1994) 15 Cr App R (S) 194 (CA).
6 See *Bradley* (1994) 15 Cr App R (S) 597 (CA); *Lowry,* above.

2.29 Mr David Maclean, Minister of State, indicated that the phrase 'exceptional circumstances' is intended to include the circumstances of the offender and of the offence, and any other background circumstance.[1] In doing so, he broadly was reiterating what are now the terms of s 1(2), which provides that in determining whether or not it would be appropriate not to impose a life sentence, the court shall have regard to the circumstances relating to either of the offences or to the offender.

Irrespective of whether the case-law on s 22 of the 1973 Act[2] is followed, it is clear that a narrow approach is to be taken to the question of 'exceptional circumstances'. Simply because there are mitigating factors will not suffice, although these will be relevant to the tariff to be set by the trial judge when a life sentence is imposed under s 28 of the new Act.[3] A sentencer may thus be in a position of imposing a life sentence, but prescribing a low tariff.

1　See para **2.25**, and HC Committee, cols 40–41.
2　See para **2.28**.
3　Or, pending the coming into force of Pt II of the Criminal Justice Act 1991, s 34.

2.30 The question remains: what *are* exceptional circumstances? The Minister of State adopted with approval[1] the extra-judicial comment of the Lord Chief Justice[2] to the effect that 'exceptional circumstances' clearly means 'very unusual at the very least ...'. 'Exceptional circumstances' might include cases where exceptional help has been given to the police.[3] However, despite being pressed to give examples, no others were forthcoming during debates in Parliament. Ministers consistently declined to be drawn further on what would fall within the test. Clearly, the circumstances of the two or more offences are to be taken into account (s 1(2)). Factors which are commonplace in relation to the types of offences which fall within the definition of 'serious offence' will not justify the application of the 'exceptional circumstances' exception, because that would negate the very purpose of s 2. So, too, with the circumstances of the offender. These are relevant (s 1(2)),[4] but courts may find difficulty in differentiating between the circumstances which justify an application of the exception, and factors that simply mitigate the tariff. However, it is submitted that the exception is an appropriate way of dealing with the obvious injustices highlighted by the hypothetical examples quoted earlier,[5] where the earlier offence or offences was committed in early youth, and many years previously. That conclusion itself, however, presupposes that courts will not take a restrictive approach to the words 'to either of the offences or to the offender'. The period of time between the two or more serious offences is, on one view, neither a matter relating to the offences themselves, nor a matter relating to the offender. The issue also arises as to whether the phrase 'circumstances of the offender' can be construed beyond the personal situation of the offender so as to include the risk the offender poses, or may pose, to the public. It probably can, and arguably should, be so continued.

1　HC Committee, col 41.
2　Lord Bingham CJ made these comments on a breakfast television programme, *Frost on Sunday*.

3 Mr David Maclean, MP, ibid, col 45. This example was given at a stage when the 'exceptional circumstances' test applied not only to the mandatory sentence provision in s 2 but also to the minimum sentence provisions in s 3 and s 4.
4 See para **2.29**.
5 See para **2.19**.

Mental illness

2.31 Mental illness of itself is not to be regarded as an exceptional circumstance,[1] unless the mental illness is such as to have a direct bearing on the culpability of the offender.[2] If culpability is established, the mandatory life sentence inevitably follows: if it is not, then the medical evidence may well justify a finding of 'exceptional circumstances'.

Attempts were made during the passage of the Act to specifically provide that the existence of identifiable psychiatric illness should provide 'exceptional circumstances' sufficient to warrant the making of a hospital order under s 38 of the Mental Health Act 1983, and which would justify the non-imposition of the mandatory life sentence.[3] Such an approach would be in accordance with the basic principle that, when a person is diagnosed as suffering from such a disease, he is treated, not punished. Such an approach was rejected by the Government, Baroness Blatch, Minister of State, arguing that people who have a history of committing offences which fall within s 2 repeatedly, for whatever reason, should receive supervision for life.[4] A disposal under the Mental Health Act 1983 would frustrate that.[5] Such persons can receive treatment, either by transfer to hospital on the recommendation of doctors, under s 47 of the 1983 Act, or be the subject of a hospital direction pursuant to s 45A of the 1983 Act.[6]

1 Baroness Blatch, HL Report, col 824.
2 Ibid, col 826.
3 Lord Hacking, HL Report, cols 818–820. He relied on the advice given by the joint Mental Health and Disability sub-committee of The Law Society and Royal College of Psychiatrists, which believed that the proposed arrangements would result in a likelihood that persons released would pose a greater risk to the community than those who had received orders under the 1983 Act.
4 See Baroness Blatch, HL Committee, col 416.
5 Baroness Blatch, HL Report, col 824.
6 See para **6.9**. This power will apply only to those suffering a psychopathic disorder, but s 45A (10) of the 1983 Act permits the Secretary of State to extend the scope of this power.

Credit for guilty plea

2.32 There is no provision in the new Act that specifically allows credit to be given for a guilty plea. Section 48 of the Criminal Justice and Public Order Act 1994 requires a court, in determining what sentence to pass on an offender who has pleaded guilty to an offence, to take into account the stage in the proceedings at which an indication of an intention to plead guilty was given, and the circumstances in which it is given. Clearly, this provision cannot operate in a situation where the sentencing court has no discretion, but an argument might be made to the effect that, in the right case, a timely indication of an intention to plead guilty could amount to 'exceptional circumstances'. If exceptional help to the police can amount to 'exceptional circumstances', why should not exceptional help to other parts of the process, by a very early indication of a plea that spares a victim considerable anguish, likewise count? Such an argument, of course, would have the effect of driving a coach-and-horses through the legislation, and will not succeed, because there is in fact evidence of clear parliamentary intent to the contrary. Section 55 of, and Sch 4, para 17, to the new Act amend s 48 of the 1994 Act so as to ensure that such a reduction is available in cases falling within s 3 or s 4 of the new Act. If Parliament had intended such a reduction to be given in the context of s 2, it clearly could, and would, have said so.

MINIMUM SENTENCE FOR CLASS A DRUG OFFENCES

The mandatory sentence

2.33   Section 3 requires the imposition of a minimum sentence of imprisonment of seven years for those convicted of a third Class A drug trafficking offence. The rationale underpinning this provision is that: 'Those who deal in "hard drugs" are a menace to society and they must know that if they continue offending they will go to prison for a very long time'.[1] For this reason, they are singled out[2] for mandatory minimum sentences.

Where the pre-conditions contained in s 3(1) are satisfied, a court must impose a custodial term of least seven years unless the court is of the opinion that there are specific circumstances relating to either of the offences or to the offender and which would make the prescribed custodial sentence unjust in all the circumstances (s 3(2)). In relation to a person under 21,[3] a custodial sentence means a sentence of detention in a young offender institution (s 3(6)). In either case, credit can be given for a guilty plea by virtue of s 48 of the Criminal Justice and Public Order Act 1994,[4] the court being entitled to make a reduction of up to 20 per cent of the otherwise appropriate sentence.

---

1 Baroness Blatch, Minister of State, Home Office, HL Second Reading, cols 969–970. See also White Paper, op cit, para 11.2, p 49.
2 As are persistent domestic burglars; see paras **2.47–2.59**.
3 See general annotations.
4 As amended by s 55 of, and Sch 4, para 17, to the new Act. See para **2.32**.

2.34   The minimum seven-year term of imprisonment applies where the pre-conditions in s 3(1) are satisfied, irrespective of whether the offence seriousness criteria in s 1(2) of the Criminal Justice Act 1991[1] are satisfied. This is because s 55 of, and Sch 4 to, the new Act amend s 1 of the 1991 Act to exclude from the operation of s 1 cases which fall within the minimum sentence provisions of s 3 of the new Act. The seven-year term also applies, as a minimum, irrespective of whether it is proportionate with the actual seriousness of the offence, Sch 4, para 15, likewise amending s 2 of the 1991 Act. However, if the reality is that the minimum term required by s 3 of the new Act is disproportionate to the actual level of seriousness, that in itself, may justify the application of the exception to the mandatory minimum sentence contained in s 3(2).[2] However, if the courts in fact take that view, a significant exception to the minimum sentence provisions will have been created.

---

1 See para **2.14**, fn 2.
2 See para **2.42**.

2.35 Nothing in s 3 prevents a court from imposing a sentence greater than that prescribed in s 3. Offences under s 4(3) and s 5(3) of the Misuse of Drugs Act 1971 carry a potential term of imprisonment (if the offender is convicted on indictment) of life imprisonment, and such offences often attract a long custodial sentence depending on the nature and quantity of the drugs involved, the amount of trafficking and degree of involvement.[1]

The sentence required, as a minimum, by s 3 must be viewed in the context of the provisions of Pt II, Ch I of the new Act which deals with the period of time to be served as part of a sentence of imprisonment.[2] Section 26 of the new Act states that a court shall impose a term of imprisonment equal to two-thirds of the term which it would have been appropriate to have been imposed if the offence had been committed after the commencement of Ch I. It follows, therefore, that a term of seven years is equivalent to approximately 10½ years in respect of a sentence passed prior to the commencement of Ch I.[3] However, the question arises as to the relationship between Pt I of the new Act and Pt II, Ch I. The former applies in respect of any offence committed after the commencement of s 3 (s 3(1)(a)); the latter applies in respect of an offence committed after the commencement of Ch I (s 9(1)(a), s 26(1)(b)). The dates of commencement may, of course, not coincide. This does not matter, because s 26(2) provides that its terms are subject to s 3(2) (s 26(2)). The seven-year term therefore is an absolute one, not to be reduced by virtue of s 26.

---

1 For guideline judgments see: *Aramah* (1983) 76 Cr App R 190 (CA); *Bilinski* (1987) 9 Cr App R (S) 360 (CA); *Satvir Singh* (1988) 10 Cr App R (S) 402 (CA); *Aranguren and others* (1994) 99 Cr App R 347 (CA); *Warren and Beeley* [1996] 1 Cr App R 120 (CA). Importing drugs such as heroin usually attracts sentences in the range of 6–10 years.
2 See para **3.7**.
3 See para **3.2**.

The pre-conditions

2.36 The pre-conditions for the requirement in s 3 are contained in s 3(1). These are as follows:

(a) a person is convinced of a class A drug trafficking offence[1] committed after the commencement of s 3;

(b) at the time when that offence was committed, he was aged 18 or over[2] and had been convicted in any part of the UK[2] of two other Class A drug trafficking offences; and

(c) one of those other offences was committed after he had been convicted of the other.

Thus, before s 3 can 'bite' there needs to have been a conviction for a Class A offence on at least three occasions, the conviction for the last offence being in respect of an offence committed after the commencement of s 3. The two earlier offences must have been committed in series[3] because of the terms of s 3(1)(c) which require the commission of one of those earlier offences after the date of conviction for the other earlier offence. The date of conviction of each offence must be prior to the commission of the third offence (s 3(1)(b)). A conviction on an earlier occasion for two such offences will not suffice. Nor will three convictions on the same occasion. The third such offence must be committed by a person when aged 18 or over.

If the relevant earlier convictions for Class A drug trafficking offences are quashed, notice of appeal against the mandatory sentence imposed under s 3 may be given within 28 days from the date of that quashing (s 5(1)).

---

1 See annotations to s 3, and para **2.38**. An equivalent offence under service law will suffice: s 7(1).

2 See general annotations.

3 Although other offences may intervene.

2.37   As already noted,[1] the offence for which the offender is being sentenced, and which, potentially, attracts the minimum sentence must have been committed on a date when the offender was aged 18 or over.[2] It is not sufficient that the offence was committed before this date, but that the offender was sentenced after the attainment of that age.

The earlier offences may have been committed as a juvenile. No restriction is placed on the age of the offender at the time he was convicted of the earlier offence, and, as was the case in respect of the mandatory sentence provisions in s 2,[3] it is irrelevant that those earlier convictions become 'spent' for the purposes of the Rehabilitation of Offenders Act 1974.

---

1 See para **2.36**.

2 See general annotations.

3 See para **2.12**.

2.38   A 'Class A drug trafficking offence' is defined by s 2(5). This provides that:

'Class A drug' has the same meaning as in the Misuse of Drugs Act 1971;[1] 'Drug trafficking offence' means a drug trafficking offence within the meaning of the Drug Trafficking Act 1994, Proceeds of Crime (Scotland) Act 1995 or the Proceeds of Crime (Northern Ireland) Order 1996.[1]

---

1 See annotations to s 2. By s 7(1), equivalent offences under service law amount to a 'Class A drug trafficking offence'.

2.39   The effect of these provisions is to target the mandatory minimum sentence provision in a way that goes beyond offenders recognised as 'dealers in hard drugs'. In respect of such persons, sentences of between 12 and 20 years are not uncommon. However, the terms of s 4 and s 5 of the Misuse of Drugs Act 1971 are extremely wide. A person commits an offence under s 4 by supplying or offering to supply a controlled drug to another. 'Supply' includes 'distributing',[1] but does not require any proof of payment or reward. Such an offence can be tried summarily, with a maximum term of imprisonment of six months, but, at the other end of the spectrum, if tried on indictment attract a possible punishment of life imprisonment.

A person commits an offence under s 5 by possessing a controlled drug with intent to supply. Such an offence can also be tried summarily, with a similar maximum term of imprisonment, and again, the potential for a life term if tried on indictment. Thus if a 19-year-old, who has twice been convicted of possession of small quantities of ecstasy to share, for pleasure with his friends, in respect of which he has elicited financial contributions from his friends, buys two ecstasy tablets, one for himself and one for his friend, he commits a third Class A drug trafficking offence and is subject to the minimum sentence provision in s 7, subject only to the court being able to conclude, under s 3(2)(b),[2] that such a sentence would be unjust in all the circumstances.

---

1 1971 Act, s 37(1)).
2 See para **2.42**.

2.40 The conviction for the earlier offence may have been by a court in Scotland or Northern Ireland, provided the offence falls within the relevant definition of the Scottish or Northern Irish offences, as defined by the sources set out in s 3(5). Clearly, the last such offence must have been committed in England and Wales, because s 3 does not apply to Scotland or Northern Ireland, and an offence committed in Scotland or Northern Ireland will be tried there.

Proof of the earlier conviction

2.41 The terms of s 6 were noted in para **2.24**, in the context of the mandatory life sentence provisions of s 2. Section 6 applies equally in respect of s 3. By s 6(1), where:

(a) on any date after the commencement of s 6 a person is convicted in England and Wales of, inter alia, a Class A drug trafficking offence;[1] and
(b) the court by or before which he is so convicted states in open court that he has been convicted of such an offence on that date; and
(c) that court subsequently certifies that fact,

the certificate shall be evidence, for the purposes of s 3 that he was convicted of such an offence on that date.

Further, such a certificate which certifies a statement in open court that the offence was committed on a particular day or over, or at some time during, a particular period, will similarly be evidence of such matters (s 6(2)).

The issues identified earlier[2] about the limits of s 6 apply equally in the context of s 3.

---

1 See annotations to s 2 and para **2.24**.
2 See para **2.24**.

The exception

2.42   Section 3(2) creates an exception to the general obligation to impose a minimum term of seven years. A court need not impose such a sentence if it is of the opinion that there are specific circumstances relating to any of the offences or to the offender which would make the prescribed custodial sentence unjust in all the circumstances. If it is of that opinion, it shall state so in open court, and state what the specific circumstances are (s 3(3)). In determining whether it would be appropriate not to impose a term of seven years, the court shall have regard to the specific circumstances relating to either of the offences or to the offender, and which would make the seven-year prescribed term unjust (s 1(3)). Unlike the case in respect of s 2, the circumstances do not have to be 'exceptional'.

2.43   The meaning of 'specific' both in s 1(3) and s 3(3) is unclear, but this word appears to be intended to limit the meaning of the expression 'unjust in all the circumstances'. What is unclear is the extent and effect of that limitation. 'Specific' means, presumably, 'identifiable', although the Minister of State, Baroness Blatch, was struggling to ascribe a meaning to this word.[1] It is difficult to envisage the difference between 'specific' and non-specific circumstances. Insofar as any meaning is discernible, arguably it requires a court to focus on the particular case, not upon the nature of the offence in the abstract.

Nor is the meaning of 'unjust in all the circumstances' particularly clear, although it is beyond doubt that it confers a discretion on the court. It appears to permit the sentencing judge to impose whatever penalty is in fact just, thus in effect negating the whole purpose of the mandatory minimum sentence. This phraseology resulted from the House of Lords, at Committee stage, accepting amendments, against the Government's wishes, amendments that survived because of the Government's desire to obtain parliamentary approval for the Bill prior to the dissolution of Parliament in March 1997. The Home Secretary, Michael Howard, described the changes as 'driving a coach and horses' through the provisions dealing with drug dealers and persistent burglars.[2] Certainly there would appear to be force in this conclusion. After all, it is clearly the case that judges have always imposed the sentences they considered 'just', where permitted to do so by Parliament. Lord Bingham CJ indicated, in relation to a virtually identical provision, that: 'We shall be back to the present position', a conclusion accepted as correct by Mr Howard.[3]

However, arguably, s 3 must mean something more. The effect of s 3 may well be that there has been created a presumption that a term of seven years is to be regarded as, in the general run of things, the appropriate minimum tariff.

1 See para **2.25**.
2 HC Consideration of Lords' Amendments, col 982.
3 Ibid.

Mental illness

2.44   It was noted that, in the context of s 2, an offender's mental state did not, of itself, usually amount to exceptional circumstances.[1] The different wording in s 3(2) may lead to a different conclusion, it patently not being just to impose a term of imprisonment in circumstances where an order under the Mental Health Act 1983 is more appropriate. However, the same conclusion can be reached by an application of the specific terms of the new Act. Paragraph 12(2) of Sch 4 to the new Act creates a new s 37(1A) of the Mental Health Act 1983. This provides that nothing in s 3(2) or s 4(2) of the new Act shall prevent a court from making a hospital order under s 37(1) of the 1983 Act. Thus, a hospital order may be made instead of the imposition of a minimum term of seven years under s 3(2) of the new Act. This was the clear intention of the Government.[2]

Further, in addition to the imposition of a term of imprisonment, the sentencing court may make a hospital direction order under s 45A of the new Act.[3]

1 See para **2.31**.
2 Baroness Blatch, Minister of State, Home Office, HL Reports, col 826.
3 See para **6.9**.

Credit for not guilty plea

2.45   Credit may be given for a timely plea of guilty, pursuant to s 48 of the Criminal Justice and Public Order Act 1994. Schedule 4, para 17, to the new Act amends s 48 by providing that nothing in s 3(2) or s 4(2) of the new Act prevents a court from imposing any sentence which is not less than 80 per cent of that specified in those sections. Therefore, credit can be given up as considered appropriate by the sentencing court, provided the minimum term is not less than 67.2 months. In reality, because courts do not generally sentence in parts of months the maximum discount off the minimum sentence is rather less than 20 per cent.

Although there is no hard-and-fast rule, the courts have generally regarded a discount of one-third as appropriate.[1] Clearly, the scope for discount in the context of s 3 is more narrow than that permitted generally by the courts, and significant attempts were made, unsuccessfully, to persuade the Government to bring the provisions of the new law into line with current practices of the courts. There is, however, no rule that restricts the court from awarding a discount greater than 20 per cent, on a sentence that is in fact greater than seven years, provided the effect of the discount is not to reduce the length of the sentence to lower than seven years less 20 per cent.[2]

---

1 See Lord Taylor CJ in *Buffrey* (1993) 14 Cr App R (S) 511 (CA). The discount may be
substantially reduced if the offender is a person from whom the public require protection,
although, even then, some credit should be given: *Stabler* (1984) 6 Cr App R (S) 129 (CA);
Pennington (1995) 16 Cr App R (S) 409 (CA).
2 Baroness Blatch, HL Report, col 843.

Consequential procedural change – mode of trial

2.46   Where a Class A drug trafficking offence would be triable either way, and
the circumstances are such that that person could, if convicted, be sentenced to
a minimum term of seven years under s 3(2), that offence shall be triable only
on indictment (s 3(4)). For that reason, where a person charged with such an
offence is before a magistrates' court in mode of trial proceedings, the court
will need to satisfy itself that the pre-conditions set out in s 3(1) do not apply.

MINIMUM SENTENCE FOR DOMESTIC BURGLARY

The minimum sentence

2.47   Section 4 introduces a scheme of minimum term sentences in respect of
certain offences of domestic burglary. That scheme is similar to that already
discussed in respect of Class A drug trafficking offences albeit with important
differences. Many of the general issues that have already been discussed apply
equally to this provision, modified appropriately to take account of the
different terms of s 4.

Where the pre-conditions contained in s 4(1) are satisfied, a court must impose
a custodial term of least three years unless the court is of the opinion that there
are specific circumstances relating to either of the offences or to the offender
and which would make the prescribed custodial sentence unjust in all the
circumstances (s 4(2)). In relation to a person under 21,[1] a custodial sentence
means a sentence of detention in a young offender institution (s 3(6)). In
either case, credit can be given for a guilty plea by virtue of s 48 of the Criminal
Justice and Public Order Act 1994. Section 55 of, and Sch 4, para 17 to, the new
Act amend s 48 of the 1994 Act, to permit the making of a reduction under s 48
of up to 20 per cent of the otherwise appropriate sentence.[2]

---

1 See general annotations.
2 See para **2.45**.

2.48   The mandatory minimum sentence applies in respect of a domestic
burglary committed after the commencement of s 4(1). This may not occur
until after the commencement of Pt II, Ch I, relating to length of sentence, and
may not happen until at least October 1999, if at all. However, s 26(2), which
deals with the length of sentence to be imposed, and requires a court to impose
a term of two-thirds of the term which would have been imposed immediately

prior to the commencement of Pt II, Ch I, states specifically that s 26(1) is to be subject to s 4(2). The minimum term of three years is therefore equivalent to a term of 4½ years imposed before the coming into operation of Pt II.

2.49   Current sentencing policy for burglary serves only to demonstrate that the nature of the crime varies considerably in seriousness. The relevant principles were reviewed by Lord Taylor CJ in *Brewster*,[1] where he observed:

(1)   burglary of a dwellinghouse, occupied or unoccupied,[2] was not necessarily and in all cases an offence of such seriousness that a non-custodial sentence could not be justified;

(2)   the decision whether or not to impose a non-custodial sentence depended on the aggravating and mitigating factors and, usually, to a lesser extent, the personal circumstances of the offender. Thus in one of the cases before the court, *H(R)*,[1] the personal circumstances of the offender were 'tragic', he having become addicted to crack cocaine. Although drug addiction was not of itself mitigation if the motive for the burglary was drug-related, in an exceptional case a non-custodial supervision order could be justified. *H(R)* was such a case;

(3)   the court generally should reflect the abhorrence with which the public regarded those who burgle the houses of others.

At one end of the spectrum, burglary might involve an impulsive act in stealing an object of little value, reaching through a window to take a bottle of milk or stealing a can of petrol from an outhouse. At the other extreme, it might involve a planned organisation directed at objects of high value, or be deliberately aimed at the elderly, infirm or disabled. It might be accompanied by vandalism. Offenders may, on occasion, lack premeditation or deliberation. On the other hand, a pattern of repeat offending might exist. In short, the circumstances of the crime could vary infinitely, and sentences would reflect that. In the cases before the court sentences ranging from nine years to a non-custodial supervision were approved by the court.

---

1   A conjoined appeal in the cases of *Brewster, Thorpe, Ishmail, Blanchard, Woodhouse, H(R)* (1997) *The Times*, 4 July.
2   Cf *Edwards, Brandy* (1996) *The Times*, 1 July.

2.50   Section 4 should also be viewed in the context of statistics which show that the average custodial sentence for burglary on a first-time offender is 16 months, which rises after some seven or more convictions to some 19 months. The 1995 Criminal Statistics[1] show that even in cases where the offender pleaded guilty, the average length of sentence was 23 months, and that an immediate term of imprisonment was imposed in only 72 per cent of cases.[2] In the magistrates' court, 61 per cent of offenders with seven or more convictions for burglary are not sent to prison at all. Some argue that these figures serve to prove the need for the mandatory minimum sentence, others that the new provisions will result in disproportionate sentences.

1 (HMSO, 1995).
2 Ibid, p 154, para 7.36, Table 7D.

The pre-conditions

2.51 Section 4(2) applies where the pre-conditions in s 4(1) are satisfied. These are as follows:

(a) a person is convicted of a domestic burglary committed after the commencement of s 4;

(b) at the time when that burglary was committed, the offender was 18 or over[1] and had been convicted in England and Wales[1] of two other domestic burglaries; and

(c) one of those other burglaries was committed after he had been convicted of the other, and both of them were committed after the commencement of s 4.

The offence for which the offender is being sentenced must have been committed when the offender was 18 or over. The fact that he is 18 at the time of sentence is irrelevant if he was under 18 at the time of commission of the offence. Further, he must at the time of commission have already have been convicted in England and Wales[1] of two other domestic burglaries. Again, these two or more convictions must already exist at the time of commission of the last offence; the fact that they had already been committed is irrelevant if the offender had not been sentenced. Thus, s 4(2) does not apply if the offender is sentenced for two other burglaries after commission of the last offence, or is sentenced for those two offences at the same time as for the last offence.

1 See general annotations.

2.52 The two earlier domestic burglaries must have been committed after the commencement of s 4, and on different occasions. In particular, the second offence must have been committed after the offender had been convicted of the first offence. Section 4(1) therefore requires domestic burglaries on at least three separate occasions. The convictions for the two earlier domestic burglaries must be on at least three separate occasions. The age condition relates to the age of the offender as at the date of the commission of the third domestic burglary. The convictions for the earlier offences may have occurred at an age below 18. The fact that the offender may have been a juvenile is irrelevant.

The age of the previous convictions is irrelevant, save to the extent described above. In particular, the fact that such convictions fall within the terms of the Rehabilitation of Offenders Act 1974 is irrelevant.[1]

1 See para **2.12**.

2.53 If the relevant earlier convictions for domestic burglary are quashed, notice of appeal against the mandatory sentence imposed under s 4 may be given within 28 days from the date of that quashing (s 5(1)). This will apply not only where all of the earlier burglary convictions are quashed but in respect of any of them that have been counted for the purposes of determining whether the mandatory minimum sentence under s 4 should be imposed.

2.54 The term 'domestic burglary' is defined by s 2(5) as meaning a burglary committed in respect of a building or part of a building which is a dwelling.[1] The term 'dwelling' is a wide one, and includes not only the particular part of a building lived in but also other parts of that building. Thus, the burglary of a garden shed attached to a house, and the theft therefrom of a can of petrol, garden tools or lawnmower will each be a domestic burglary. So too will the stealing of a pint of milk from inside a storm porch, because there will have been entry for the purposes of the law of burglary.[2] However, arguably, the simple taking of a bottle of milk from an open porch, or the taking of newspapers from a letterbox does not amount to a burglary. A 'domestic burglary' may amount to one or more offences within the generic classification, 'burglary'. In particular, it can amount to aggravated burglary. Although the new Act does not explicitly say so, it is inconceivable that such a variant of the basic offence is excluded. Such a conclusion would be absurd, and nothing in s 4 demands such a conclusion. The minimum sentence provision therefore applies to all variants of the burglary offence that involve burglary of a dwelling.

---

1 By s 7(1), equivalent offences under service law amount to a 'domestic burglary'.
2 *Collins* [1973] QB 100 (CA).

Proof of the earlier convictions

2.55 By s 6(1), where:

(a) on any date after the commencement of s 6 a person is convicted in England and Wales[1] of, inter alia, a domestic burglary; and

(b) the court by or before which he is so convicted states in open court that he has been convicted of such an offence on that date; and

(c) that court subsequently certifies that fact,

the certificate shall be evidence, for the purposes of s 4 that he was convicted of such an offence on that date.

Further, such a certificate which certifies a statement in open court that the offence was committed on a particular day or over, or at some time during, a particular period, will similarly be evidence of such matters (s 6(2)).

Such a certificate is not conclusive proof and the issues identified in para **2.12** relating to the proof of the fact of conviction apply equally to proof under s 6 of a conviction for the purposes of s 4.

---

1 See general annotations.

The exception

2.56 Section 4(2) creates an exception to the obligation it places on a sentencing court to impose a minimum term of imprisonment of three years. It need not impose such a term if it is of the opinion that there are specific circumstances relating to any of the offences or to the offender which would make the prescribed custodial sentence unjust in all the circumstances. If it is of that opinion, it shall state so in open court, and state what the specific circumstances are (s 4(3)). In determining whether it would be appropriate not to impose a term of three years, the court shall have regard to the specific circumstances relating to either of the offences or to the offender, and which would make the three-year prescribed term unjust (s 1(3)). Unlike the case in respect of s 2, the circumstances do not have to be exceptional.

2.57 The uncertain meaning of the term 'specific' both in s 1(3) and s 4(3) has already been noted.[1] As was argued in the context of s 3, it requires a court to focus on the particular case, not upon the nature of the offence in the abstract.

Nor is the application of the 'unjust in all the circumstances' test particularly clear. It appears to permit the sentencing judge to impose whatever penalty is in fact just, and thus would appear in one sense to negate the whole purpose of the mandatory minimum sentence. The factors considered relevant in the context of s 3 apply equally here.[2] However, the fact that s 4 has been enacted, even with a broader exemption than that originally proposed by the Government, arguably creates a presumption that the period of three years is to be regarded as the 'tariff'.

---

1 See para **2.25**.
2 See para **2.43**.

2.58 The three-year term may be reduced by up to 20 per cent of a plea of guilty. The reasons for that, and the effect of that provision, was considered at paras **2.45** and **2.47**.

Consequential procedural change – mode of trial

2.59 Where a domestic burglary would be triable either way, and the circumstances are such that that person could, if convicted, be sentenced to a minimum term of three years under s 3(2), that offence shall be triable only on indictment (s 4(4)). For that reason, where a person charged with such an offence is before a magistrates' court in mode of trial proceedings, the court will need to satisfy itself that the pre-conditions set out in s 4(1) do not apply.

Chapter 3

DETERMINATE SENTENCES – LENGTH, EARLY RELEASE AND POST-RELEASE SUPERVISION

The existing regime – transitional arrangements – length of sentence to be served – credit for time on remand – early release – additional days – supervision after release

INTRODUCTION

3.1　Chapter I of Pt II of the new Act introduces a new scheme for determining the length of time in respect of a sentence of imprisonment which is to be served. It also introduces new early release arrangements, some six years after the passage of the Criminal Justice Act 1991, which itself effected a radical change in the law. Sections 33 to 51 of that Act are repealed by s 56(2) of, and Sch 6 to, the new Act, although transitional arrangements have the effect of continuing in effect most of those provisions in respect of sentences to which Ch I does not apply (s 56(1) and Sch 5).[1] The new Act contains provisions relating to supervision after release from custody.[2]

1　See para **3.11**.
2　See para **3.38**.

Commencement

3.2　The provisions of Ch I will come into effect on such date as the Home Secretary may by order appoint (s 57(2)). No such commencement order had been made as at the date of going to press, and it is unlikely that Ch I will be brought into effect, if at all, before 1999, because of the effect it will have on the size of the prison population and the need, potentially, to make additional prison space available. In the various provisions in Ch I, the term 'prisoner' is used. Section 8(2) states that the word 'prisoner' means any person who is sentenced to imprisonment for a term in respect of an offence committed after the commencement of Pt II. As a result, there will be a considerable period of time after commencement, stretching over a period of many years, during which two distinct sets of provisions will be in operation. The 1991 Act will apply in respect of pre-commencement offences (irrespective of the date of conviction) and the new Act will apply in respect of post-commencement offences. It is even possible to envisage cases where an offender is being sentenced at the same time for two offences to which different early release regimes apply. To deal with such cases, transitional arrangements are introduced by s 56 and Sch 5.[1] The calculation of sentence length and operation of the release provisions have not in the past proved easy.[2] The two-system approach may well serve to compound those difficulties.

1 See para **3.11**.
2 See the case-law cited at para **3.18**.

Background – the existing regime

3.3 The present arrangements for early release of persons serving determinate sentences are contained in Pt II of the Criminal Justice Act 1991. Section 33 of that Act distinguishes between a 'short-term' and a 'long-term' prisoner. The former is defined by s 33(5) of the 1991 Act as a person serving a sentence of imprisonment for a term of less than four years, the latter as a person serving a term of imprisonment of four years or more. The length of a sentence is to be calculated by aggregating terms of imprisonment which are consecutive, in whole or in part, the overall total of the consecutive elements being regarded as a single term (1991 Act, s 51(2)).

3.4 The basic rules contained in s 33(1) of the 1991 Act are as follows:

(a) A short-term prisoner is released unconditionally after having served one-half of his sentence, in the case of a term of imprisonment of less than 12 months (1991 Act, s 33(1)(a)). A prisoner sentenced to nine months thus serves 4½ months prior to release.

(b) A prisoner sentenced to a term of at least 12 months but less than four years is released automatically on licence (automatic conditional release) after one-half of his sentence, this licence extending in duration until the expiration of three-quarters of the sentence (1991 Act, s 33(1)(b), s 37(1)(a)). A prisoner sentenced to three years imprisonment thus serves 18 months, is on licence for a further nine months, and at liberty unconditionally for a further three months. He remains subject to potential return to prison if convicted of a further imprisonable offence during the remaining period of the total sentence (1991 Act, s 40(1)), or for breach of the terms of the licence (1991 Act, s 38(1)).

(c) A prisoner sentenced to four years or more becomes eligible for conditional release after serving one-half of his sentence (discretionary conditional release) (1991 Act, s 35(1)). This discretionary conditional release is dependent on a recommendation for release by the Parole Board, and, if granted, extends until the expiration of three-quarters of the sentence (1991 Act, s 37(1)). If the prisoner is refused discretionary conditional release on licence, automatic conditional release occurs at the two-thirds point, the licence expiring at the three-quarters point. A prisoner sentenced to a term of six years must thus serve a minimum of three years before release. He may then be granted discretionary release, but in any event must be granted automatic conditional release after four years. Any release becomes unconditional after four years, six months. The prisoner may be returned to prison if convicted of a further imprisonable offence during the remaining period of the total sentence (1991 Act, s 40(1)), or if revocation of the licence is recommended by the Parole Board, or is expedient in the public interest (s 39(1), (2)).

(d) Special rules apply in respect of young offenders (1991 Act, s 43), sexual offenders (1991 Act, s 44), fine defaulters and contemptors (1991 Act, s 45), persons liable to removal from the UK[1] (1991 Act, s 46) and persons extradited to the UK[1] (1991 Act, s 47).

(e) The calculation of sentence length can take into account remand time (1991 Act, s 41) and additional days for disciplinary offences (1991 Act, s 42).

---

1 See general annotations.

Rationale for change

3.5   The stated objective of the changes made by Pt II, Ch I, of the new Act is to achieve 'greater transparency' to the sentencing process.[1] The then Government considered that offenders sentenced to custody should serve the full term ordered by the court, so that the offender, and the public, know that, broadly, the sentence imposed is that which will be served.[2] Its intention was that limited exceptions to this principle should exist, through early release provisions intended to reward prisoners for good behaviour and co-operation.

These changes have been introduced despite the fact that the pre-existing regime had itself only been introduced in 1991. As already noted,[3] that system, based on the recommendations of the Carlisle Report[4] was based on a system of early release, usually on licence, with the supervision of offenders other than those who are serving a term of imprisonment of less than 12 months. The 'time served' did not necessarily correspond with the sentence imposed. Thus, a person sentenced to a term of two years would, under the 1991 Act regime serve 12 months, six months more than an offender sentenced to a term of 12 months, who would have served six months.

---

1 Mr Michael Howard, MP, QC, Home Secretary, 4 November 1996.
2 White Paper, op cit, para 9.6, p 44.
3 See para **3.4**.
4 *The Parole System in England and Wales* (HMSO, 1988) Cm 532. See also *Crime, Justice and Protecting the Public* (HMSO, 1990) Cm 965.

Length of sentence

3.6   The Government considered the pre-existing arrangements to be 'complicated'.[1] In many cases, offenders would serve only 50 per cent of the term imposed. As a result, the White Paper concluded: 'the public, and sometimes even the courts, are frequently confused and increasingly cynical about what prison sentences actually mean'. The scheme, as originally proposed, was based on the principle that prisoners should serve the whole of the term imposed, subject to a maximum of six days per month being earned for good behaviour during sentences of less than three years. These earned days could be taken away as punishment for offences against prison discipline. New supervision arrangements for offenders sentenced to 12 months or more, and representing 15 per cent of the term originally imposed (or three months, whichever was greater) were proposed. This scheme has, in principle, been enacted by Ch I of Pt II of the new Act, albeit with some changes in the detail.

---

1 White Paper, op cit, para 9.3.

3.7 In the absence of any specific provision the effect of the changes made by the new Act would be to significantly increase the length of time actually served by prisoners as part of their sentence. It was calculated that, in the absence of provisions to reduce sentence length, the effect of the provisions as originally proposed in the Government White Paper would be to increase the prison population by some 24,000 prisoners.[1] This is not the intention of Parliament. To avoid this result, s 26 contains provisions intended to ensure that approximately the same time in prison is served by a person sentenced to a term of imprisonment in respect of an offence:

(a)   to which s 26 applies; and
(b)   which is committed after the commencement of Ch I (s 26(1)).

Section 26 applies to any offence other than one:

(a)   which did not subsist, or was not punishable with imprisonment, immediately prior to the commencement of Ch I; or
(b)   for which the maximum sentence of imprisonment that may be imposed has been varied after commencement (s 26(3)).

Where s 26 does apply, then, subject to s 3(2) and s 4(2) of the new Act (minimum terms of imprisonment),[2] the sentencing court shall impose a term which is equal to two-thirds of the term which, at that time, it would have considered to be appropriate if the offence had been committed immediately prior to commencement (s 26(2)).

---

1 Penal Affairs Consortium – Sentencing and Early Release: The Home Secretary's Proposals (Penal Affairs Consortium, 1995).
2 See paras **2.33–2.59**.

3.8 Such an approach is not novel. A similar situation potentially arose when the early release provisions of the Criminal Justice Act 1991 were introduced. As a result, Lord Taylor CJ issued a Practice Direction[1] stressing the necessity for a judge, when passing a custodial sentence in the Crown Court, to have regard to the actual period likely to be served and to the potential that an offender could serve substantially longer periods in custody under that new scheme compared with the then prevailing scheme. This exhortation did not appear to have had any apparent effect in reducing sentencing levels.

The wording of what is now s 26 was a matter of controversy during the passage of the new Act, with the Government substantially revising the drafting of s 26 in an attempt to achieve clarity of meaning. The exercise judges are required to undertake by s 26(2) is to calculate what sentence it would have imposed immediately prior to commencement, and then reduce that sentence by one-third. It is not entirely clear whether the arithmetic has to be exact; but such a conclusion is unlikely given the odd mathematical products that would arise. For instance, a pre-commencement sentence of five years reduces to three years four months. Courts may well avoid the problem by the pitching of the starting point for the calculation at a convenient number, divisible by three! More worryingly, on a literal interpretation of s 26 the effect could be to effectively freeze sentence levels at pre-commencement levels. The appropriate tariff will be that applied by the courts at commencement, unless the maximum punishment has been altered by statute after commencement (s 26(3)). This is not, in its absolute form, to be regarded as the intention of parliament.[2] It is clear that s 26(2) should be read in the context of the general statement of intent contained in s 26(1), namely that lengths of periods of custody are not to increase simply because of the changes to the early release provisions. One possible approach would be to construe s 26(2) as requiring a sentence to be two-thirds of the length that sentencing policy would otherwise justify, from time to time. This conclusion accords with parliamentary intent[2] and, although the words 'at that time' give no support for such an approach, it is clear that the courts should adopt a purposive approach, not creating potential absurdity by a literal reading of s 26(2). No doubt the problem can be resolved in practice in the light of the relative flexibility of sentence tariffs.

---

1 *Practice Statement (Crime: Sentencing)* [1992] 2 WLR 948.
2 Baroness Blatch, HL Report, col 801.

3.9 Equally open to criticism is the detailed application of s 26. It applies only in respect of offences *committed* after the commencement of Ch I, and not in respect of offences in respect of which the prisoner is sentenced after commencement but which were committed before. It is quite possible to envisage an accused being sentenced for virtually identical offences committed over a period of time, with some being pre-commencement and some post-commencement. These seemingly identical offences may attract significantly different periods of custody. Of course, the period of time actually served should, approximately, be the same, because of the different rules to be applied, but nevertheless such a situation does little to create credibility and an acceptance of the principle that sentencing is clear and open.

Application of Part I, Chapter I

3.10 The new provisions apply to those serving determinate sentences in respect of offences committed after the commencement of Ch I. It applies to a 'prisoner', defined as any person who is sentenced to imprisonment for a term in respect of an offence committed after the commencement of Ch I (s 8(2)). The expression 'sentence of imprisonment' includes an activated suspended sentence (s 9(8)), but does not include a committal of imprisonment for default of payment of any sum of money (s 27(1)). Nor does it include committal for want of sufficient distress to satisfy any sum of money, or for failure to do, or abstain from doing, anything required to be done or left undone (s 27(1)).

Section 19 deals with the application of Ch I to young offenders. A 'sentence of imprisonment' includes detention in a young offenders institution and to a determinate sentence under the Children and Young Persons Act 1933, s 53. The provisions of s 9 (periods of detention on remand) also apply to those who are liable to serve a secure training order (s 19(3)).

TRANSITIONAL ARRANGEMENTS

3.11 Section 56(1) and Sch 5 make transitional provision in respect of offences committed before the commencement of Ch I. Schedule 5, para 1, continues in force certain provisions of the Criminal Justice Act 1991, in respect of persons sentenced to determinate sentences of imprisonment committed before the commencement of Ch I. The provisions which continue in force in this way are ss 33, 35 to 47, 49 to 51 and 65, subject to certain amendments made by Sch 5. The effect of this is that the pre-existing early release and supervision regime continues in force in respect of pre-commencement offences.

No problem arises where all the offences for which the prisoner is sentenced occurred pre-commencement, or, indeed, if they all occurred post-commencement. However, transitional arrangements are needed to deal with situations where there are sentences, either concurrent or consecutive, in respect of offences which were committed both before and after the commencement of Ch I. Those transitional arrangements are contained in Sch 5, and are discussed at paras **3.12–3.15**. The effect of them is shown, in summary, in Table 1, below.

Table 1: Summary of transitional arrangements under Schedule 5

	Length	*Credit for days on remand*	*Release*	*Licence*	*Source*
Consecutive sentences for offences before and after commencement	Length of sentence determined by appropriate rules for each sentence	Against sentence for offence for which on remand – no double counting	After time for final sentence	Under rules applicable to final sentence Length under Ch I, aggregating sentence length CJA 1991, s 35 does not apply	Sch 5, para 2
Concurrent sentences for offences before and after commencement	Length of each sentence determined by appropriate rules for each sentence	Against sentence for offence for which on remand – no double counting	After time for final sentence	Under rules applicable to final sentence	Sch 5, para 3

Consecutive sentences for offences committed before and after that commencement

3.12 Where such consecutive terms are imposed, Sch 5, para 2, applies. The time to be served in respect of each sentence is calculated by whichever set of rules is applicable to that offence, ie under the provisions contained in the 1991 Act in respect of the pre-commencement offence or offences, and under the provisions of Ch I in respect of post-commencement offences (para 2(2)). The prisoner is released when he has served the 'final sentence' (para 2(5)).

Which sentence is the 'final sentence' for this purpose must be judged from time to time, and means, at any given time, the sentence which at that time falls to be served after the other or others (para 2(8)). In determining this, regard must be had to the relevant early release arrangements: in the case of a pre-commencement offence the rules set out in para **3.4** will, with one exception, apply. In the case of a post-commencement offence, the length of detention will be calculated under the new scheme. The one exception to this is that s 35 of the 1991 Act (discretionary conditional release for long-term prisoners) does not apply unless that sentence is the 'final sentence' (para 2(4)). Clearly, it would be absurd for the Home Secretary to agree to the release of such a prisoner when that prisoner has, in fact, longer to serve in respect of other offences.

The actual length of the term to be served for each offence will take into account days on remand. On release the offender may be subject to licence provisions. Whether this is in fact so will depend on the rules that apply to the 'final sentence' (para 2(6)). If no licence provisions apply in respect of release for the final offence, then there is no question of licence after release irrespective of whether licence conditions might have applied in respect of other offences had one of them constituted that 'final sentence'. However, irrespective of which regime applies, the length of the supervision period is to be calculated as if each of the terms of imprisonment were imposed for post-commencement offences (para 2(7)). In short, the provisions of the 1991 Act may determine whether supervision occurs, but, if it does, the length of that supervision period is to be determined under s 16 of the new Act.

3.13 The effect of the above provision can be demonstrated by three examples

EXAMPLE 1

X is sentenced to nine months for a pre-commencement offence (A). He will serve, for that offence, 4½ months. For an identical post-commencement offence (B), he is sentenced to a consecutive term of six months (application of s 26).[1] The length of time to be served for offence B is determined by the new rules, and, assuming best behaviour leading to the award of early release days (s 11),[2] is likely to be approximately five months, 24 days. The total time served will be approximately 10 months, nine days.

EXAMPLE 2

X is sentenced to three years for a pre-commencement offence (A). He will serve, for that offence, 18 months then being released on automatic conditional release.[3] For an identical post-commencement offence (B), he is sentenced to a consecutive term of two years (application of s 26).[2] The length of time to be served for offence B is determined by the new rules, and, assuming best behaviour leading to the award of early release days (s 11), is likely to amount to approximately 20 months. The total time served thus will be approximately three years, two months. When released, X will be subject to a release supervision order of 15 months, this being 25 per cent of the aggregate of the two terms of imprisonment (s 16(2)(a), s 27(2)), and governed by the provisions of s 16 and s 17.[4]

If X had spent three months on remand in custody in respect of both offences, and the court makes a direction that such days shall count as part of the sentence (s 9(1)),[5] those days count against the sentence for offence B. The length of period of custody for offence B will thus be approximately 17 months.

EXAMPLE 3

X is sentenced to four years for a pre-commencement office (A). He will serve, for that offence, 28 months before being entitled to automatic conditional release for that offence.[3] For an identical post-commencement offence (B), he is sentenced to a consecutive term of 28 months (application of s 26).[1] The length of time to be served for offence B is determined by the new rules, and, assuming best behaviour leading to the award of early release days (s 11), is likely to be approximately 23 months five days. The 'final sentence' will be offence B. When released, X will be subject to a release supervision order of 19 months, being 25 per cent of the aggregate of the two sentences (s 16(2)(a) s 27(2)), and governed by the provisions of s 16 and s 17.[4]

If X had spent three months on remand in custody in respect of both offences, and the court makes a direction that such days shall count as part of the sentence (s 9(1)),[5] those days count against the sentence for offence B. The length of the sentence for offence B will thus be 25 months.

---

1 See para **3.7**.
2 See para **3.27**.
3 See para **3.3**.
4 See para **3.38**.
5 See para **5.21**.

Concurrent sentences for offences committed before and after commencement

3.14 Where concurrent terms are imposed, Sch 5, para 3, applies. The period of time to be served in respect of each sentence is calculated by whichever set of rules is applicable to that offence, ie the 1991 Act in respect of the pre-commencement offence or offences, and Ch I in respect of post-commencement offences (para 3(2)). The prisoner is released when he has served the 'final sentence' (para 3(4)). The term 'final sentence' is defined by para 3(8). In this context,[1] for the purposes of the concurrent sentence rules, it means, in relation to any time, the sentence which at that time will have the later or latest release date, making certain assumptions. These assumptions are as follows:

(a)   the time to be served in respect of a post-commencement offence is equal to the term imposed by the court less the number of days (if any) directed by the court to count as time served as part of the sentence (under s 9); and

(b)   the time to be served in respect of a pre-commencement offence is equal to the appropriate proportion of the term imposed by the court less any period by which the sentence falls to be reduced under s 67 of the Criminal Justice Act 1967. The 'appropriate proportion' is one-half in the case of a term of less than four years and two-thirds in respect of a term of four years or more. Section 67 of the 1967 Act provides that the length of any custodial sentence is treated as reduced by any period during which the offender was in custody solely because of a court order concerned with the proceedings relating to the sentence (ie on remand).[2]

In determining which sentence is the 'final sentence', regard must be had to the relevant early release arrangements. In the case of a pre-commencement offence, the rules set out in para **3.4** will apply. In the case of a post-commencement offence, the length of the period of detention will be calculated under the rules contained in the new Act. Thus, in making the calculation as to the later or latest release date, regard will have to be given to days awarded for good behaviour, awarded in respect of each assessment period.[3] Thus a post-commencement office may initially be the 'final sentence', and be governed by the new Act, but as time passes and early release days are awarded having the effect of shortening the period of detention under that term, such a sentence may in fact cease to be the 'final sentence'.

Regard must also be had to additional days awarded to the offender. However, provisional additional days[4] awarded are to be had regard to only for the purposes of the post-commencement offence and not under sentence length calculation under the 1991 Act (para 3(3)).

---

1   See para **3.11**, for its meaning in a different context.
2   See para **3.18**.
3   See para **3.27**.
4   See para **3.32**.

3.15   On release, the offender may be subject to licence provisions. Whether this is so will depend on which set of rules apply to the 'final sentence' (Sch 5, para 5(5)). If no licence provisions apply in respect of the position on release for the final offence, then there is no question of licence after release irrespective of whether licence conditions might have applied in respect of the sentences for other offences, if any of them had constituted the 'final sentence'. However, irrespective of which regime applies, the length of the period of supervision is to be calculated as if each of the terms of imprisonment were imposed for post-commencement offences (para 3(6)). In short, the 1991 Act may require a period of supervision, but the length of that period of supervision is to be determined under s 16 of the new Act, in accordance with the length of the longer or longest sentence (s 27(2)).

3.16   The effect of the above again can be demonstrated by three examples:

EXAMPLE 1
X is sentenced to nine months for a pre-commencement offence (A). He will serve, for that offence, 4½ months. For an identical post-commencement offence (B) he is sentenced to a concurrent term of six months (application of s 26).[1] The length of time to be served for offence B is determined by the new rules, and, assuming best behaviour leading to the award of early release days (s 11),[2] is likely to be approximately five months, 24 days, which will therefore be the period served.

EXAMPLE 2
X is sentenced to three years for a pre-commencement offence (A). He would serve, for that offence, 18 months before being eligible for automatic conditional release.[3] For an identical post-commencement offence (B) he is sentenced to a concurrent term of two years (application of s 26).[1] The length of time to be served for offence B is determined by the new rules, and, assuming best behaviour leading to the award of early release days (s 11),[2] is likely to be approximately 20 months, which will therefore be the period served. The total time served will be approximately three years, two months. When released, X will be subject to a release supervision order of nine months, this being 25 per cent of the longer of the two terms of imprisonment (s 16(2)(a), s 27(2)), and governed by the provisions of s 16 and s 17.[4]

If X had spent three months on remand in custody in respect of both offences, and the court makes a direction that such days shall count as part of the sentence (s 9(1)),[5] those days count against the sentence for offence B, or against offence A, but not both. The question then arises as to which is the final sentence. Offence A has a release date some 15 months after sentence (one-half of three years less three months) (para 3(8)). The sentence for offence B is reduced to approximately 17 months, and is thus always the final sentence.

EXAMPLE 3
X is sentenced to four years for a pre-commencement offence (A). He would serve, for that offence, 28 months before being entitled to automatic conditional release[3] for that offence. For an identical post-commencement offence (B), he is sentenced to a concurrent term of 28 months (application of s 26).[1] The length of time to be served for offence B is determined by the new rules, and, assuming best behaviour leading to the award of early release days (s 11),[2] is likely to be approximately 23 months five days. The 'final sentence' will be offence B. When released, X will be subject to a release supervision order of 12 months, being 25 per cent of the longer of the two sentences (s 16(2)(a) s 27(2)), and governed by the provisions of s 16 and s 17.[4] If X had spent three months on remand in custody in respect of both offences, and the court makes a direction that such days shall count as part of the sentence (s 9(1)),[5] those

days count against the sentence for offence B, or against offence A, but not both. The question then arises as to which is the final sentence. Offence A has a release date some 29 months after sentence (two-thirds of four years less three months) (para 3(8)). Offence A will always be the final sentence, and thus the release date will be calculated by reference to the rules applicable to that sentence (para 3(2), (4)). The terms of para 3(8) require an assumption to be made for determining which is the 'final sentence' not sentence length.[6] X is entitled to automatic conditional release after 28 months.

---

1 See para **3.7**.
2 See para **3.27**.
3 See para **3.3**.
4 See para **3.38**.
5 See para **3.21**.
6 See para **3.15**.

LENGTH OF SENTENCE TO BE SERVED

3.17 A legal right to release arises when the prisoner has served his sentence (s 8(1)). The term 'prisoner' means any person who is sentenced to imprisonment for a term in respect of an offence committed after the commencement of Ch I (s 8(2)). Chapter I does not apply to offences committed prior to commencement. The transitional arrangements as to how the period of custody served is to be calculated are set out in Sch 5, and discussed at paras **3.11–3.16**.

In determining the length of a term of imprisonment, consecutive terms and terms which are wholly or partly concurrent are to be treated as a single term (s 27(2)), subject only to the one exception contained in s 27(4) relating to extended periods of supervision.[1] The principle of treating terms of imprisonment as one single term is not, of course, new, s 27(2) broadly replicating the terms of s 51(2) of the 1991 Act.[2] In this context, references to terms of imprisonment are to the terms of imprisonment imposed by the court, not to the periods of time actually served under such terms. This principle was explicitly stated by s 67 of the Criminal Justice Act 1967, not only in respect of enactments passed before the commencement of the 1967 Act but also in respect of those which are passed thereafter. This put beyond any doubt the meaning of the equivalent words in s 51(2) of the 1991 Act. Section 67 of the 1967 Act has now been repealed (s 56(2) and Sch 6), but the principle is surely beyond real doubt and unaffected by this repeal.

The length of time served in respect of any term of imprisonment may be shortened by credit being given for periods of remand in custody (s 9), by the award of early release days for good behaviour (s 11), by early release on the recommendation of the Parole Broad (s 12) or by compassionate early release (s 10). Conversely, the time actually served (but not the length of the sentence) may be increased by the award of additional days for disciplinary offences (s 14).

1 See para **3.39**.
2 Section 51(2) of the 1991 Act states:

> 'For the purposes of any reference in this Part, however expressed, to the term of imprisonment to which a person has been sentenced or which, or part of which, he has served, consecutive terms and terms which are wholly or partly concurrent shall be treated as a single term.'

Credit for periods of remand in custody

3.18   The position regarding the credit which is to be given for periods spent in custody prior to sentence has been a confusing one. Under pre-existing law, periods of time spent on remand are automatically credited to the prisoner, and thus a lengthy period spent on remand may lead to the immediate release of that offender, or, at any rate, a substantial reduction in the period of time served after sentence. However, in a series of cases[1] the courts grappled with how this principle should be applied in the context of consecutive and concurrent terms. The relevant statutory provision governing pre-existing law is s 67 of the Criminal Justice Act 1967.

Section 67(1) of the Criminal Justice Act 1967[2] stated that the length of any sentence of imprisonment imposed on an offender by a court shall be reduced by any relevant period. The expression 'relevant period' was defined, by s 67(2), as meaning:

(a)   any period during which the offender was in police detention in connection with the offence for which the sentence was passed; or
(b)   any period during which he was in custody:
    (i)   by reason only of having been committed to custody of an order of a court made in connection with any proceedings relating to that sentence or the offence for which it was passed or any proceedings from which those proceedings arose; or
    (ii)   by reason of his having been so committed and having been concurrently detailed otherwise than by order of a court.

Clearly, credit is to be given in respect of a period of remand in custody for an offence when the offender is being sentenced for that offence. Problems have arisen, however, where an offender is sentenced for more than one offence. The principle that different terms shall be treated as a single term has already been noted.[3] Section 51(2) of the 1991 Act states that. Further, s 104(2) of the 1967 Act, provides that any references to the:

> 'term of imprisonment or other detention to which a person has been sentenced or which, or part of which he has served, consecutive terms which are wholly or partly concurrent shall be treated as a single sentence.'

Section 104(2) remains in force despite the enactment of s 51(2) of the 1991 Act, a fact overlooked in some of the subsequent case-law. It also survives the passage of the new Act.

1 See para **3.19**.
2 As amended by the Police and Criminal Evidence Act 1984, s 49.
3 See para **3.17**.

3.19 These statutory provisions were considered in a series of four cases.[1] Each was concerned with a prisoner who had been sentenced to concurrent terms of imprisonment. In each of those cases, the courts concluded that the intention of s 67 of the 1967 Act was to link the periods of time spent in custody to particular sentences for particular offences (ie the periods spent in custody or remand should be deducted from each of the particular sentences to which these periods relate before calculating the release date by reference to the total sentence). The court in those cases rejected the 'aggregate' approach, namely, the aggregation of the periods in custody on remand, the release date being calculated by deducting that total aggregate from the sentence length.

1 *Governor of Blundleston Prison, ex parte Gaffney* [1982] 2 All ER 492, [1982] 1 WLR 696 (DC); *Secretary of State for the Home Office, ex parte Read* (1987) 9 Cr App R (S) 206 (DC); *Governor of HM Prison Styall, ex parte Mooney* [1996] 1 Cr App R (S) 74 (DC); *Secretary of State for the Home Department, ex parte Woodward and Wilson* (24 June 1996, unreported) (DC).

3.20 This position was the subject of significant criticism in two decisions in 1996. In *Secretary of State for the Home Department, ex parte Naughton*,[1] a Divisional Court considered whether, in respect of consecutive terms of imprisonment, periods of time spent on remand in respect of two separate offences should be deducted from each sentence, or whether they should be aggregated and deducted from the total sentence. The court concluded that the words 'sentence of imprisonment' in s 104(2) were, like the expression 'term of imprisonment', to be construed as referring to the aggregate of any consecutive sentences imposed at the same trial on the offender. The periods of time spent on remand were thus to be aggregated. This conclusion was reached by rejecting as absurd the approach to the interpretation of s 67 which would have required the deduction from the period to be served under each consecutive sentence of the period spent on remand for each offence. However, to reach that conclusion the Divisional Court felt bound to cast doubt on the line of authority described above.

In *Governor of Brockhill Prison, ex parte Evans* (and the companion case *Governor of Onley Young Offender Institution, Rugby, ex parte Reid*),[2] the Divisional Court considered the different situation where the sentences were concurrent rather than consecutive. It concluded that where a defendant spent time in custody on remand awaiting trial for more than one offence, and, on conviction, was sentenced to more than one term of imprisonment, to be served concurrently, the period of the sentence is to be reduced by the total period of time that the defendant spent in custody before being sentenced, not merely the period of time spent on remand in respect of the offence for which the longest sentence was passed, or which would expire last. However, any such remand period cannot be taken into account more than once, nor can any period of time during which the defendant was in custody for some reason unrelated to the offences for which he was sentenced be taken into account for the purposes of calculation of sentence length. The court distinguished *ex parte Naughton* as correct on its facts, but cast doubt as to whether the conclusion in that case that the earlier authorities were wrong was itself necessary for the decision that that court had in fact reached in respect of consecutive sentences. The court, in *ex parte Evans*, concluded that s 51(2) of the 1991 Act and s 104(2) of the 1967 Act focused attention on the overall term, thus making it inconsistent to adopt a particular approach. For that reason, it adopted the aggregate approach described at para **3.19** and disapproved of the earlier case-law.

---

1 [1997] 1 All ER 426.
2 Both reported at [1997] 1 All ER 439.

3.21 The position in respect of credit for periods in custody is now to be governed by s 9 of the new Act. Section 9 extends to detention in custody not only in prison but, as before in police detention (s 9(9), (10)). Credit for periods of time spent in custody prior to sentence may be given under s 9, even if the offender:

(a) has also been remanded in custody in connection with other offences; or
(b) has also been detained in respect of other matters (s 9(2)).

Section 67 of the Criminal Justice Act 1967 is repealed by s 56(2) and Sch 6. Curiously, s 67 of the 1967 Act is not preserved by the transitional arrangements for pre-commencement offences in Sch 5, para 1. At first sight, therefore, the basis for the award credit for periods in custody for pre-commencement offences simply does not exist.

The explanation as to the position in respect of pre-commencement offences may lie in the terms of Sch 5, para 4. The terms of this provision are themselves baffling. Schedule 5, para 4 to the new Act states that, in relation to any time between the commencement of s 9 and the commencement of Ch I, ss 34, 41 and 47 of the 1991 Act shall have effect as if any reference (however expressed) to a relevant period by which a sentence falls to be reduced under s 67 of the 1967 Act were a reference to a number of days directed under s 9 of the new Act to count as time served as part of a sentence. Two observations can be made. The first is as to how any period of time can arise between the commencement of s 9 and the commencement of Pt II, Ch I. Section 9 is part of Ch I. If the Chapter is not brought into effect, s 9 does not apply. Secondly, even if para 4 is construed as meaning 'the commencement of other parts of Chapter I' (presupposing that different commencement days are set), the problem remains. None of the provisions of the 1991 Act actually authorise the giving of credit for remand days. In particular, s 41 of the 1991 Act merely requires days credited under s 67 of the 1967 Act to count for the purposes of determining the proportion of sentence that has been served. Clearly, it was not the intention of Parliament in passing the new Act to deny credit for periods in custody in respect of pre-commencement offences, but this is apparently what, by a sidewind, has been achieved. It remains to be seen how the courts will justify a conclusion that is clearly correct, namely, that, in respect of pre-commencement offences credit should be given for periods of time on remand.

3.22 Section 9(1) defines the circumstances in which the provisions of s 9 are to apply. It applies to where:

(a)   a court sentences an offender to imprisonment for a term in respect of an offence committed after the commencement of s 9; and

(b)   the offender has been remanded in custody in connection with the offence or for a related offence, that is to say, any other offence the charge for which was founded on the same facts or evidence.

Subject to the exceptions contained in s 9(4), the sentencing court shall direct that the number of days for which the offender was remanded in custody in connection with an offence or a related offence shall count as time served by him as part of the sentence (s 9(3)). The reason for the new arrangement, requiring the giving of a direction, is based on the concept of transparency in sentencing. The White Paper[1] explained that 'offenders sentenced to a term of imprisonment can sometimes be released after a very short time – or even walk out of the court straight away – because of the time they have already spent in custody on remand, without this being apparent when the sentence is announced in court'.

Despite the seemingly clear words of s 9(3) that the direction shall specify the number of days spent on remand, in fact a court may give a direction in respect of a lesser number of days than the length of the actual period of remand if the test in s 9(4)(b) is satisfied. This is not explicitly stated, but clearly flows from the terms of s 9(5)(b), and from those of s 9(6), which speaks of a 'number of days less than that for which the offender was remanded in custody ...'. In giving a direction, the court must state in open court the number of days for which the offender was remanded in custody, and the number of days in relation to which the direction is given (s 9(5)).

---

1 Op cit, para 9.7.

3.23   Section 9(4) empowers a court not to give a direction:

(a)   to give effect to regulations made by the Home Secretary in respect of custody wholly or partly concurrent with a term of imprisonment, or in respect of sentences of imprisonment which are consecutive or wholly or partly concurrent; or

(b)   where in the opinion of the court it is just in all the circumstances not to give a direction.

The power not to give a direction contained in s 9(4)(a) clearly addresses the issue of whether credit should be given for periods of time spent on remand concurrent with the service of a term of imprisonment for other offences. The wording of s 9(4) is such that the presumption will be that such a period can potentially count, for otherwise there would be no need for s 9(4) to be framed in the form of an exception to the general rule. The exception, if there is one in this context, will be contained in rules made by the Home Secretary. No such rules had been made as at the date of going to press.

The power in s 9(4)(b) sets out the criteria on which the decision not to give a direction or, by implication from s 9(6), a decision to award a lesser number of days is to be based. These criteria apply equally to a direction of a lesser number of days (s 9(6)). The reason for the failure to give a direction, or for a direction for a lesser number of days, must be stated in open court (s 9(6)).[1]

---

1 See annotations to s 3.

3.24 The question remains as to the extent to which the new Act overcomes the issues relating to concurrent and consecutive sentences, and periods spent on remand, raised by the case-law discussed earlier.[1] Section 9(3) of the new Act requires a court to make a direction in respect of time served as part of the 'sentence', subject only to s 9(4). Although a 'term of imprisonment' is defined by s 24(2), the term 'sentence' is not defined. The 'sentence' is to be 'imprisonment for a term in respect of an offence' (s 9(1)(a)). Section 27(2) states that for the purposes of any references in Ch I, however expressed, to the term of imprisonment to which a person has or could be sentenced, consecutive terms and terms which are wholly or partly concurrent shall be treated as a single term. As already noted, this, in effect, replicates s 51 of the 1991 Act, and s 104(2) of the 1967 Act. This latter provision is not, in fact, repealed and remains in place. The key issue is the meaning, in s 9(3) of the word 'offence'. This is expressed in the singular, and therefore suggests that, in respect of each offence, the court should direct how many days on remand should count. The singular of any word in a statute includes the plural, unless a contrary intention appears from the context.[2] It is submitted that a no such contrary intention is evident from s 9. In s 9(1)(b), the expression 'related offence' is used in a way that may fit other charges for which the offender is being sentenced at the same time. In the context of s 67(1A) of the 1967 Act the singular 'offence' was held to include the plural.[3] Arguably, a court is required, under s 9(3) to state the total period to be spent on remand, and to be deducted from the time to be served, such a period to be calculated in accordance with the aggregate approach identified at para **3.19**, and approved in *ex parte Evans*.

---

1 See paras **3.19–3.20**.
2 Interpretation Act 1978, s 6.
3 *Governor of Brockhill Prison, ex parte Evans* [1997] 1 All ER 439 at 453.

3.25 Section 13 contains complex provisions designed to ensure that early release days can be earned, provisionally, during periods on remand. Thus an offender can not only gain credit for the time on remand, but, during that period, earn early release days. This is dealt with at para **3.32**.

EARLY RELEASE

3.26 Despite the desire of the Government to ensure that, broadly, the period of time served is that to which the offender is sentenced, the term of imprisonment imposed by the sentence court will not, generally, be that actually served. Like the 1991 Act before it, the new Act, in ss 10–13, creates a scheme for early release, although the intention is that the period actually served should correspond more closely with that actually awarded. Early release can be based on compassionate grounds. By s 10, the Home Secretary may at any time release a prisoner if he is satisfied that exceptional circumstances exist which justify the prisoner's release. In such cases involving prisoners serving a term of three years or more there is a duty to consult the Parole Board, unless the circumstances are such as to render consultation impracticable (s 10(2)).

The provisions of s 10 replicate the repealed s 36 of the 1991 Act, and no new principles or issues are involved.

Early release days for terms less than three years

3.27 A prisoner who is serving a term of imprisonment of more than two months and less than three years may be awarded early release days for good behaviour (s 11(1), (2)). Such days may be earned in respect of periods of time calculated by reference to an 'assessment period'.

What constitutes an 'assessment period' is dealt with by s 11(9). This subsection defines 'assessment period' as meaning:

(a) the period of two months beginning with the day on which the prisoner is sentenced; and

(b) each successive period of two months ending before his release.

Section 11(9) also defines the phrase 'initial assessment period' as meaning an assessment period beginning less than 12 months after the day on which he was sentenced. Thus, every period of two months during the first 12 months of the sentence will amount to an 'initial assessment period' and such periods thereafter will be 'subsequent assessment periods'.

3.28 It is intended that a prisoner can earn a number of early release days in each assessment period, up to a specified maximum. The prisoner will do so through good behaviour and compliance with the prison regime. In order to implement this regime, the Home Secretary is authorised, by s 11(6), to make prison rules[1] which may:

(a) require determinations as to early release days to be made at prescribed times, and to be notified to the prisoners concerned in the prescribed manner; and

(b) make provision for enabling prisoners to appeal against such determinations to prescribed persons.

This provision is framed in permissive, non-mandatory terms, but clearly the discretion that exists is as to *what* rules are made, not whether such rules should be made. The whole scheme of legislation in Ch I presupposes that a scheme of early release will exist and, self-evidently, that requires a detailed scheme to be put in place. Who will be the 'prescribed person' for these purposes will be one of the matters of detail to be dealt with in those prison rules. The concept of the award of additional days is not new,[2] and therefore the converse arrangement (ie the award of early release days) is a change in approach but not novel in concept.

1 By statutory instrument (s 27(5)).
2 See Criminal Justice Act 1991, s 42.

3.29 What number of days, if any, are awarded for each assessment period will be determined by the prescribed person in the light of the extent to which the prisoner's behaviour has attained the 'prescribed minimum standard' (s 11(2), (3)). That standard will likewise be specified in prison rules, but the intention of the Government was expressed in its White Paper which stated[1] that 'attainment' will be demonstrated by showing co-operation, and those who can show positive good behaviour, including hard work and diligent and effective compliance with prison programmes related to their offending behaviour, will be likely to be judged to have exceeded that standard.

The prescribed person may make the following awards:

(a)   for each initial assessment period, such number of days not exceeding 12 as he may determine having regard to the extent to which the prisoner's behaviour during that period has attained the prescribed minimum standard (s 11(2));

(b)   for each subsequent assessment period, the prescribed person may award the prisoner such number of days, not exceeding six, as he may determine having regard to the extent to which the prisoner's behaviour during that period has attained the prescribed minimum standard (s 11(3)(a)), and such number of days, not exceeding six, as he may determine having regard to the extent to which the prisoner's behaviour has exceeded that standard (s 11(3)(b)).

Although s 11 does not explicity say so, there is no provision in the Act which authorises the taking away of days which the prisoner has earned. However, the prisoner may be awarded additional days to add to the period to be served. That is dealt with at para **3.36**.

The effect of s 11(3) is that early release days may be awarded which amount to a maximum (but theoretical) potential remission of sentence of 20 per cent of sentence. In reality, the percentage is less because of the on-going process leading to early release.[2] Because the time served is reduced by the number of early release days earned and credited (s 11(5)), the theoretical number of assessment periods during which such days can be earned is reduced.

1 Op cit, para 9.9, p 45.
2 Ibid, para 9.6.

3.30 The physical effect of these rules can be seen from the following example.

EXAMPLE

A prisoner serving a term of two years will, assuming best behaviour, have accumulted 120 early release days after serving 20 months (ie 12 days per assessment period × 10 assessment periods). The actual period of time to be served is reduced by that amount and the prisoner will have completed, or almost completed, the period of imprisonment. The reduction amounts to approximately 16 per cent of the term imposed.

3.31 Various matters of detail are dealt with by s 11. No entitlement to early release arises before the day after that on which an award is made (s 11(5)). Further, in some situations assumptions are made that such days have been earned.

The first such assumption is in respect of a case where a determinate sentence of three years or more, or a life sentence, has been imposed but is set aside or varied on appeal. In that situation, if the sentence that ultimately results is one to which s 11 applies (ie is less than three years), the prescribed person is required to assume that the maximum number of early release days has been earned by the prisoner (s 11(3)).

The second assumption relates to young offenders. Where the prisoner is:

(a)   under 16;[1] or
(b)   detained in local authority accommodation, or a home provided by the Home Secretary under s 82(5) of the Children Act 1989,[2]

the prescribed person is required to assume that the prisoner's behaviour had been such as to entitle him to the maximum number of early release days available under s 11 (s 19(4)).

Other assumptions arise in the context of the award of provisional early release days. These are dealt with at paras **3.32–3.33**.

---

1 See general annotations.
2 See annotations to s 19.

Provisional early release days

3.32 Special provisions are contained in s 13 relating to the earning, provisionally, of early release days during periods on remand for offences alleged to have been committed after the commencement of Ch I, and in respect of such offences which the person on remand is liable to imprisonment for more than two months. In such cases, the assessment period is calculated differently. It is assumed that the assessment period began on the day the prisoner was remanded in custody, that he had been convicted on that date and sentenced to a term of imprisonment of more than two months and less than three years, and that the relevant period is not two months but 60 days (s 13(2)). In the calculation of the period of 60 days, days when the accused was not on remand in custody are disregarded (s 13(2)(b)).

If the court which sentences the offender for a term of imprisonment of more than two months but less than three years in respect of the offence, or a related offence, and that court makes a direction under s 9(3) (credit for periods in custody), the court may make an award of provisional early release days (s 13(3), (8)). A 'related offence' is any other offence the charge for which was founded on the same facts or evidence (s 9(1)(b)).

Each of these conditions must be satisfied, in the light of the wording of s 13(3) which uses the expression 'if, and only if, each of the following conditions is fulfilled'. However, it should be borne in mind that in reality there is a further pre-condition. Section 13 only applies if the court makes a s 9 direction (s 13(3)(c)). A court may only make a s 9 direction if the pre-conditions contained in s 9(1) are satisfied. Thus, in addition to the conditions explicitly stated in s 13(3), the further condition exists that the offender must be sentenced to a term of imprisonment in respect of an offence committed after the commencement of s 9 (s 9(1)).

3.33 The effect is that the period of a sentence of imprisonment actually served will be reduced not only by the days on remand specified in the s 9 order but also by such additional days earned whilst on remand. Such days are provisionally awarded for each assessment period (as defined by s 11(3) and s 13(2)). Obviously, they cannot be formally awarded until there is a sentence of imprisonment against which they can count. Thus, the days are deemed to be awarded on the day the direction under s 9 is made. Clearly, however, the possibility exists that a court, in making a s 9 direction, may direct that only some of the days spent on remand should attract credit. It would be odd if, nevertheless, the prisoner was entitled to full credit for the early release days provisionally awarded. It is to deal with that situation that s 13(6)(a) provides that the prisoner should be entitled to the appropriate proportion of those days. 'Appropriate proportion' is defined by s 13(8) as the proportion which the number of days in relation to which the direction under s 9 is given bears to the number of days for which the accused was remanded in custody. The resulting product is rounded up to the nearest day (s 13(6)).

Thus, if credit was only given under s 9 for 90 out of 180 days spent on remand, then the prisoner will be entitled to credit for only 18 out of the 36 early release days (50 per cent of 12 × three assessment periods of 60 days).

The provisions of s 13 also address the question as to what credit should be given for periods spent, not in prison, but in police detention. The prisoner is deemed to have been in prison, and it is assumed that his behaviour had attained, but not exceeded, the prescribed minimum standard (s 13(7)). The prisoner in police detention is not disadvantaged by this assumption, because the assumption made is that the prisoner has fully complied with the standard applicable for full award of such days during the first 12 months of a sentence.[1]

---

1 See para **3.29**.

Early release for prisoners sentenced to at least three years

3.34 In respect of a prisoner serving a determinate term of imprisonment of three years or more, s 12 applies. As soon as the prisoner has served five-sixths of his sentence, the Secretary of State shall, if recommended to do so by the Parole Board, release him. That release is subject to the release supervision order arrangements contained in s 16. This arrangement replaces the provisions relating to long-term prisoners contained in s 33 and s 35 of the 1991

Act. Under that provision, it was possible for the Home Secretary to release such a prisoner after one half of his sentence (s 35(1)), on the recommendation of the Parole Board, and he was obliged to release the prisoner conditionally after two-thirds of that sentence. Thus, an offender who was sentenced to a term of six years, could be released after three years, and was entitled to be released after four years. The equivalent sentence under the new Act would be four years (s 26(1)). The prisoner would be eligible to be released, on the recommendation of the Parole Board, after five-sixths of that term, ie after three years four months, and entitled to be released after four years.

3.35   The new early release provisions relating to prisoners sentenced to three years or more mark a change of heart by the Government. The White Paper did not propose any such arrangement for this section of the prison population, it being firmly based on the concept that the offender should, broadly, serve the term to which he is sentenced. However, second thoughts by the Government led to the introduction of s 12 during the passage of the Act through Parliament, it recognising that such provision was necessary to ensure that the prison population was not increased beyond levels considered to be manageable.

Additional days

3.36   Section 42 of the 1991 Act made provision for the award of additional days for disciplinary offences under the prison rules.[1] Where such additional days were awarded, the length of time to be served by the prisoner was thereby increased. However, such days did not increase the total length of the sentence, but merely extended the period of time within that sentence which was to be served. On release at the half-sentence stage, together with the additional days, the prisoner was then subject to the normal period of licence.

That remains the position under the new Act. Section 42 of the 1991 Act is replaced by the provisions of s 14 of the new Act. Section 14(3) makes it clear that such additional days cannot have the effect of extending the period of detention beyond the end of the prisoner's sentence. At the end of the period of detention, the offender may then be subject to a release supervision order under s 16. Nothing in s 14 prevents that order being for the normal period under that provision: the period of supervision is not reduced by the additional time served.

---

1 See annotations to s 11.

3.37   Just as early release days could be earned provisionally during a period of remand in custody, so too with additional days. This, too, is not new in concept. Section 42(1)(b) of the 1991 Act stated that provision might be made for the award of additional days conditionally on their subsequently becoming such prisoners, to persons on remand. The new Act deals with the point in s 15, which applies where an accused is remanded in custody in connection with one or more offences:

(a)   which are alleged to have been committed after the commencement of Ch I; and

(b)   in respect of which he would be liable, if convicted, to a life sentence or to a term of imprisonment for a term of more than two months (s 15(1)).

Where an accused is so remanded in custody the prison rules made by virtue of s 15(2) have effect as if the accused had been convicted, and sentenced to a term of more than two months on the day he was remanded in custody (s 15(2)). Additional days may be awarded provisionally.

The effect of that provisional award depends on whether the pre-conditions in s 15(3) are satisfied. If they are, the days provisionally awarded are treated as having been awarded on the day a s 9 direction is made (ie the day of sentence). The pre-conditions for the award of additional days provisionally awarded are to be found in s 15(3), and are as follows:

(a)   the offender is convicted of the offence, or any of the offences;

(b)   he is sentenced to imprisonment for a term more than two months; and

(c)   a direction has been given under s 9 of the new Act (crediting periods of remand in custody).

If no direction under s 9 has been made, there is no basis for confirming the award of provisional additional days: clearly, if the remand period itself does not count towards the period to be served under the sentence ultimately imposed, there is no justification for the award of additional days. If, by contrast, a s 9 direction is given for period of days less than the period spent on remand, the proportion of the additional days provisionally awarded that will actually be treated as actually awarded should be the same as the proportion of the remand period directed to count towards sentence bears to the total remand period. Thus, if a court makes a direction that 50 per cent of remand time shall count towards sentence, then 50 per cent of the provisionally awarded additional days are deemed actually to have been awarded on the day the s 9 direction was given (s 15(5)).

However, this is subject to the proviso that those days cannot extend the period to be served beyond the end of the prisoner's sentence (s 14(3)). Whatever his behaviour, a prisoner serving a determinate sentence of two years cannot be detained for longer than two years.

SUPERVISION AFTER RELEASE

3.38   Sections 16 to 18 of the new Act introduce a new scheme for supervision after release. The licence provisions of the 1991 Act were summarised at para **3.4**, but will not apply to cases to which s 16 of the new Act applies. It is intended that supervision resources should be concentrated on those whose need for supervision is greatest. Under the provisions of the 1991 Act a 'short term prisoner' was automatically released on licence after one half of sentence, the licence extending until the expiration of three-quarters of the term of imprisonment.[1] In respect of long-term prisoners, discretionary licence arose at the one-half stage, extending to, again, three-quarters term.[2] The new provisions potentially have the effect of shortening the supervision period generally, but impose potentially longer periods on sex offenders or violent offenders.

---

1 See para **3.4**.
2 Ibid.

3.39 Section 16 operates where one of the following paragraphs of s 16(1) applies:

(a) an offender who has been sentenced to imprisonment for a term of 12 months or more in respect of an offence committed after the commencement of Ch I is released otherwise than under the compassionate release provisions of s 10;

(b) an offender who has been so sentenced is released under s 10; or

(c) an offender who has been sentenced to imprisonment for a term of less than 12 months in respect of an offence committed after the commencement of Ch I is released.

On release in one of these sets of circumstances set out above the offender will be subject to a release supervision order. One exception to that is in respect of an offender who is liable to removal from the UK (s 24(1)(b)). In such a case, it is for the Home Secretary's discretion as to whether the offender is subject to such an order. The other exception to the general rule is in respect of persons committed to prison for fine default or for contempt of court (s 23).

The length of that order is determined in accordance with the provisions of s 16(2), subject to special provisions dealing with length which are contained in s 19(6) (young offenders), s 20(2) (sexual offenders) and s 21(2) (violent offenders). In particular, in the case of violent or sexual offenders, the terms of s 27(4) should be noted, if that offender is subject to concurrent or consecutive terms.

For convenience, a summary of the effect of these provisions is contained in Table 2, below, the detailed provisions, and their effect, being discussed at paras **3.41–3.47**. The effect of a release supervision order is prescribed by s 16(2)–(7) and ss 17–19. Such an order, made by the Home Secretary, provides that the offender shall be under the supervision of a probation officer, and shall comply with such conditions as are specified (s 16(3)).

3.40 Table 2 – Length of period of supervision

Type of sentence and offence	Length of supervision	Paragraph
12 months' imprisonment or more on offender aged 22 or over (s 16(1)(a), s 19(6))	25% of term of imprisonment or 3 months (whichever greater) (s 16(2)(a))	**3.41**
Offender sentenced to 12 months' imprisonment or more and released under s 10 (s 16(1)(b))	25% of term of imprisonment or 3 months (whichever greater) + remainder of term not served because of s 10 release, taking account of early release or additional days (s 16(2)(b))	**3.41**
Offender aged 22 or over sentenced to less than 12 months imprisonment and released under s 10 (s 16(1)(c), s 19(6))	Remainder of term not served because of s 10 release, taking account of early release or additional days (s 16(2)(c))	**3.42**
Offender aged under 22 sentenced to term of imprisonment (s 16(1)(a), s 19(6)(a))	25% of term of imprisonment or 3 months (whichever greater) + remainder of term not served because of any s 10 release, taking account of early release or additional days (s 16(2))	**3.43**
Offender sentenced to term of imprisonment for a term in respect of a sexual offence committed after commencement (s 20(1))	Period of supervision specified by court under s 20(3) amounting to (a) 50% of total sentence or 12 months (whichever is longer); or (b) such longer period (not exceeding 10 years) as the court may determine under s 20(6) + remainder of term not served because of s 10 release, taking account of early release or additional days (ss 16(2), 21(2))	**3.44**
Offender sentenced to term of imprisonment for a term of 3 years or more in respect of a violent offence committed after commencement, and the court gives direction under s 21(3) (s 21(1))	Period of supervision specified by court under s 21(3) + remainder of term not served because of s 10 release, taking account of early release or additional days (ss 16(2), 21(2))	**3.46**

Length of supervision – sentence of 12 months or more

3.41 Where a person aged 22 or over is sentenced to a term of imprisonment of 12 months or more for a post-commencement offence, the length of the period of supervision is 25 per cent of the term of imprisonment (rounded up to the nearest day), or three months, whichever is greater (s 16(2)(a)). Special rules apply to violent or sexual offenders.[1] The effect of this change can be gauged by considering the case of a person convicted for burglary. Under the provisions of the 1991 Act, such a person, sentenced to two years, would have been released on licence after having served 12 months, the licence lasting for a period of six months. Under the new Act, the equivalent sentence should be 16 months (s 26).[2] The length of the period of the release supervision order will be 25 per cent, namely four months. There is thus a reduction in the supervision period.

If the offender is released earlier than the normal date for release, on compassionate grounds under s 10, the period of supervision is extended by the period of time after release that the offender would have otherwise had to have served, but for the compassionate release (s 16(2)(b)). Thus, in the example above, if the offender was released one month early, for compassionate reasons, the four-month release licence period would be extended by a further month.

---

1 See paras **3.46** and **3.44**.
2 See para **3.7**.

Length of supervision – sentence of less than 12 months

3.42 No release supervision order applies unless the offender is subject to compassionate release under s 10 (s 16(1)(a)), or is aged under 22[1] (s 19(6)(a)). If the offender, aged 22 or over, is released under s 10, the period of supervision amounts to the period of time he would otherwise have served (taking into account early release or additional days). There appears to be no minimum period of supervision. If an offender serving a term of imprisonment of six months is released after four months, on compassionate grounds, a supervision period of approximately five weeks appears to result. This is because, assuming best behaviour, the offender will have earned some 24 early release days, and he would in any event have been released after approximately five months, six days. It is difficult to conceive of any meaningful purpose such a period of supervision would serve. It would have been preferable to exclude such cases from the release supervision requirements.

---

1 See general annotations.

Length of supervision – offenders aged under 22

3.43 The effect of s 19(6) is that any such offender will be subject to a period of supervision of 25 per cent of sentence or three months, whichever is greater, irrespective of the length of sentence (s 19(6)). Despite somewhat difficult wording, this is the clear effect of the modifications made to s 16(1)(a) by s 19(6), although it must be borne in mind that the length of that supervision period may be extended by virtue of the fact that the offender is a violent or sexual offender.[1] Section 19(6) only modifies s 16(1), not the provisions of s 20 or s 21.

Thus, under the 1991 Act, such a young offender sentenced to nine months' imprisonment, or detention, would have received no supervision on release. He would not have fallen within the special arrangements contained in s 43 of the 1991 Act. That section, which deals with young offenders, does not require a supervision period in respect of a young offender serving a term of 12 months or less. Only in respect of young persons serving a term of more than 12 months does s 43(4)(b) create a power to release on licence. Under s 16 of the new Act, as amended by s 19(6), such an offender will now be subject to supervision for a period of three months (s 16(2)(a)).

---

1 See paras **3.46** and **3.44**.

Length of supervision – sexual offenders

3.44　Where an offender has been sentenced to a term of imprisonment, for a sexual offence[1] committed after the commencement of Ch I, a court may give a direction under s 20(3) that s 20 shall apply (s 20(1)). The effect of giving such a direction is to put in place a longer supervision period. In principle, this is no different from the longer period of licence that was provided for, in the case of sexual offenders, by s 43 of the 1991 Act. That section increased the licence period so that it extended from the time of release (potentially at half sentence) to the time when the whole of that sentence would have been completed. However, the potential will now exist under s 20 of the new Act to extend significantly the period of supervision beyond the time when the sentence would have been served.

The power to give such a direction arises irrespective of the length of the term of imprisonment to which the offender was sentenced, and is not confined to cases where a term of 12 months or more was imposed (s 20(2)(a)). A court is obliged to give such a direction unless it is of the opinion that exceptional circumstances exist which justify it not doing so (s 20(3)).

The effect of a direction is that the length of supervision period shall be as specified in the direction (s 20(5)). That period is specified by s 20(6), as:

(a)　a period equal to 50 per cent of the offender's term of imprisonment (rounded up to the nearest whole day) or a period of 12 months, whichever is longer; or

(b)　if the court considers a longer period necessary for the purpose of preventing the commission by the offender of further offences and of securing his rehabilitation, such longer period, not exceeding 10 years, as it may determine.

The period of supervision specified in the direction under s 20(6) may be further increased by the balance of sentence which was due to be served but for early release on compassionate grounds under s 10 (taking into account early release[2] or additional days (s 16(2))[3] (as substituted for this purpose by s 20(2)). The period of supervision is also increased by the supervision period appropriate to any part of any term of imprisonment which runs consecutively to the term in respect of which the direction under s 20 was made (s 27(4)).

---

1 See annotations to s 20.
2 See para **3.26**.
3 See para **3.36**.

3.45 The clear intention of Parliament is that a sexual offender should be subject to supervision. What amount to exceptional circumstances for the purposes of s 20(3) is unclear. The meaning of the same expression, in the different context of s 2 of the new Act, was considered at paras **2.25–2.32**. It should be noted that the qualifications 'to either of the offences or to the offender' to be found in s 2(2) are not to be found in s 20. It is not clear what, if any, the significance of this difference is. Factors which are characteristic of sexual offences or of sexual offenders ought not to be regarded as 'exceptional circumstances', for otherwise the extended supervision provisions would have little purpose. However, factors might exist which show the offender to be a person who, exceptionally, does not pose a risk or where the facts of the offence are such as to mark out the offence as different from the normal run of sexual offences. Reasons will need to be established. This is because the court, if it decides not to give a direction, shall state in open court[1] that it is of the opinion that there are exceptional circumstances which justify its not doing so, and shall state what those exceptional circumstances are (s 20(4)).

---

1 See annotations to s 3.

Length of supervision – violent offenders
3.46 Special rules apply to violent offenders. The term 'violent offence' has the same meaning as in Pt I of the Criminal Justice Act 1991 (s 21(5)).[1]

Where a term of imprisonment is imposed of less than 12 months, no release supervision order is made, unless in respect of a term of imprisonment imposed for an offence committed after commencement, the offender is released early under the compassionate release provisions of s 10 (s 16(1)). In that case, the period of supervision is the period the offender would have been liable to serve but for his early release (s 16(2)(c)).

Where the term is 12 months or more, in respect of an offence committed after commencement, the provisions of s 16(1) apply, as set out in para **3.41**. To that general rule there is, however, one exception. In respect of offenders sentenced to a term of three years or more in respect of a post-commencement offence, s 21(1) introduces, for the first time, a special power to extend the period of supervision in respect of violent, non sexual, offenders. This is part of the intended targeting of supervision resources on violent and sex offenders. Section 20(1) gives the power to a court to make a direction under s 20(3). If no direction is made, then the normal rules apply. However, if a court makes a direction, then s 21(2) modifies the effect of s 16(2). The modified s 16(2) states that a violent offender shall be subject to a release supervision order of such length as is specified in the direction, plus a further period in respect of any period the offender would have been liable to serve but for an early, compassionate, release under s 10 should that have occurred (s 16(2), as modified by s 21(2)).

The pre-condition for the making of such a direction is that the court must consider a longer release supervision period necessary for the purpose of preventing the commission by the offender of further offences and of securing his rehabilitation (s 21(3)). There appears to be no requirement of pro-portionality[2] between the nature of the offence for which the term of imprisonment was imposed and the length of the supervision period. However, the extended supervision period is for the purpose stated in s 21(3). Arguably, a disproportionate supervision period goes beyond what is necessary for that purpose, and is, perhaps, challengeable on that basis. However, it is difficult to imagine that an appeal court will readily accept an argument that an extended supervision period imposed on a violent offender, and within the limits permitted by the new Act, is excessive.

---

1 See annotations to s 11.
2 For proportionality in respect of longer than commensurate sentences under s 2(2)(b) of the 1991 Act, see para **2.3**.

3.47 The length of that supervision period shall be such period, not more than 50 per cent of the offender's term of imprisonment, as is specified in the direction (s 21(4)).

The effect of this can be gauged by comparing the position before and after the coming into operation of Ch I. In the case of an offender sentenced to six years for a violent offence committed before commencement, the offender would be eligible for release after three years, would be under conditional licence for a further 18 months, and liable to recall if convicted of further offences during the remaining 18-month period. For the same offence committed after commencement of Ch I, the appropriate sentence would be four years (s 26).[1] The offender would be eligible for release after three years, four months (s 12(6)) and potentially subject to a release supervision order of 12 months (s 16(2)(a)). However, if a court were to make a direction under s 21(1)(b), the supervision period could be for such period not exceeding two years as the court considered necessary (s 21(3)).

---

1 See para **3.7**.

The release supervision order

3.48 Such an order will be made by the Home Secretary (s 16(3)). By s 16(3), it shall provide that, throughout the release supervision period the offender, so long as he is at large:

(a)   shall be under the supervision of a probation officer; and

(b)   shall comply with such conditions as are for the time being specified in the order.

The limitations on what conditions can be specified are contained in s 16(4). The Home Secretary:

(a)   shall not specify any condition which:
    (i)   requires the offender to live in an approved probation hostel;[1] or
    (ii)   makes such provisions as is made by a curfew order,[1]
    except in accordance with recommendations of the Parole Board made after an oral hearing at which the offender had the opportunity to be heard or represented; and

(b)   in the case of an offender who has been sentenced to imprisonment for a term of three years or more, shall not specify any other condition except in accordance with recommendations of the Parole Board.

In this respect the new Act broadly mirrors the pre-existing position. Under s 37(5) of the 1991 Act, the Home Secretary could not impose conditions on the licence of a long-term or life prisoner except after consultation with the Parole Board. That equates with the provisions of s 6(4)(b) of the new Act. The new limitation is that contained in s 16(4)(a).

---

1 See annotations to s 16.

Offence – breach of conditions of release supervision order

3.49   Section 17 of the new Act creates a criminal offence, of failing, without reasonable excuse, to comply with any of the conditions of the order. It supersedes s 38(1) of the 1991 Act, which made a breach of condition of a licence imposed on a short-term prisoner an offence triable summarily. Section 38(1) did not apply in respect of long-term prisoners, nor did it contain a defence of 'reasonable excuse'. 'Long-term prisoners' are, under s 39 of the Criminal Justice Act 1991, subject to possible revocation of licence and return to prison. Further, both 'short-term' and 'long-term' prisoners are liable to return to prison if a further offence was committed during the currency of the original sentences (1991 Act, s 40). Those provisions are not replicated by the new Act, and therefore in respect of the offender who is subject to Pt II, Ch I of the new Act, the sanction for breach of licence is the offence under s 17. However, the commission of a further offence is likely to amount to a breach of the terms of the licence.

3.50   Section 17(1) states that if any offender in respect of whom a release supervision order is in force fails without reasonable excuse to comply with any of the conditions of the order, he shall be liable:

(a)   on conviction on indictment, to imprisonment for a term not exceeding the relevant period or a fine or both;

(b)   on summary conviction, to imprisonment for a term not exceeding the relevant period or a fine not exceeding level 3 on the standard scale[1] or both.

The 'relevant period' is defined by s 17(6) as:

(a)   on conviction on indictment, so much of the release supervision as falls after the day on which the offender failed to comply with the condition;

(b)   on summary conviction, so much of that period as so falls or six months, whichever is the shorter.

Special provisions apply to young offenders. In respect of a released offender, who is aged under 22 and whose sentence:

(a)   was a sentence of detention in a young offender institution, or a sentence of detention under s 53 of the Children and Young Persons Act 1933, for a term of less than 12 months; and

(b)   was not imposed in respect of a sexual offence committed after the commencement of Ch I,

the relevant period is 30 days.

---

1 See general annotations.

3.51   The offence under s 17(1) is only triable on indictment if the relevant period would be longer than six months, or the act or omission in question constitutes another offence which is punishable with imprisonment and is triable on indictment (s 17(2)). Clearly, in the latter case, in determining whether the offence under s 17(1) should be tried summarily or on indictment a court will have regard to the mode of trial that is being adopted in respect of that other offence. It would be absurd to consider trying the s 17 offence on indictment if the other offence were to be tried summarily. If the s 17(1) offence is tried summarily, and could have been tried in indictment, the magistrates' court may commit the offender, either in custody or on bail, for sentence (s 17(3)). In that case, the Crown Court may impose whatever sentence as could have been imposed if the offender had been convicted on indictment under s 17(1)(a). The question remains: can and should a court impose a custodial sentence for an offence under s 17? The offence seriousness criteria in s 1 or s 2 of the 1991 Act will not apply (s 17(5)).[1] Nor will the restrictions on the imposition of a community sentence contained in s 6 of the 1991 Act (s 17(5)). The one limitation is that contained in s 17(4). By s 17(4), a court shall not impose a sentence of imprisonment for an offence under s 17(1) unless:

(a)   it considers it expedient to do so in the interests of protecting the public from serious harm from the offender; or

(b)   the offender's failure to comply with the condition in question consisted of the commission of an offence punishable with imprisonment.

In order to facilitate the enforcement of the conditions in a release supervision order, s 18 confers a power of arrest on a constable without warrant, and s 18(2) confers a power on a magistrate to issue a warrant authorising entry to premises for the purpose of arresting a person liable to be arrested for an offence under s 17(1).

Where a person has been sentenced to a term of imprisonment for an offence under s 17, the normal rules about periods of release, and release supervision orders apply. One exception to this is where an offender under 22 years of age is sentenced to detention in a young offenders institution, or a sentence of detention under s 53 of the 1933 Act. In such cases, a release supervision order does not follow release from such detention (s 19(9)).

---

1 See para **2.14**, fn 2.

EFFECT OF THE PROVISIONS OF PART I

3.52   The following examples demonstrate the likely effect of implementation of the provisions outlined above. Each example assumes good behaviour by a prisoner, and release at the earliest date possible.

EXAMPLE 1
An adult sentenced to 12 months' imprisonment for theft prior to the 1997 Act would serve:

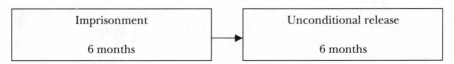

Under the new Act, the equivalent sentence is 8 months (s 26(2)) served as follows:

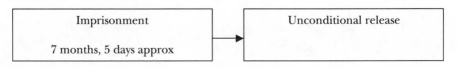

EXAMPLE 2
An adult sentenced to 4 years' imprisonment for fraud prior to the 1997 Act would serve:

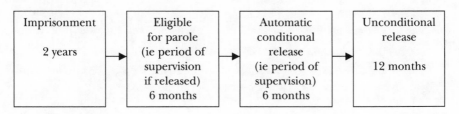

Under the 1997 Act, the equivalent sentence is 2 years, 8 months (s 26(2)) served as follows:

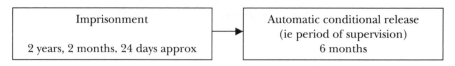

EXAMPLE 3

An adult sentenced to 6 years' imprisonment for rape prior to the 1997 Act would serve:

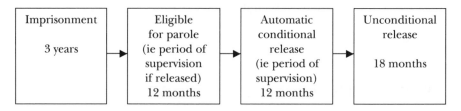

Under the 1997 Act, the equivalent sentence is 4 years served as follows:

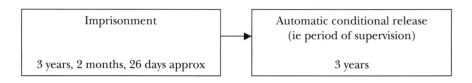

Chapter 4

LIFE SENTENCES – RELEASE ON LICENCE

Reasons for change – definition of life prisoner – the duty to release – licence and recall – transferred prisoners

INTRODUCTION

4.1   Chapter II of Pt II of the new Act deals with the release on licence of life prisoners, and is the second major legislative intervention on this issue in some six years. The pre-existing law is contained in ss 33 to 51 of the Criminal Justice Act 1991, which are repealed by the new Act (s 56(2) and Sch 6). The new Act broadly maintains the scheme for the release of life prisoners created by the 1991 Act, but with significant changes in respect of offenders aged under 18[1] serving a sentence of detention during Her Majesty's Pleasure, pursuant to s 53(1) of the Children and Young Persons Act 1933. These changes are intended to give effect to several rulings of the European Court of Human Rights,[2] in which the UK was found to be in breach of the European Convention.

Commencement

Chapter II will come into effect on such day as the Home Secretary may appoint by order (s 57(2)). No such order has been made as at the date of going to press.

---

1 See general annotations.
2 See paras **4.4–4.6**.

4.2   Where a person is convicted of murder, and is aged 21 or over,[1] a court is obliged to impose a life sentence.[2] In respect of those under 18[1] at the date of commission of an offence of murder, the appropriate order is one of detention during Her Majesty's Pleasure,[3] and, in respect of those between 18 and 20 years old,[1] the appropriate order is one of custody for life under s 8(1) of the Criminal Justice Act 1982. A life sentence imposed under s 2 of the new Act is not, for this purpose, a sentence which is fixed by law (s 2(4)).

Besides the offence of murder, for which the life sentence is mandatory, a range of other offences permit a life sentence to be imposed (hitherto known as 'discretionary life sentences').[4] The imposition of such a sentence is in accordance with principles developed by the Court of Appeal.[5] In *Hodgson*,[6] the Court of Appeal stated that a sentence of life imprisonment would be justified where three conditions were satisfied:

(a)   the offence or offences are in themselves grave enough to require a very long sentence;

(b)   it appears from the nature of the offence or from the defendant's history that he is a person of unstable character likely to commit such offences in the future; and

(c)   if the offences are committed, the consequences to others may be specially injurious.

In essence, an indeterminate sentence is being imposed so that 'the prisoner's progress may be monitored ... so that he will be kept in custody only so long as public safety may be jeopardised by his being let loose at large'.[7]

Persons sentenced to a term of imprisonment for life, irrespective of whether the sentencing court was obliged to impose that term or not, have a tariff set in relation to that period of imprisonment. This tariff represents the period it is considered that the prisoner should serve in order to satisfy the requirements of retribution and deterrence, and is calculated by reference to the term that the offender would in fact have served had he been made the subject of a determinate sentence.[8] At the end of that period the prisoner becomes eligible for release on licence, in accordance with provisions that have, hitherto, been contained in Pt II of the Criminal Justice Act 1991.[9] Under s 34(3) of the 1991 Act, the Home Secretary is under a duty to release a 'discretionary life prisoner' when he has served the part of his sentence set as the tariff by the court, pursuant to s 34(2), but then only after the Parole Board has directed his release. The Parole Board may consider a case only where, under s 34(4) the Home Secretary has referred the case to the Board. The Board may direct his release where it is satisfied that it is no longer necessary for the protection of the public that the prisoner should be so confined. A discretionary life prisoner may require the Home Secretary to refer his case to the Board at any time after the expiration of the tariff period, and, if there has been a previous reference to the Board, after the end of the period of two years beginning with the disposal of that reference.

---

1 See general annotations.
2 Murder (Abolition of Death Penalty) Act 1965, s 1(1).
3 Pursuant to Administration of Justice Act 1933, s 53(1).
4 But now see para **4.8**.
5 See, generally, para **2.8** and annotations to s 2.
6 52 Cr App R 113 (CA).
7 *Wilkinson* (1983) 5 Cr App R (S) 105, at 108.
8 Criminal Justice Act 1991, s 34. See *O'Connor* (1994) 15 Cr App R (S) 473 (CA).
9 These, in turn, superseded provisions in the Criminal Justice Act 1967.

4.3   In the case of mandatory life prisoners, different considerations apply. Section 35(2) of the 1991 Act provides that the Home Secretary may, after consultation with the Lord Chief Justice together with the trial judge if available, release on licence a life prisoner who is not a 'discretionary life prisoner'. The duty to release following a recommendation by the Parole Board does not apply in the case of a mandatory life sentence.

4.4 The 1991 Act provisions were introduced to bring the then pre-existing law into line with the requirements of the European Convention on Human Rights. In 1990, the European Court of Human Rights in *Thynne, Wilson and Gunnell v United Kingdom*[1] held that the system then in place for dealing with the release of discretionary life prisoners contravened the Convention. That Court held that once the prisoner had served the part of the life sentence attributable to retribution and deterrence he was entitled to have the remaining period of detention under judicial control. That, hitherto, had not been the case, and it was for this reason that the procedures requiring release following a recommendation by the Parole Board[1] were introduced.

The position was different in respect of those serving mandatory life sentences. The power to release offenders convicted of murder remained in the hands of the Home Secretary, 'because in their case the punishment for the offence of murder was considered to require life imprisonment which was not necessarily the case with discretionary life sentences where the sentence could be imposed because of the mental instability or the risk of further offending on the part of the defendant'.[2] That change did not extend to those detained during Her Majesty's Pleasure, which was regarded as equivalent to a mandatory life sentence in a case of murder by an adult.[3]

---

1 (1990) 13 EHRR 666 (ECHR).
2 See para **4.2**.
3 Ibid. See also *Secretary of State for the Home Department, ex parte Furber* (1997) *The Times*, 11 July (CA).

4.5 The 1991 Act radically changed the rules relating to both discretionary and mandatory life prisoners, and also introduced a new system of release on licence in respect of those serving determinate sentences.

As noted at para **4.3**, a tariff is set, indicating the period to be served to reflect the period of detention required for the purposes of deterrence and retribution. That tariff, is, in the case of a discretionary life sentence, set by the trial judge. However, different procedures apply in the case of a mandatory life sentence for murder. Since 1983, the trial judge in such a case, and the Lord Chief Justice, make a recommendation to the Home Secretary on the appropriate length of the tariff period which the offender must serve in order to meet the requirements of retribution and deterrence. The final decision on the tariff is that of the Home Secretary, who does not have to accept either of the judicial recommendations. The same procedure applies in cases where a juvenile has been convicted of murder, and sentenced to detention during Her Majesty's Pleasure. It was this that was the subject of challenge in *Venables*,[1] the trial judge recommended an eight-year tariff period, the Lord Chief Justice recommended a period of 10 years, but the Home Secretary set the tariff at

15 years. When doing so, he stated he had taken into account the judicial recommendations as well as other factors including the circumstances of the case, levels of public concern and the need to maintain confidence in the criminal justice system, a decision ultimately found to be unlawful.[2]

At the end of the tariff period, the Parole Board considers the case and makes recommendations as to whether the offender can safely be released. The Home Secretary is not obliged to accept a recommendation for release.

---

1 See *Secretary of State for Home Department, ex parte Venables; Secretary of State for Home Department, ex parte Thompson* [1997] 3 All ER 97 (HL).
2 See para **4.12**.

4.6   In February 1996, the European Court of Human Rights held in two cases, *Hussein v United Kingdom* and *Singh v United Kingdom*,[1] that the system for making release decisions at the end of the tariff period of a juvenile sentenced under s 53(1) of the Administration of Justice Act 1933, contravened Art 5(4) of the European Convention on Human Rights. The new Act is intended to bring English law into line with that ruling. It does not bring the setting of the tariff in such a case within the remit of judicial determination, despite attempts during the passage of the Act to do so,[2] and despite doubts as to whether detention during Her Majesty's Pleasure could properly be equated with a mandatory term of life imprisonment imposed on an adult.[3] The removal of the setting of the tariff from the Home Secretary was resisted by Baroness Blatch, Minister of State, on the grounds that for a judge to fix the tariff 'would downgrade the unique seriousness of the offence. It would mean that the penalty for murder committed by juveniles would operate in exactly the same way as the life sentence for those offences where it is the maximum rather than the only remedy'.[4]

---

1 (1996) 22 EHRR 1 (ECHR). See para **4.1**.
2 See, eg, Lord Meston, HL Committee, cols 818–819.
3 See para **4.12**.
4 Baroness Blatch, Minister of State, Home Office, HL Committee, cols 819–820.

4.7   Section 28 of the new Act provides for the release on licence of what have been known as 'discretionary life prisoners'.[1] Where s 28 does not apply,[2] release is governed by s 29, which replicates the terms of s 35(2) and (3) of the 1991 Act. By s 29(1), the Home Secretary may, if recommended to do so by the Parole Board and, after consultation with the Lord Chief Justice together with the trial judge if available, release on licence a life prisoner to whom s 28 does not apply. The Parole Board may not make a recommendation under s 29(1) unless the particular case, or class of case to which that case belongs, has been referred to it by the Home Secretary.

---

1 See para **4.9**.
2 Ibid.

DEFINITION OF 'LIFE PRISONER'

4.8   Part II of Ch II applies to life prisoners, who are defined by s 34(1) as persons serving one or more life sentences. The definition of life sentence effectively is unchanged: a 'life sentence' is a sentence of imprisonment for life, a sentence of detention during Her Majesty's Pleasure or for life under s 53 of the Administration of Justice Act 1933, or a sentence of custody for life under s 8 of the Criminal Justice Act 1982 (s 34(2)). This is so irrespective of whether the sentence was imposed for an offence committed before or after the commencement of Ch II.

Although the definition of 'life prisoner' and 'life sentence' remain the same, couched in different terms, the effect of Ch II is to recast the rules relating to 'mandatory' and 'discretionary' life prisoners. The latter term was specifically used by s 34 of the 1991 Act, but is not so used by the new Act. The reason for this is, no doubt, that the terms of s 28 of the new Act go beyond the pre-existing category of discretionary life prisoners to include those serving a term of detention during Her Majesty's Pleasure, and who have hitherto been equated with those serving a mandatory life term.[1] For this reason the term is not used hereafter, but, for ease of exposition, the term 'mandatory life sentence' and 'mandatory life prisoner' are used to denote cases to which s 28 does not apply and which are governed by s 29.

Part II also applies, subject to modifications, to life prisoners transferred to England and Wales (s 33). This is discussed at paras **4.20–4.23**.

---

1   But now see *Secretary of State for the Home Department, ex parte Venables; Secretary of State for the Home Department, ex parte Thompson* [1997] 3 All ER 97 (HL); *Secretary of State for the Home Department, ex parte Furber* (1997) *The Times*, 11 July 1997 (CA).

THE APPLICATION OF SECTION 28

4.9   Section 28 identifies the cases that would have, hitherto, been categorised as 'discretionary life sentences'. It is wider than the pre-existing provision in s 34(1) of the 1991 Act. Section 34 defined a discretionary life prisoner as one where the sentence was imposed for a violent or sexual offence the sentence for which is not fixed by law, and where the court by which he was sentenced for that offence ordered that s 34 should apply to him as soon as he had served a part of his sentence specified in the order. The new s 28 is not so limited to violent or sexual offences.

The pre-conditions for the operation of s 28 of the new Act are prescribed by s 28(1). The first pre-condition is that the conditions in s 28(2) apply. If that subsection is not satisfied, the second, alternative, pre-condition is contained in s 28(1)(b).

Section 28(2) is wider than its predecessor in s 31 of the 1991 Act. The conditions in s 28(2) are:

(a) that the prisoner's sentence was imposed for an offence the sentence for which is not fixed by law; and

(b) that the court by which he was sentenced for that offence ordered that s 28 should apply to him as soon as he had served a part of his sentence specified in the order.

Thus the main change in this provision is that s 28(2) does not confine the sentence to one in respect of an offence which amounted to a violent or sexual offence.[1] Subject to that, in any case where s 28(2)(a) applies, and the court has specified the tariff under s 28(2)(b), the duties and rights contained in s 28(5)–(7) apply.[2] In setting that tariff under s 28(2)(b), the court shall, by s 28(3), take into account:

(a) the seriousness of the offence, or the combination of the offence and any other offences associated with it[3] (see s 28(9)); and

(b) the effect of any direction which it would have given under s 9 of the new Act (credit for periods in custody)[4] if it had sentenced him to a term of imprisonment.

In the absence of an order under s 28(2)(b), a case will be governed by s 28(4), which provides for a direction to be made by the Home Secretary setting the tariff. However, this is not intended to confer a general power to set the tariff in non-mandatory life cases: that would run counter to the ruling of the European Court of Human Rights in *Thynne v United Kingdom,* and run counter to the intent of Parliament when passing the 1991 Act. That Act was, after all, intended to bring English law into line with the European Convention.

---

1 See annotations to s 2.
2 See para **4.14**.
3 See para **2.11**, fn 2.
4 See para **3.18**.

4.10   The second, alternative pre-condition is contained in s 28(1)(b), which is new. That pre-condition is that the prisoner was aged under 18[1] at the time when he committed the offence for which his sentence was imposed. The effect of this change is thus to bring persons detained during Her Majesty's Pleasure, pursuant to s 53 of the Administration of Justice Act 1933, within what, hitherto, were known as the discretionary life imprisonment provisions. In so providing, English law is, to this extent, being brought into line with the decision of the European Court of Human Rights in *Hussein v United Kingdom*[2] that persons serving terms of detention during Her Majesty's Pleasure should be treated, for the purposes of determining the date when release should occur after expiration of the tariff, as discretionary life prisoners, and with the same procedural rights as such prisoners. The effect of s 28(1)(b) is to achieve this.

---

1 See general annotations.
2 (1996) 22 EHRR 1 (ECHR).

4.11   Section 34(1) contains an important limitation to the broad application of s 28, a limitation that effectively replicates the terms of s 34(7) of the 1991 Act. By s 34(1)(a) of the new Act, a person serving two or more life sentences is not to be treated as a life prisoner to whom s 28 applies unless the requirements of s 28(1) are satisfied as respects each of those sentences. Thus, if not all of the life sentences fall within s 28 the duty to release which is imposed on the Home Secretary by s 28(5), and the right of the prisoner to require referral of the case to the Parole Board, conferred on that life prisoner by s 28(7), do not apply until such time as the conditions in s 28(1) are satisfied in respect of all such life sentences (s 34(1)(b)).

4.12   Where the condition in s 28(1)(b) has brought the case within the ambit of s 28, there will have been no tariff set pursuant to s 28(2)(b). It is for this reason that s 28(4) provides that, in any case where s 28 applies and the conditions in s 28(2) are not fulfilled, the Home Secretary shall direct that s 28 shall apply as soon as the life prisoner has served a part of his sentence specified in the direction. In other words, the Home Secretary sets the tariff.

It was this issue that was at the heart of one part of the judicial disagreements to be found in *Secretary of State for the Home Department, ex parte Venables* and *ex parte Thompson*.[1] The facts have already been stated.[2] In that case, the House of Lords, by a majority overturned a majority decision of the Court of Appeal[3] which itself doubted the view of a Divisional Court on the nature of the sentence, although concluding, on grounds of procedural unfairness, that the Divisional Court had been right to decide that the Home Secretary had acted unlawfully in his setting of the tariff. The Divisional Court held that a sentence of detention during Her Majesty's Pleasure should not be equated with a mandatory term of life imprisonment imposed on an adult convicted of murder, and thus the decision of the Home Secretary that such offenders should, like an adult, serve an identified penal element before their release could be considered was unlawful. The Court of Appeal, by a majority (Lord Woolf MR dissenting), by contrast considered that where an offender was sentenced to detention during Her Majesty's Pleasure under s 53(1) of the 1933 Act, or detention for life under s 53(2), he remained subject to that sentence for the rest of his natural life, and was thus in the same position as an adult offender sentenced to a mandatory life sentence. That was the case even though the conditions of detention differ. For that reason, the court held that the two cases were governed by s 35 of the 1991 Act, which dealt with the release of mandatory life prisoners, and which conferred on the Home Secretary in such case the power to set the tariff required for retribution and deterrence, but concluded that the Home Secretary had acted in a way that was procedurally unfair.

In the House of Lords, the majority of the Law Lords found that a sentence of detention during Her Majesty's Pleasure imposed on a child was not the same as a mandatory life sentence imposed on an adult, since an order of detention involved merely an authority to detain indefinitely and meant that the Home Secretary had to decide from time to time, taking into account the punitive element whether detention was still justified, whereas imprisonment for life involved an order of custody for life which meant that the Home Secretary had to consider whether release was justified. The House accepted that detention of a child carried a punitive element, but by applying a tariff scheme which took no account of the saviour and development of the child after sentence he was acting unlawfully. By a majority, the House also found that the Home Secretary had acted in a way that was procedurally unfair.

---

1 [1997] 3 All ER 97 (HL).
2 See para **4.5**.
3 [1997] 1 All ER 327 (CA).

4.13 In the light of this decision, it is far from clear that the existing law, replicated by the new Act, complies with the European Convention on Human Rights. In the original complaint by Hussein to the European Commission on Human Rights, the applicant complained of the secretive and unfair manner in which his tariff had been established. In the light of the fact that the tariff period had in fact expired, the court found it unnecessary to determine that aspect of the complaint. The ruling of the court was confined to the post-tariff position, but, in that context, the court concluded that the applicant's sentence was more comparable to a discretionary life sentence, a position echoed by Lord Woolf in his dissenting judgment in the Court of Appeal *ex parte Venables* and recognised in other case-law. Indeed, Lord Woolf MR was of the opinion that English law might not comply with the European Convention if the arguments of the Home Secretary in that case were accepted. In the view of Lord Woolf MR, and the majority of the House of Lords, a distinction exists between a mandatory life sentence, where a discretion exists to bring custody to an end, and detention during Her Majesty's Pleasure where there is a discretion to continue custody even though that may last for life. On this basis, any tariff set by the Home Secretary under s 28(4), may be open to challenge under the Convention. Whether it is challengeable in the domestic courts is more debatable. Parliament did not have the decision of the House of Lords in *Venables* before it when considering the terms of the new Act. It could be argued, that, in line with the general presumption that Parliament is presumed to intend to comply with its international obligations, it should be so construed. Against that, the words of s 28(4) are clear.

The duty to release

4.14 The Secretary of State is under a duty to release a life prisoner to whom s 28 applies once he has served the relevant part of his sentence attributable to the purposes of retribution and deterrence, and the Parole Board had directed his release (s 28(5)). The Parole Board will not consider the case unless either s 28(6) or (7) apply. Section 28(6), which replicates s 34(5) of the 1991 Act, provides that the Board shall not make such a direction unless the Secretary of State has referred the prisoner's case to the Board, and it is satisfied that it is no longer necessary for the protection of the public that the prisoner be confined. Section 28(7) is in its terms different from the pre-existing s 34(5) of the 1991 Act, the changes reflecting the new release provisions that apply in respect of determinate sentences.

Section 28(7) provides that a life prisoner to whom s 28 applies may require the Home Secretary to refer his case to the Parole Board at any time:

(a)   after he has served the relevant part of his sentence (ie the tariff period); and

(b)   where there has been a previous reference after the end of the period of two years beginning with the disposal of the reference; and

(c)   where he is also serving a determinate term, after the time when, but for his life sentence, he would be entitled to be released.

No account is taken of time during which the prisoner was unlawfully at large. As noted above, the wording of s 28(7)(c) reflects the fact that the release at half-sentence stage provisions in the 1991 Act have now been replaced by a new system of early release.

Mandatory life sentences

4.15   As noted at para **4.8**, the new Act does not use the expression 'mandatory life sentence'. Nevertheless, that term is a convenient one to use to describe the cases to which s 29 applies. Section 29 in fact applies in respect of all life prisoners to whom s 28 does not apply. It replicates s 35(2) and (3) of the 1991 Act. Any such prisoner will, if released on licence, be subject to the provisions in s 31 and s 32 in respect of licences and recall.

Compassionate release

4.16   Section 30 provides for compassionate release. By s 30(1), the Home Secretary may at any time release a life prisoner on licence if he is satisfied that exceptional circumstances exist which justify the prisoner's release on compassionate grounds. Before any such release, the Home Secretary shall consult the Parole Board, unless the circumstances are such as to render such consultation impracticable.

These provisions are in identical terms to the pre-existing s 36 of the 1991 Act, and the case-law thereon will remain relevant.

LICENCES AND RECALL

4.17   The duration and conditions of a life sentence were dealt with by s 37(3)–(7) of the 1991 Act, and these provisions are replicated, with minor drafting changes, by s 31 of the new Act.

The licence remains in force until the death of the life prisoner, unless revoked under s 32(1) or (2) (s 31(1)). The life prisoner must comply with the conditions of that licence (s 31(2)). The Home Secretary may make rules for regulating the supervision of any description of such persons, and, subject to the exception set out in para **4.18**, any life licence shall include conditions as to his supervision by a probation officer. Thus, for example, a licence might include a condition of attendance of a sex offender at a specified treatment programme or provide that such an offender should attend such programmes as may be required by the supervising probation officer.

4.18　The one exception to the requirement that the licence shall include conditions relating to his supervision is in respect of prisoners liable to removal from the UK (s 31(6)). A prisoner is liable to removal from the UK if one of the four situations set out in s 24(2) exists. These are as follows:

(a)　he is liable to deportation under s 3(5) of the Immigration Act 1971 and has been notified of a decision to make a deportation order against him;

(b)　he is liable to deportation under s 3(6) of the 1971 Act;

(c)　he has been notified of a decision to refuse him leave to enter the UK; or

(d)　he is an illegal immigrant within the meaning of s 33(1) of the 1971 Act.

Again, this provision replicates equivalent provisions in the 1991 Act (1991 Act, s 46(2), (3)). The fact that s 31(6) amends s 31(2) in such a way as to remove the duty to impose such conditions does not, of course, prevent the imposition of such conditions by way of discretion.

Such conditions may be specified in the licence on the grant of release on licence, or inserted into that licence subsequently. The words 'for the time being' in s 31(2) provide confirmation that the conditions of a licence may be varied or cancelled, or new conditions inserted, a fact confirmed by the terms of s 31(3) and (4). However, in the case of any life prisoner who falls within the terms of s 28, then any condition, its variation or cancellation must be in accordance with the recommendations of the Parole Board. In cases that fall under s 29, such assertion, variation or cancellation must occur only after consultation with the Board (s 31(3)). Such consultations can be about an individual case, or be in respect of proposals of a description to be applied generally or to a particular class of case (s 31(4)).

A licence may be revoked under s 32(1). It may be revoked on the recommendation of the Parole Board (s 32(1)), or without such a recommendation where it appears to him that it is expedient in the public interest to recall that person before such a recommendation is practicable (s 32(2)). Once a licence is revoked under s 32, the life prisoner is liable to be detained and, if at large, shall be deemed to be unlawfully at large (s 32(6)).

4.19　The procedure to be followed, and the right to make representations, is governed by s 32(3) and (4). Section 32(3) provides that a life prisoner recalled to prison under s 32(1) or (2):

(a)　may make representations in writing with respect to his recall; and

(b)　on his return to prison, shall be informed of the reasons for his recall and of his right to make representations.

Where recall occurs under s 32(1), and the life prisoner makes representations under s 32(3), or where the recall is under s 32(2), the Home Secretary must refer the case to the Parole Board (s 32(4)). In a case to which s 28 applies, the Parole Board can direct the release of the life prisoner, and the Home Secretary must give effect to that direction (s 32(5)). There is no discretion to disregard it. In a case to which s 29 applies, the Parole Board may recommend release (s 32(5)(b)). The wording of s 32(5)(b) is curious. The nature of a recommendation is that it may be adopted or not, as the case may be, provided the Home Secretary follows proper procedures and addresses his mind to all relevant matters. However, the wording of s 32(5)(b) is that: 'the Secretary shall give effect to the direction or recommendation'. It cannot be the case that the word 'shall' governs the word 'recommendation', for this would negate the very distinction being drawn by s 32(5)(b).

LIFE PRISONERS TRANSFERRED TO ENGLAND AND WALES

4.20 It has already been noted that Pt II applies, with modifications, to transferred life prisoners. Section 33 of the new Act replicates s 48 of the 1991 Act, with minor drafting changes to reflect the amended scheme of release created by Pt II.

A 'transferred life prisoner' is defined by s 33(4) as a person:

(a) on whom a court in a country or territory outside England and Wales[1] has imposed one or more sentences of imprisonment or detention for an indeterminate period; and

(b) who has been transferred to England and Wales, in pursuance of:
  (i) an order made by the Home Secretary under Sch 1, para 1, to the 1997 Act, or under s 2 of the Colonial Prisoners Removal Act 1884; or
  (ii) a warrant issued by the Home Secretary under the Repatriation of Prisoners Act 1984,

  there to serve his sentence or sentences or the remainder thereof.

Section 41 of, and Sch 1 to the new Act provide for the transfer of prisoners within the British Islands. Under para 1(1), the Home Secretary may, on the application of:

(a) a person remanded in custody in any part of the UK in connection with an offence; or

(b) a person serving a term of imprisonment in any part of the UK,[1]

make an order for his transfer to another part of the UK or to any of the Channel Islands, there to be remanded in custody pending his trial for the offence or, as the case may be, to serve the whole or any part of the remainder of his sentence, and for his removal to an appropriate institution there.

Paragraph 1(2) entitles a transfer order to be made, without application, in respect of a person remanded in custody, or sentenced to imprisonment, in any of the Channel Islands.

These provisions clearly include the transfer of a life prisoner. Further, s 42 of, and Sch 2 to the new Act amend the Schedule to the Repatriation of Prisoners

Act 1984. The amendments, of an extremely detailed nature, are necessary to adjust the 1984 Act to the different regime for sentence length and early release created by the 1997 Act. In particular, para 4(5) of Sch 2 substitutes a new para 3 for the pre-existing para 3 of the Schedule to the 1984 Act. The new para 3 has the effect, in a life imprisonment case to which s 29 of the new Act would apply (ie falls to be treated as a mandatory life sentence), of permitting release on the recommendation of the Parole Board after consultation with the Lord Chief Justice, but without consultation with the trial judge. The difficulties of consultation with a trial judge in a different jurisdiction are self-evident.

---

1 See general annotations.

4.21　Where a life prisoner is transferred to England and Wales, that prisoner will be subject to the terms of s 33(3) if the pre-conditions in either s 33(1) or (2) are satisfied. The first set of pre-conditions is contained in s 33(1). This provides where the Home Secretary, after consultation with the Lord Chief Justice, certifies his opinion that, if:

(a)　the prisoner's offence had been committed after the commencement of Ch II; and

(b)　he had been sentenced for it in England and Wales,[1]

the court by which he was so sentenced would have ordered that s 28 should apply to him as soon as he had served a part of his sentence specified in the certificate.

It should be noted that the sentencing principles that will apply are those that apply in England and Wales. Clearly, the principles set out at para **2.8** as to the imposition of a discretionary life sentence will apply. So, too, will the pre-conditions relating to a mandatory life sentence for a second serious offence under s 1 of the new Act. Although a mandatory sentence, it is not to be regarded as a sentence which is fixed by law (s 1(4)) and thus falls within s 28. In that context, the wording of s 33(1) clearly requires the court to impose a mandatory sentence only if the conviction for the previous serious offence occurred in a UK court. Section 33(1) does not entitle any assumption to be made that previous convictions were by a court or courts in the UK.

---

1 See general annotations.

4.22　The second pre-condition is contained in s 33(2). This provides that s 33 applies where, in the case of a transferred life prisoner, the Home Secretary certifies his opinion that, if:

(a)　the prisoner's offence had been committed after the commencement of Ch II; and

(b)　he had been sentenced for it in England and Wales,

the Home Secretary would have directed that s 28 should apply to him as soon as he had served a part of his sentence specified in the certificate.

It has already been seen that the Home Secretary may only make such a direction where the conditions in s 28(2) are not satisfied. This means that the chief purpose of s 33(2) is in respect of persons aged under 18 at the time of the commission of the offence and thus detained during Her Majesty's Pleasure.

4.23 Where either s 33(1) or (2) has the effect of bringing s 33 into operation, s 33(3) brings into operation in such a case the provisions generally of Ch II, except s 29. The transferred life prisoner is to be regarded as a life prisoner to whom s 28 applies, with the tariff being that part of the sentence specified in the Home Secretary's certificate. The one exception to that is contained in s 33(5). If there are two or more such sentences, the prisoner is not to be treated as a life prisoner unless the requirements in s 33(1) or (2) are satisfied in respect of each of those sentences.

Chapter 5

SEX OFFENDERS

Introduction – Sentencing and release arrangements – Notification requirements of Sex Offenders Act 1997 – Offences – Sex tourism – Other provisions

INTRODUCTION

5.1 In June 1996, the Government published a consultation document, canvassing the range of measures which might increase public protection against sex offenders.[1] It focused on a range of possible measures, including the supervision of convicted sex offenders following release from custody,[2] the registration of convicted sex offenders, increased powers to DNA test offenders, prohibitions on employment in certain occupations and proposals for criminal conviction and criminal intelligence checks.

Following that consultation process, recent legislation has implemented important parts of that group of proposals.

1 *Sentencing and Supervision of Sex Offenders: A Consultation Document* (HMSO, 1996) Cm 3304.
2 The Crime (Sentences) Act 1997: see para **3.44**. Other legislation passed in 1997 is referred to by name, in full or in abbreviated form. See, in particular, the Sex Offenders Act 1997.

5.2 The expression 'sex offender' is used to describe those who have committed a sexual offence. The expression 'sexual offence' is defined by s 31 of the 1991 Act, in the broadest of terms.[1] The sexual offences which trigger the mandatory sentence requirements of s 2 of the new Act are more narrow in extent,[2] whilst the Sex Offenders Act 1997 (SOA 1997) defines 'sexual offence' and 'sex offender' in terms which are not only different from those set out in s 31 of the 1991 Act, but also include offences for which a person has been cautioned, albeit not convicted.[3]

1 See annotations to s 27 of the new Act.
2 See para **2.16**.
3 See para **5.19**.

5.3 The range of provisions that have been introduced, and which relate to sex offenders, directly or indirectly, is set out below.

First, the provisions in s 2 in respect of mandatory life sentences for a second violent or sexual offence are a direct legislative response to the problems caused, inter alia, by sex offenders. Extended supervision arrangements are put in place[1] in respect of those offenders who are being released from custody having served a term of imprisonment for a sexual offence.[2]

Secondly, SOA 1997 provides for a scheme of registration for those convicted of a sexual offence, and also contains measures designed to curb 'sex tourism'.

Thirdly, Pt VI of the Police Act 1997 introduces measures designed to facilitate enhanced criminal conviction and criminal intelligence checks, which will facilitate employers in sensitive areas, including voluntary bodies in respect of their volunteers, to check on those seeking to work with them.

Fourthly, the Protection from Harassment Act 1997 creates new civil powers, and new criminal offences, in respect of conduct that often, although not always, has a sexual element.

Fifthly, the Sexual Offences (Protected Material) Act 1997 regulates access to victim statements in sex offence cases.[3]

Finally, the Criminal Evidence (Amendment) Act 1997 extends police powers to obtain DNA tests for all convicted sexual offenders still serving a sentence.[4]

---

1 See para **3.44–3.45**.
2 See annotations to s 2.
3 See para **5.61**.
4 See para **5.60**.

5.4   These new provisions are part of a deliberate strategy designed to protect the public from the dangers of sexual offenders targeting children.[1] In part, that strategy is based on the principle that custody is the appropriate, and primary, means of protecting the public. There has been a significant increase in the use of immediate custody in respect of those offenders convicted of, or pleading guilty to, sexual offences. In 1993, some 44 per cent of sentences for sex offences dealt with on indictment involved immediate custody, compared with only 20 per cent of such offences in 1983.[2] The Government's strategy was also based on the belief that on-going work needs to be undertaken with sex offenders both during the period in custody[3] and on release. It is for this reason that the new Act contains extended supervision powers. Finally, it is believed that a scheme of registration will assist in making the police aware of the whereabouts of those likely to pose a significant risk in the community, which, in combination with a more developed DNA database, will assist in the prevention and detection of crime.

---

1 Mr David Maclean, MP, Minister of State, Home Office, speaking during the Second Reading of the Sex Offenders Bill, 27 January 1997, HC Deb, vol 289, no 50, col 23.
2 D West, 'Sexual Molesters', in *Dangerous People*, ed Walker (Blackstone Press, 1996).
3 For the limitations of sex offender programmes within prisons, see Sarah Ward, 'Responses to Sex Offenders – A Flawed Approach' *Journal of Contemporary Issues in Law* (1996) Vol II, Issue 3, p 53.

SENTENCING AND RELEASE ARRANGEMENTS FOR SEX OFFENDERS

5.5 The new legislation identified above[1] builds upon, but does not, generally, replace the sentencing scheme created by the Criminal Justice Act 1991 and which deals, inter alia, with sex offenders. In such cases, the normal rules relating to offence seriousness contained in s 1 of the 1991 Act apply. Irrespective of the level of risk the pattern of offending by the offender demonstrates, the offence for which the offender is being sentenced must, either on its own or in combination with one or more associated offences,[2] be so serious[3] that only such a sentence can be justified for that offence (1991 Act, s 1(1)(a)). Only if the custody threshold is crossed can the courts consider the imposition of a term of imprisonment longer than is commensurate with the seriousness of the offence,[4] under s 2(2)(b) of the 1991 Act. Such a sentence may be justified in the case of a person who is considered to be a danger to the public. That judgment may be reached in the light of reports presented to the sentencing court, in the light of expert opinion evidence as to the level of risk posed by the offender to the public, but may also be a judgment reached by a judge even where such evidence is lacking.[5] That danger does not have to be to the public generally, but may be to a single person or small group of persons.[6] Thus the offender who has targeted a specific woman, or child, or group of children, may be the subject of a longer than commensurate sentence if the danger to that person, or persons, is regarded as on-going. However, it must be noted that that sentence must be proportionate to the offence for which the offender has been sentenced, and that s 2(2)(b) does not provide a general power to detain offenders for whatever period is necessary to prevent future harm. The extent to which the Mental Health Act 1983 provides a basis for continued detention in such a case is discussed below.[7]

---

1 See para **5.3**.
2 See para **2.11**.
3 In *Bradbourn* (1985) 7 Cr App R (S) 180 (CA), Lawton LJ described this as: 'The kind of offence which when committed by a young person would make all right-thinking members of the public, knowing all the facts, feel that justice had not been done by the passing of any sentence other than a custodial sentence.' This test was applied in *Baverstock* [1993] 1 WLR 202 (CA), and in *Cox* [1993] 1 WLR 188 (CA).
4 See para **2.3**.
5 See para **2.3**.
6 *Hashi* (1995) 16 Cr App R (S) 121, CA.
7 See para **5.6**.

5.6 There is no power generally to detain a person who creates a risk of the commission of a serious sexual offence, or to order his continued detention after a term of imprisonment has been served. A person who is a sex offender may well fall within the definitions of 'mental disorder','severe mental impairment', 'mental impairment' or psychopathic disorder' contained in s 1 of the Mental Health Act 1983.[1] However, the making, and therefore the continuance, of a hospital order,[2] with or without restriction, under s 37 of the 1983 Act will presuppose that the terms of s 37(2) of the 1983 Act are satisfied.

The key prerequisite in this context is that 'in the case of psychopathic disorder or mental impairment, that such [medical] treatment is likely to alleviate or prevent a deterioration of his condition' (1983 Act, s 37(2)(a)(i)). It is often the case that medical practitioners are unable to state that treatment will, or might, have this effect. There is thus a significant gap in the law in respect of which the Government is considering what further measures, if any, are appropriate.

---

1 See annotations to s 46.
2 See para **6.3**.

5.7   Where a person is imprisoned for a sexual offence,[1] the court has hitherto been entitled, under s 44 of the 1991 Act, to extend the period of supervision that follows release from the three-quarters stage which generally applies, but until the end of the sentence. In deciding whether to so extend that period of supervision, the court has to have regard to the need to protect the public from serious harm, and the desirability of preventing further offences by offenders and of the needs to secure rehabilitation.

As noted earlier,[2] s 44 of the 1991 Act will cease to apply in respect of offences to which Ch I of Pt II of the new Act applies. The new supervision regime is contained in s 20 of the Crime (Sentences)Act 1997, and, in its length, may extend for a period of time of up to 50 per cent of the term of imprisonment imposed (not, it should be noted, the length of time actually served), or for a period of 12 months (whichever is longer), or for such longer period, not exceeding 10 years, as the court considers necessary for the purpose of preventing the commission by the offender of further offences and of securing his rehabilitation.[3]

This provision is one of the three alternative approaches canvassed by the Government at Consultation stage.[4] The Government specifically considered, but rejected approaches that would have allowed a court to specify a supervision period as part of its sentencing discretion, without specific limits, and also rejected an approach that would have permitted an extension of a supervision period for a determinate period, subject to regular review by an independent body, such as the Parole Board, or by a court.

---

1 See annotations to s 20.
2 See para **3.44**.
3 Crime (Sentences) Act 1997, s 20(3).
4 Sentencing and Supervision of Sex Offenders, op cit.

5.8   The new Act sets the potential parameters within which a court may act. Within them, there are no limits as to the period of supervision that may be imposed. In this respect, the wording of s 20(3) is similar to that contained in s 44 of the new Act. However, in exercising the power in s 44 of the 1991 Act a court has to have regard to the matters contained in s 32(6)(a) and (b) of the 1991 Act. Those matters are:

(a)   the need to protect the public from serious harm from offenders; and

(b)   the desirability of preventing the commission by them of further offences and of securing their rehabilitation.

Section 20(3) of the new Act does not require the court to have regard to 'protecting the public from serious harm'. However, s 44 of the 1991 Act merely permitted the extension of the supervision period until the end of the total period of the sentence.

Section 20(3) of the new Act raises wider issues than s 44 of the 1991 Act because of the potential length of a supervision period, and the question as to the relationship between the offence for which the offender is being sentenced and the period of supervision. It is submitted that the further period of supervision does not in any sense have to be proportionate to that offence, unlike the position in respect of longer than commensurate sentences,[1] but has to be proportionate to the *risk* identified by the court that that offence establishes in the light of the offender's background and antecedents, and other offences which the offender has admitted. This approach is consistent with the intent of the proviso, namely to prevent, or reduce, the risk of future offending. On this basis, it would be illogical to relate the period of extended supervision to the instant offence.

---

1 See para **2.3**.

5.9   The new Act creates a presumption that an extended supervision period will be imposed. Section 20 requires a court which is sentencing an offender for a sexual offence to which Ch I applies to give a direction as to the extended supervision period unless there are exceptional circumstances which justify its not doing so.[1] In the light of this presumption, there appears to be no specific need for a court to require expert evidence as to the degree of risk posed by an offender in any individual case. It will be open to a judge to reach this conclusion in the light of the evidence put before the court during trial, or from the depositions, and in pre-sentence reports and other reports prepared or submitted in respect of the offender. By contrast, the existence or otherwise of 'exceptional circumstances' is surely a matter that should be established by evidence.[2]

However, the fact that a risk assessment report is not *required* does not mean to say that such a report cannot, or should not, be obtained. There is, of course, nothing to prevent a judge from calling for a risk assessment report from those, whether in the prison service, probation service or working with specialist units dealing with sex offenders, and who are in a position to make some judgment as to the degree of risk an offender poses. It is submitted that a judge should always do so in a case where an extended supervision period under s 20(3)(b) is being contemplated. Such a supervision order is inherently coercive in that it will impose requirements or restrictions on the offender, and make the offender potentially liable to criminal proceedings for failure to comply.[3] No mechanism to secure release from such an extended supervision order is created by s 20: the power vested, by s 16(5) of the new Act, in the Home

Secretary to make rules regulating the supervision of offenders under s 16[4] cannot extend to reducing the period of supervision in fact ordered by the court under s 20(6)(b). Finally, the length of any such period extended by virtue of s 20(6)(b) is surely a matter reviewable on appeal. For all of these reasons, it is important that an evidential basis establishing the levels of risk that justify the length of the extended period should exist, and, by analogy with the position in respect of longer than commensurate sentences under s 2(2)(b) of the 1991 Act, it is arguable that the sentencer should give the advocate for the offender notice that he is considering an extended supervision period, in order that that advocate can make submissions about the length of that supervision period and, if necessary, seek to adduce evidence as to the degree of risk that the offender poses.

---

1 See para **3.44**.

2 An analogous situation is the position in respect of inferences from failure to testify, under the Criminal Justice and Public Order Act 1994, s 35, where it has been held that an evidential basis establishing the factual basis justifying the non-drawing of an inference should be established: *Cowan* [1996] 1 Cr App R 1 (CA).

3 See para **3.49**.

4 Although s 20 deals with the length of period of supervision, that supervision order itself is made pursuant to s 16.

5.10 The new provisions relating to extended supervision periods for sex offenders are not without difficulty.[1] The appropriate length of the supervision period can only be judged by the sentencing court in the light of the evidence, information and judgments as to risk available to it at the time of sentence. That court cannot, and will not, be aware of the offender's response to imprisonment, to any response by him to a sex offender treatment programme in which he has participated, and of the availability of treatment programmes after release. These matters are ones to which regard could have been had had the Government adopted the indefinite licence period approach noted earlier.[2] Further, the sanction for breach of the supervision requirements is not recall to prison, but potential prosecution for a specific offence.[3]

---

1 See Sarah Ward, 'Responses to Sex Offenders – A Flawed Approach' (1996) *Journal of Contemporary Issues in Law* Vol II, Issue 3, para **5.4**.

2 See para **5.7**.

3 See para **3.49**.

5.11 The release supervision order may specify such conditions as the Home Secretary may consider necessary. These may require the attendance at community-based treatment programmes,[1] provided, in the case of an offender sentenced to a term of imprisonment of three years or more, that that is recommended by the Parole Board (s 16(4)(b)). The supervision order may (subject to recommendations of the Parole Board) require residence at an approved probation hostel[2] (s 16(4)(a)) and (by implication from the terms of s 16(4)(a)), may include restrictions equivalent to a curfew order.[3] This can include requirements in respect of electronic tagging of offenders, a step advocated by the Government in its Consultation Paper,[4] and achieved through the definition of curfew order in s 16(7) of the new Act and through the terms of ss 12 and 13 of the 1991 Act. The last provision states that 'a curfew order may ... include requirements for securing the electronic monitoring of the offender's whereabouts...'.

Although the power to make a curfew order contained in s 12 of the 1991 Act is confined to a person aged 16[5] or over at the date of conviction, no such age restriction is contained in s 16 of the new Act, which is hardly surprising in the light of the fact that s 16 does not positively create a power to impose conditions having like effect as a curfew order. Nor does there appear to be any explicit limitation on the curfew provisions that might be imposed by virtue of licence provisions, unlike s 12 of the 1991 Act which proscribes certain specified curfew conditions.[3] Section 12(2) of the 1991 Act states that any curfew order shall not specify:

(a)   periods which fall outside the period of six months beginning with the day on which it is made; or
(b)   periods which amount to less than 2 hours or more than 12 hours in any one day.

Further, the requirements in a curfew order shall, as far as practicable, be such as to avoid:

(a)   any conflict with the offender's religious beliefs or with the requirements of any other community order to which he may be subject; and
(b)   any interference with the times, if any, at which he normally works or attends school or other educational establishment.

There is a strong argument for concluding that any curfew-type conditions imposed as part of a release supervision order should comply with the limitations in the 1991 Act, s 16(7) of the new Act specifically providing that the expression 'curfew order' has the same meaning as in the Criminal Justice Act 1991. It would surely be wrong for the safeguards envisaged by Parliament when creating the order to be negated by the way in which the power has been extended to supervision arrangements.

---

1   Consultation Paper, op cit, para 24.
2   See annotations to s 16.
3   Ibid.
4   Op cit, para 38.
5   See general annotations.

5.12   The consent of the offender is not required in respect of any conditions imposed as part of a release supervision order. Thus, provided the appropriate recommendation of the Parole Board exists, an offender can be required to attend at a treatment group, reside at a probation hostel or comply with curfew and monitoring requirements.

Although it may be open to question as to whether such participation in the absence of consent freely given is likely to be effective, given that such programmes are often based on philosophies based on offender willingness to accept and recognise the nature and consequences of his behaviour,[1] this position is consistent with other provisions of the new Act, which remove the need for an offender to consent before requirements are included in a community order.[2]

What is unclear is how such requirements will in reality be enforced if consent or willingness to comply are absent. The release supervision order will, generally, be made at a time when the offender will be entitled to release from custody. There is no question that the offender's unwillingness to participate or comply, or the lack of consent to any condition or requirement, can in any way delay the date of release beyond the expiration of the period when an offender is entitled to be released. Only in a case where an offender is serving a term of three years or more, and where release is being considered under s 12, on the recommendation of the Parole Board,[3] does any discretion exist, in which case the offender's willingness to participate or comply would, of course, be relevant.

Where such requirements are imposed, no recall provisions exist as a sanction for failing to comply with, or to co-operate with, such programmes. The sanction for breach or non-co-operation is prosecution for a criminal offence under s 17(1).[4] In this context the provisions of s 17(4) are of importance. That sub-section permits a term of imprisonment to be imposed, inter alia, where the court considers it expedient to do so in the interests of protecting the public from serious harm from the offender. An offender who continues to present a serious risk to the public may thus be sentenced to a term of imprisonment for failing to comply with requirements which may well have been imposed for that very same purpose. It is unclear what the effect of such imprisonment is on the release supervision order. Because the imprisonment is for a specific offence, there is no automatic revocation of that supervision order, and no revocation powers are conferred by the new Act. At first sight, the order remains in force. Such a conclusion appears to accord with the general scheme of the new Act. An offender might be fined for breach of condition[5] but clearly this should not negate on-going supervision. If it did, then no further supervision requirements would exist, because a s 17 offence is not itself a sexual offence attracting a supervision period. Nor would such an offence necessarily attract a supervision period, even if the punishment for the offence amounted to a term of imprisonment.[6]

However, a contrary conclusion might be justified by an examination of the terms of s 17(6), which deals with the meaning of the phrase 'relevant period'. The concept of 'relevant period' is important in determining the potential maximum period of imprisonment for failing to comply with the requirements of a release supervision order. The fact that the definition of 'relevant period' in s 17(6) equates this maximum with the remaining period of time of the supervision order as falls after the date of failure to comply with the condition lends support to the view that the imprisonment is intended to be in substitution for the supervision order. However, it is submitted that a better view is that the supervision order remains in force.

1 See Goring and Ward, 'Group Work with Sex Offenders – The Legal Problem' (1990) *Journal of Social and Welfare Law* 193.
2 See para **7.23–7.24**.
3 See para **3.34**.
4 See para **3.49**.
5 Ibid.
6 See para **3.39**.

5.13 One further problem arises in the context of determining the date a breach of a requirement contained in a release supervision order actually occurs. It has already been noted that this will be important for determing the potential length of imprisonment available to a court to punish such a breach.[1] In the case of a sex offender, where the breach may comprise a failure to comply with the requirements of an offender treatment programme the problem may be acute. The failure may result from a course of conduct over a period of time. In such circumstances, it is unfortunate that s 17 chooses to use the date of failure to comply rather than the date of conviction as the relevant date. As this is a penal provision, it should be construed restrictively, with ambiguities being resolved in favour of an accused. On this basis, the relevant date is, arguably, the date when the offender was informed he was in breach.

1 See paras **5.8** and **3.49**.

NOTIFICATION REQUIREMENTS FOR SEX OFFENDERS

5.14 Part I of the Sex Offenders Act 1997 creates a scheme whereby those convicted of sex offences against children, and other serious sexual offences, are required to register their name and address, and any subsequent changes, with the police. Part I of this Act comes into force on 1 October 1997.[1]

1 Sex Offenders Act 1997 (Commencement) Order 1997, SI 1997/1920.

5.15 These provisions, first proposed by the Police Superintendents Association,[1] are intended primarily to ensure that the information contained within the police national computer is fully up to date.[2] It is likely that some 6,000 names will be put on the register immediately, with another 3,500 per year being added.[3] Until the Act comes into force, the address held in police records is the last one known to police. This may be the address where the offender was residing at the time of being taken into custody, although it should also be remembered that the police are notified by the prison service of persons leaving prison who have been convicted of serious offences. Further, life prisoners may have conditions imposed as part of their life licences that they should notify the police of any change of address. Nevertheless, save in that latter situation there is no requirement on an individual to tell the police that he is moving, or that he has moved.

---

1 Mr David Maclean, LC Second Reading, HC Deb, vol 289, no 50, col 23, 27 January 1997.
2 Ibid, col 24.
3 (1997) *The Times*, 12 August.

5.16 Offenders generally do not have to notify their whereabouts to the police, and these new notification requirements have been criticised that they are selective, and do not extend to other groups of offenders who may pose a danger to the community.[1] However, the Government regarded paedophiles[2] as being in a special category: 'We can distinguish their sexual activity from that of violent criminals, muggers or other serious criminals because ... usually paedophiles are highly manipulative and clever and often their offending behaviour intensifies as they get older. They are in a particularly dangerous category...'.[3]

---

1 See Sir Patrick Cormack, MP, HC Second Reading, op cit, col 25.
2 The term is used widely in the debates into the Bill, but it should be noted that the SOA 1997 is not confined to sexual offences against children: see para **5.27**.
3 Mr David Maclean, MP, Minister of State, Home Office, HC Second Reading, op cit, col 25.

Commencement

5.17 The Act comes into effect on such days as may be appointed (SOA 1997, s 10). The appointed day is 1 October 1997.[1] The Act will not apply to those convicted of a sex offence prior to the commencement of Pt I, and thus there will be a group of persons who are believed to create a serious risk to the public who will not be subject to the notification requirements.[2]

---

1 Sex Offenders Act 1997 (Commencement) Order 1997, SI 1997/1920.
2 See para **5.15**. See, eg, *The Times*, 5 July 1997, for disquiet about the failure of the notification requirements to extend to known paedophiles.

Extent of operation

5.18 Part I of SOA 1997 applies to England and Wales, Scotland and Northern Ireland (s 10). This chapter is concerned only with its operation in England and Wales. However, it should be noted that the application of the Act, even in England and Wales, may occur because of a conviction for an offence in Scotland or Northern Ireland (s 1(9) and Sch 1). It does not apply in respect of persons convicted of a sexual offence abroad.[1] Although s 7 and Sch 2 identify certain conduct committed abroad as an offence under English law, that does not extend the notification provisions to persons who have engaged in such conduct but who have not been tried and convicted in the UK.

---

1 Mr David Maclean, MP, Minister of State, Home Office, HC Second Reading, op cit, cols 29–31.

Persons subject to notification requirements

5.19   The notification requirements apply to the persons who fall within one of the three sets of pre-conditions contained in s 1. The first set of pre-conditions is contained in s 1(1). By s 1(1), a person is subject to the notification provisions if, after commencement of Pt I of the Act:

(a)   he is convicted of a sexual offence[1] to which Pt I applies;

(b)   he is found not guilty of such an offence by reason of insanity, or to be under a disability[2] and to have done the act charged against him in respect of such an offence; or

(c)   in England and Wales[3] or Northern Ireland, he is cautioned by a constable in respect of such an offence which, at the time when the caution is given, he has admitted.

1 See para **5.26**.
2 See para **5.22**.
3 See general annotations.

5.20   Secondly, by s 1(2), an offender is subject to those requirements if, at commencement:

(a)   he has been convicted,[1] but not dealt with for a sexual offence to which Pt I applies; or

(b)   he was found not guilty of such an offence by reason of insanity, or to be under a disability and to have done the act charged against him in respect of such an offence, but has not been dealt with in respect of the finding.

1 This includes a finding in summary proceedings, under the Mental Health Act 1983, s 58(3), or equivalent Scottish or Northern Irish legislation, that the accused did the act charged (SOA 1997, s 6(2)).

5.21   A third set of circumstances is contained in s 1(3). By s 1(3), a person is subject to the requirements of Pt I if, in respect of such an offence:

(a)   he is serving a sentence of imprisonment or a term of service detention, or subject to a community order in respect of a sexual offence to which Pt I of SOA 1997 applies;

(b)   he is subject to supervision,[1] having been released from prison after serving the whole or part of a term of imprisonment for such an offence;

(c)   he is detained in a hospital,[2] or is subject to a guardianship order,[3] having been convicted of such an offence; or

(d)   he is detained in a hospital,[2] having been found not guilty of such an offence by reason of insanity, or to be under a disability and found to have done the act charged against him in respect of such an offence.

1 'Supervision' means supervision in pursuance of an order made for the purpose or, in the case of a person released from prison on licence, in pursuance of a condition contained in his licence: SOA 1997, s 6.

2 'Detained in a hospital' means detained in a hospital under:

   (a) Part III of the Mental Health Act 1983, Mental Health (Scotland) Act 1984, s 71, Pt VI of
        the Criminal Procedure (Scotland) Act 1995 or Pt III of the Mental Health (Northern
        Ireland) Order 1986;
   (b) Schedule 1 to the Criminal Procedure (Insanity and Unfitness to Plead) Act 1991; and
   (c) regulations made under the Army Act 1955, s 116B(3), Air Force Act 1955, s 116B(3), or
        the Naval Discipline Act 1957, s 63B (SOA 1997, s 6).

   It includes detention or admission under the Criminal Procedure (Insanity and Unfitness to
   Plead) Act 1991, Sch 1 and under Sch 1 to the Criminal Procedure (Insanity) Act 1964, as
   well as admission or detention under equivalent Scottish, Northern Irish or service
   legislation.
3 'Guardianship order' means a guardianship order under the Mental Health Act 1983, s 37,
   Criminal Procedure (Scotland) Act 1995, s 58, or Mental Health (Northern Ireland) Order
   1986, art 44.

Persons under a disability

5.22 It has been seen that the three sets of conditions in s 1 deal, inter alia,
with a person who is under a disability. This includes a person:

(a)   who is unfit to be tried for such an offence;
(b)   who is, or has been, found to be insane so that his trial for such an offence
      cannot or could not proceed; or
(c)   who is unfit to be tried and to have done the act charged against him in
      respect of such an offence.[1]

It may be the case that a person is found to be under a disability, and found to
have done the act charged against him in respect of a sexual offence, but later is
tried for the offence. In such cases, the original finding, and any order made in
respect thereof, is to be disregarded for the purposes of s 1.[2] The result appears
to be that a fresh notification requirement arises on conviction, under s 1(1),
and the original requirement arising by virtue of s 1(1)(b) or other provision
ceases to have effect. However, this does not mean that the original notification
requirement is invalid. In such a case, a person being prosecuted for a breach of
the notification requirement, under s 3, remains liable to conviction. This is
because s 1(7) states that the 'finding' (ie the previous finding) shall be
disregarded for the purposes of 'this section' (ie s 1). Arguably, this means that
it is disregarded for the purposes of whether a fresh notification obligation
arises under s 1(1) and (4). It does not require that that finding is to be
disregarded for the purposes of s 3. It would be absurd to conclude that an
intentional breach of a then subsisting requirement did not constitute an
offence under s 3.

1 SOA 1997, s 6(3).
2 Ibid, s 1(7).

Young sex offenders

5.23 Section 4 of the 1997 Act makes it clear that Pt I of the Act applies not
only to those serving terms of imprisonment, but also to those serving terms of
detention under a secure training order,[1] a sentence of detention in a young

offenders institution, a sentence of detention under s 53 of the Children and Young Persons Act 1933,[2] or a sentence of detention for life under s 8 of the Criminal Justice Act 1982.[3] Equivalent orders under Scottish, Northern Irish or service law are also included within the general scope of the term 'imprisonment'.

---

1 See annotations to s 45.
2 See annotations to s 34.
3 See annotations to s 19.

Cautions

5.24 The notification requirements apply not only to those who are, or have been, convicted of a sexual offence, but also to those who are cautioned for such an offence. The legal basis of a caution is far from clear, [1] as is the effect of such a caution. Cautioning is undertaken, not pursuant to statutory authority, but in accordance with guidance contained in Circulars 59/1990 and 18/1994. The safeguards for an individual are extremely limited: the full implications of a caution may not be apparent to those who agree to make the necessary admission upon which the caution is based, there may be little or no opportunity to obtain legal advice, and there may well be pressure on a suspect to accept the administration of a caution rather than run the risk, on trial, of acquiring a conviction.[2] The Royal Commission on Criminal Justice recommended that police powers to caution should be governed by statute, and that the keeping of records of cautions should be governed by regulations.[3] The Sex Offenders (Certificate of Caution) Order 1997[4] has now been made, which prescribes the form to be used by a constable to certify that a person has been cautioned for an offence to which Pt I of the 1997 Act applies and that the person has been so informed.

---

1 See May 'The Legal Effect of a Caution' [1997] Crim LR 491.
2 For these, and other, arguments, see Evans 'Challenging a Police Caution Using Judicial Review' [1996] Crim LR 106.
3 Cm 2263 (HMSO, 1993), Ch 5, para 57.
4 SI 1997/1921.

5.25 Although the use of cautions in respect of sexual offences has declined, [1] from some 43 per cent in 1993 to 32 per cent in 1995, the use by the police of the power to caution individuals for the purposes of triggering the notification requirements would, if used for that purpose, have potentially serious consequences. It would effectively turn cautions into 'quasi-convictions'.[2] It has been argued that the use of cautions in this way will undermine their value as a warning, and that it is inappropriate to use them to trigger the coercive requirements of the 1997 Act. On the one hand, the police may seek to use the cautioning power more often, in the light of the value claimed for the notification requirement in enhancing police data. On the other hand, the use of cautions in this way may in fact reduce the willingness of suspects to agree to accept the caution, with the result being that greater numbers of cases may well go to trial, or, possibly, lead to a greater number of challenges to cautions being undertaken by way of judicial review.

---

1 See, generally, Soothill, Francis and Sanderson 'A Cautionary Tale: The Sex Offenders Act 1997, the Police and Cautions' [1997] Crim LR 482.
2 A phrase used by Liberty in its briefing on the Sex Offenders Bill, 1997.

The sexual offences to which Part I applies

5.26   The offences to which Pt I applies are identified by s 1(9) and Sch 1. The list is extensive and includes offences in England and Wales, Scotland, Northern Ireland or under service law (SOA 1997, s 1(9)). Paragraphs 1 to 4 of Sch 1 list the relevant offences in, respectively, England and Wales, Scotland, Northern Ireland and under service law. They are intended to cover sexual offences involving children, including child pornography offences, and the 'most serious' sexual offences against adults.[1] Some of the offences have age-related exemptions. These 'focus on consensual teenage sex and adult homosexual acts', the Government being mindful of the possibility of manipulative and coercive pressure being exerted by older people on younger impressionable people.[2]

---

1 Mr David Maclean, MP, Minister of State, op cit, col 26.
2 Ibid, col 27.

5.27   The sexual offences under the law of England and Wales and to which Pt I applies, are set out in Sch 1, para 1. They include the following offences[1] under the Sexual Offences Act 1956, references to age being to the age[2] as at the date of commission of the offence (Sch 1, para 5).

(i)   section 1 (rape);

(ii)   section 5 (intercourse with a girl under 13);

(iii)   section 6 (intercourse with a girl between 13 and 16). Part I does not apply to offences committed by a person under 20 (1997 Act, Sch 1, para 1(2)(a));

(iv)   section 10 (incest by a man). Part I does not apply where the other party is aged 18 or over (Sch 1, para 1(2)(b));

(v)   section 12 (buggery). Part I does not apply to such offences committed by a person under 20 (1997 Act, Sch 1, para 1(2)(a)), or where the other party is aged 18 or over (Sch 1, para 1(2)(b));

(vi)   section 13 (indecency between men). Part I does not apply to offences committed by a person under 20 (1997 Act, Sch 1, para 1(2)(a)), or where the other party is aged 18 or over (Sch 1, para 1(2)(b));

(vii)   section 14 (indecent assault on a woman). Part I does not apply where the other party is aged 18 or over, unless the offender is, or has been sentenced to imprisonment for a term of 30 months or more, or is admitted to a hospital subject to a restriction order (Sch 1, para 1(2)(b), para 1(3));

(viii)　section 15 (indecent assault on a man). Part I does not apply where the other party is aged 18 or over, unless the offender is, or has been sentenced to imprisonment for a term of 30 months or more, or is admitted to a hospital subject to a restriction order (Sch 1, para 1(2)(b), para 1(3));

(ix)　section 16 (assault with intent to commit buggery). Part I does not apply where the other party is aged 18 or over (Sch 1, para 1(2)(b));

(x)　section 28 (causing of, or encouraging prostitution of, intercourse with, or indecent assault on, girl under 16).

Schedule 1 also identifies certain other offences, set out in para **5.28**, below.

1　These include attempts, conspiracies or incitements to commit the substantive offence (Sch 1, para 5).

2　See general annotations.

5.28　Paragraphs (b)–(f) of Sch 1 identify other offences, principally concerned with children. These are as follows:

'(b)　an offence under Indecency with Children Act 1960, s 1 (indecent conduct towards young child);

(c)　an offence under Criminal Law Act 1977, s 54 (inciting girl under 16 to have incestuous sexual intercourse). For this purpose a person shall be taken to have been under the age of 16 at any time if it appears from the evidence as a whole that [she][1] was under that age at that time (Sch 1, para 1(4)(b));

(d)　an offence under Protection of Children Act 1978, s 1 (indecent photographs of children);[2]

(e)　an offence under Customs and Excise Management Act 1979, s 170 (penalty for fraudulent evasion of duty, etc) in relation to goods prohibited to be imported under Customs Consolidation Act 1876 (prohibitions and restrictions);

(f)　an offence under Criminal Justice Act, s 160 (possession of indecent photographs of children).'

Of these offences, the offence at para (e) above (fraudulent evasion of duty, etc), does not, at first sight, sit easily with the other offences which plainly are aimed at prohibiting unacceptable conduct in relation to children. The reason for the inclusion of this offence in the category of offences that trigger the notification requirement is that in cases involving the importation of obscene material featuring children, difficulties of establishing possession under s 160 can arise. On the same facts it is often possible to secure a conviction for importation under s 170.[3]

1　The word used in para 1(4)(b), 'he', is singularly inappropriate in that the only person whose age is ever relevant for this purpose is, by definition, female. The point is, of course, of no legal significance whatsoever.

2　This includes pseudo-photographs: see Criminal Justice and Public Order Act 1994, s 84(2), which amends s 1 of the 1978 Act.

3　Mr David Maclean, MP, Minister of State, Home Office, HC Second Reading, op cit, col 27.

5.29 The above list of offences is inevitably arbitrary and open to criticism. It includes offences where no on-going risk arises. A gay man aged 20 who engages, consensually, in sexual intercourse with another gay man aged 17, is, if convicted of that offence, subject to the notification requirement. The same conduct committed abroad, for example, whilst on holiday in Europe, is not criminal[1] and thus does not attract the notification requirement. The law is also potentially discriminatory. A 19-year-old man who engages, consensually, in sexual intercourse with a 15-year-old female, is not subject to a reporting requirement, even if prosecuted for, and convicted of, unlawful sexual intercourse. Further, some[2] question whether a notification requirement should be automatically imposed on a man aged 20 who has consensual sexual relations with an aware 15-year-old. The fact that, in some of these instances a prosecution might not result is, arguably, insufficient justification for a measure of lack of selectivity. Quite apart from any arguments of principle, the notification requirements can arise following a formal caution.[3]

---

1 Provided the other party is aged over 16 the conduct does not fall within the terms of s 7 of the 1997 Act.
2 See, eg, the civil liberties organisation, Liberty.
3 See para **5.24**.

5.30 Part I of SOA 1997 does not apply to an offender whose conviction for a sexual offence was in a court in another jurisdiction outside the UK. During the passage of the Act, the Government was urged to widen its scope to include those convicted abroad.[1] This was rejected by the Government as being both impracticable and potentially contrary to the European Convention on Human Rights, because of the inevitably partial application such a rule would have.[2] It would, argued the Government, be impossible to ensure that the fact of such a conviction was known to the UK authorities. In addition, 'to place an obligation on the authorities in respect of those who have been convicted abroad would undoubtedly imply recognition of the judgment of a foreign court. It would also assume that the sentences were compatible with the sentences that would have been imposed here and that the standards of evidence and procedure in the foreign courts were compatible with ours'.[3]

---

1 See HC Second Reading, 27 January 1997, HC Deb, vol 289, cols 23–71.
2 Mr David Maclean, Minister of State, Home Office, HC Second Reading, HC Deb 289, col 30; Mr Timothy Kirkhope, MP, Parliamentary Under Secretary, Home Office, ibid, col 71.
3 Ibid, col 72.

5.31 Paragraph 2 of Sch 1 deals with the offences under Scots law, in respect of which the conviction, or caution, of an individual will trigger the notification requirement. The relevant offences[1] can be split into four categories.

The first set of offences are offences at common law, and include: rape, clandestine injury to women, abduction of a woman or girl with intent to rape, assault with intent to rape or ravish, indecent assault, lewd, indecent or libidinous behaviour or practices,[2] shameless indecency, and sodomy.

The second set comprises offences relating to indecent images of children, under the Civic Government (Scotland) Act 1982, s 52 and s 52A.

The third set are offences under ss 1 to 3, 5 to 6, 8, 10, and 13(2) of the Criminal Law (Consolidation) (Scotland) Act 1995. These are sexual offences which, broadly, but not precisely, correspond with the offences which arise in England and Wales.

Finally, there is the offence under s 170 of the Customs and Excise Management Act 1979.

---

1 These include attempts, conspiracies or incitements to commit the substantive offence (Sch 1, para 5).
2 See annotations to s 2.

5.32 In respect of offences where a person is convicted in Northern Ireland,[1] para 3 of Sch 1 specifies the following offences:

(a) rape;
(b) offences under the Offences Against the Person Act 1861, s 52 (indecent assault upon a female person), s 61 (buggery)[2] and s 62 (assault with intent to commit buggery or indecent assault upon a male person);
(c) offences under Criminal Law Amendment Act 1885, s 4 (unlawful carnal knowledge of a girl under 14) and s 5 (unlawful carnal knowledge of a girl under 17);[2]
(d) an offence under s 11 of the 1885 Act (committing, or being party to the commission of, or procuring or attempting to procure the commission of, any act of gross indecency with another male);[2]
(e) an offence under Punishment of Incest Act 1908 (incest by males);
(f) offences under Children and Young Persons Act (Northern Ireland) 1968 (causing or encouraging seduction or prostitution of a girl under 17[3]) and s 22 (indecent conduct towards a child);
(g) an offence under art 3 of the Protection of Children (Northern Ireland) Order 1978[4] (indecent photographs of children);
(h) an offence under Customs and Excise Management Act 1979, s 170 (fraudulent evasion of duty, etc), unless the prohibited goods did not include indecent photographs of persons who were under the age of 16;[3]
(i) an offence under art 9 of the Criminal Justice (Northern Ireland) Order 1980[5] (inciting girl under 16 to have incestuous sexual intercourse); and
(j) an offence under art 15 of the Criminal Justice (Evidence, etc) (Northern Ireland) Order 1988[6] (possession of indecent photographs of children).

The offences in (b), (d) and (e) do not apply where the victim, or, as the case may be, the other party to the offence was aged 18 or over.[3] There is, however, one exception to that exception. If an offence under s 52 (of indecent assault on a female) or under s 62 of the 1861 Act (indecent assault on a male) is committed, and the offender is sentenced to a term of 30 months or more, or is, or has been, admitted to a hospital subject to a restriction order, then the offence is indeed a qualifying offence for the purpose of para 3, of Sch 1 (Sch 1, para 3(3)).

1 These include attempts, conspiracies or incitements to commit the substantive offence (Sch 1, para 5).
2 Provided the offender is 20 years of age or over.
3 See general annotations.
4 SI 1978/1047.
5 SI 1980/704.
6 SI 1988/1847.

5.33 The relevant offences under service law are those offences under the Army Act 1955, s 70; Air Force Act 1955, s 70; or Naval Discipline Act, s 42, of which the corresponding civil offence would fall within para 1 of Sch 1 (Sch 1, para 4).[1]

1 See annotations to s 2.

The notification requirement

5.34 Where a person falls within the notification requirement by virtue of s 1(1), (2) or (3), that person is required to comply with the requirements contained in s 2. No court order is required, and there is no provision whereby a person may be exempt from the reporting requirement, even if no actual on-going risk is considered to exist. No doubt the lack of risk would be one factor considered by a court in determining sentence, and thus affect the period of supervision. However, should for example a 20-year-old man be prosecuted for having sexual relations, consensually, with a 17-year-old man, being given a conditional discharge, he is nevertheless to be subject to a five-year notification period. This blanket approach may have the merit of simplicity, but has surely little else to commend it.

The question of registration is not a matter for a sentencing court to address directly, although there is, no doubt, no objection to such a court taking into account the fact that an offender will have to comply with the requirements of the 1997 Act in determining what is the appropriate sentence to pass. It might, for example, persuade a court dealing with a sexual offence at the less serious end of the range that a non-custodial disposal is appropriate.

The notification requirements continue to operate for the periods specified in s 1(4). These are dealt with at paras **5.35–5.37**, below. Where sentences for more than one such offence are consecutive, the terms of imprisonment are aggregated for the purposes of calculating the notification period (s 1(6)(a)); if they are concurrent, the supervision period is calculated by reference to the length of the longer sentence (s 1(6)(b)).

The length of the notification period

5.35 The period during which the notification requirement which applies in the case of an adult offender subsists is dealt with by s 1(6) of the 1997 Act, and is related to the length of the term of imprisonment imposed, or whether a hospital order pursuant to the Mental Health Act 1983[1] has been made subject to, or without, a restriction order. The applicable period for an adult is set out in Table 3, below. For the position in respect of young sex offenders, see para **5.36**.

Table 3: Length of notification period

Description of person	Applicable period
Offender sentenced to life or term of 30 months or more	Indefinite period
Offender admitted to hospital subject to restriction order[1]	Indefinite period
Offender sentenced to term of more than 6 months but less than 30 months	10 years, beginning with relevant date
Offender sentenced to term of 6 months or less	7 years, beginning with relevant date
Admitted to hospital without restriction order[1]	7 years, beginning with relevant date
Person of any other description	5 years, beginning with relevant date

The 'relevant date' for the purpose of calculating the applicable period is defined, by s 1(8), as the relevant date of conviction, finding of disability or of the caution.

---

1 In the 1997 Act, a 'restriction order' means an order under the Mental Health Act 1983, s 41.

5.36 In respect of an offender who is under 18[1] at the relevant date,[2] the references to a period of 10 years, seven years or five years are to be construed as references to one half that period (s 3(1)). Thus the relevant notification periods are five years, three years six months, and two years six months. Again, the arbitrary nature of the provision is demonstrated. Although a strong case can be made for reducing notification periods for those who are still developing, or even for excluding offences committed as a juvenile from the notification provisions entirely, the simple formula in s 3(1) itself pays little heed to the actual or potential risk that the offender may create.

---

1 See general annotations.
2 See para **5.19**.

5.37 If an offender is sentenced to terms of imprisonment in respect of two or more offences, only one of which is a sexual offence, the relevant length of sentence is that applicable to the sexual offence, even if a consecutive term is imposed for that other offence, or those other offences. However, where a person is sentenced in respect of two or more sexual offences to which Pt I of the 1997 Act applies:[1]

(a)   to consecutive terms of imprisonment; or

(b)   to terms of imprisonment which are partly concurrent,

then the provisions of s 1(6) apply (s 1(5)).

The effect of applying s 1(6) is that, in calculating the applicable period, s 1(4) has effect as if the offender were, or had been, sentenced, in respect of each of those offences, to a term of imprisonment which:

(a)   in the case of consecutive terms, is equal to the aggregate of those terms;
(b)   in the case of concurrent terms, is equal to the aggregate of those terms after making such deduction as may be necessary to secure that no period of time is counted more than once.

In short, if an offender is sentenced to two consecutive periods of 18 months, the length of sentence for calculation of the applicable period is three years. If, however, a term of 18 months is imposed to run concurrently with another of two years (both offences being sex offenders committed after commencement of Pt I), the length of sentence for this purpose is two years.

No power exists to waive, shorten or otherwise amend or discharge the notification requirement, even if it becomes clear that the offender ceases to pose any risk to the public. The Government currently has the position of such offenders under review,[1] and it is likely that further provision will be made to deal with such cases.

---

1 Mr Alan Michael, Minister of State, Home Office, HC Deb, col 751, 7 July 1997.

Effect of notification requirement

5.38   By s 2(1), a person subject to the notification requirements shall, before the end of the period of 14 days beginning with the relevant date or, if later, the date of commencement of the Act,[1] notify to the police the following information:

(a)   his name and, where he uses one or more other names, each of those names; and
(b)   his home address.

The 'relevant date' for the purpose of s 2(1) and (3)[1] is defined by s 1(8), and is the date of conviction, of the finding of not guilty by reason of insanity or of disability, or the date of the caution.

The expression 'home address' in relation to any person means the address of his home, that is to say, his sole or main residence in the UK[2] or, where he has no such residence, premises in the UK which he regularly visits (s 2(7)). This formulation is inevitably imprecise. Whether premises are a person's 'sole or main residence' is a question of fact, but will on occasion cause difficulty. Take, for example, the hopefully rare case of a Member of Parliament convicted of a sexual offence. He may well have a 'home' in London, in his constituency and, perhaps, even elsewhere. Leaving to one side arguments that the notification requirement ought logically to extend to each such area, a court will find it difficult to make a judgment as to which is the 'sole or main residence'. Relevant factors to which regard should be had will be the length of time spent at each premises, the place where the offender's family resides and, in the case where premises are both in the UK, whether premises in the UK are regarded as the 'sole or main residence' for other purposes.

The expression, 'premises . . . which he regularly visits' is intended to deal with situations where, for example, the offender lives in France but visits the United Kingdom regularly. However, this formulation is itself unclear. An individual can 'regularly visit' premises without residing in them, even on a temporary basis. A person resident in France who regularly visits an English football club would literally fall within the notification requirements, a conclusion both absurd and unintended. The clear parliamentary intent is to ensure that the notification procedures cannot be evaded by an offender visiting regularly the home of, say, a girlfriend, or by being of no fixed abode but regularly visiting premises of friends. It was for this reason that amendments were made to the Bill as originally drafted in the form that now constitutes s 2(2), providing for notification of residence or staying at premises for a qualifying period (defined by s 2(7)). For this reason, the words of s 2(7) should be construed in the context of the term being defined, namely, 'home address', thus confining the scope of the definition to premises where the offender resides from time to time on a regular basis, irrespective of whether the premises are the whole or main residence. As Mr Timothy Kirkhope told the House of Commons,[3] 'Nor do I believe that [a requirement] to register all addresses that an offender visits – even for a period of one night – is practical. The police would be swamped with too much information. Moreover, I am not sure what the point is of recording an address that the offender has visited once and may never visit again'. However, the use of the term 'visits' in the above passage, and in s 2(7) does not make it clear that the visit must be residential in nature. The use of the terms 'resided' and 'stayed' in s 2(2) provides further support for a conclusion that a 'visit' must be a residential visit.

Finally, the 'regularly visits' test in s 2(7) provides no guidance as to how cases of multiple residences are to be dealt with. In the hypothetical Member of Parliament example, above, he *will* have a sole or main residence in the UK, and thus the 'regularly visits' test does not apply unless a court is prepared to conclude s 2(7) applies where no such sole or main residence is readily identifiable. The fact that, in such a case, *changes* in address will have to be notified[4] does not necessarily provide an answer: that would only be the case if the offender were to remain in one residence for at least 14 days. In the interests of ensuring full notification by those perceived to present a risk to the community, and in the interest of avoiding arguments such as those above, a test based simply on 'regular visits' for the purposes of residence would have had much to commend it.

1 See para **5.17**.
2 See general annotations.
3 See HC report, vol 291, no 70, col 234.
4 See para **5.39**.

5.39 By s 2(2), a person subject to the notification requirements shall, before the end of the period of 14 days beginning with:

(a)   his using a name which has not been notified to the police under s 2;
(b)   any change of his home address;
(c)   his having resided and stayed, for a qualifying period, at any premises in the UK[1] the address of which has not been notified to the police under s 2,

must notify that name, or change of address to the police within a 14-day period. The thrust of s 2(2) was discussed at para **5.38**. The term 'qualifying period' means:

(a)   a period of 14 days; or
(b)   two or more periods, in any period of 12 months, which (taken together) amount to 14 days (s 2(7)).

In calculating any period of time for the purposes of s 2(1) or (2), there is to be disregarded any time when the person in question:

(a)   is remanded in or committed to custody by an order of a court;
(b)   is serving a sentence of imprisonment or a term of service detention;
(c)   is detained in a hospital; or
(d)   is outside the UK.[1]

Surprisingly, the fact that a person is in police detention[2] is not on the list of matters that are to be disregarded. Thus, an offender who towards the end of the 14-day period for notification is taken into and remains in police detention is technically in breach of his notification requirement, but would not have been if, on the same date, he had left the UK. The point is not of practical importance because, arguably, such a person would, in those circumstances, have 'reasonable excuse' for failing to comply with the notification requirement, and thus would not be guilty of an offence under s 3(1).[3]

---

1 See general annotations.
2 See annotations to s 9.
3 See para **5.51**.

5.40   The effect of s 2(6) is that an offender who immediately goes abroad following conviction is under no obligation to notify his address abroad, nor the address of any premises that he visits in the UK unless and until he stays at those same premises for periods, singly or cumulatively, amounting to 14 days.

Thus, the combined effect of s 2(1) and (2) is that a person who 'visits' premises in the UK regularly must, within 14 days of the relevant date, notify the police of that address. If, however, he does not begin to visit those premises regularly until after the notification requirement has been complied with, then no notification requirement arises unless and until he spends a period of 14 days there (s 2(7)). It is submitted that the meaning of para (b) of s 2(2), which deal with the definition of 'qualifying period' is not such as to require the expiration of the whole of a 12-month period. The duty of notification arises once cumulatively the periods spent there amount to 14 days, those days falling within such a period of 12 months. However, if an offender spends 10-day periods with a friend and her children, or with different friends and that friend changes lodgings frequently, the notification requirement appears not to apply.

5.41 A further issue arises as to the meaning of the term 'premises'. This is not defined by SOA 1997. A convenient example of the term 'premises' is s 12 of the Criminal Law Act 1977, which includes within the meaning of 'premises' any building, or part of a building under separate occupation, any land ancillary to a building, and the site comprising any building or buildings together with any land ancillary thereto. 'Building' in this context includes any immovable structure, and any movable structure, vehicle or vessel designed or adapted for residential use (s 12(2)). Thus the notification requirements would appear to apply to residence or stays in caravans, motorhomes, caravans, houseboats and tents. Arguably, a person who lives rough, for example on park-benches, in cardboard boxes in shop doorways, or under the pier at a seaside resort in summer, is not subject to notification requirements in respect of that residence, even if it is for a period greater (individually or cumulatively) than 14 days.

The mechanics of notification

5.42 The mechanics of notification are dealt with by s 2(5). A person may give a notification:

(a) by attending at any police station in his local police area and giving an oral notification to any police officer, or to any person authorised for the purpose by the officer in charge of the station; or
(b) by sending a written notification to any such police station.

'Local police area' means the police area in which the offender's home is situated. A problem theoretically arises in respect of the offender who visits a family, on a regular basis, who live in a mobile caravan. A notification requirement arises, unless it is argued that there is no 'address' to notify, but, if the caravan is peripatetic between different police areas it is difficult to see to whom the notification should be given.

A notification must, in addition to the details prescribed in s 2(1) or (2), also state:

(a) the offender's date of birth;
(b) his name on the relevant date and, where he used one or more other names on that date, each of those names; and
(c) his home address on that date (s 2(3)).

The information supplied

5.43 Considerable debate has occurred as to the extent to which it is possible, or desirable, for the police to disclose information obtained about convicted sex offenders to other agencies involved in child protection work, to other public bodies (eg to education authorities) or communities as a whole. Such debate has occurred in a context of an awareness that in some jurisdictions in the United States the so-called 'Megan's law' has permitted full disclosure to the public of the identity of any sex offender who has taken up residence in a locality. Instances have occurred in the UK where public awareness of identity, or address, of a sex offender has led to vigilante conduct in the community.[1] Interested bodies have urged that the details on the sex offender register compiled under Pt I of the 1997 Act should not generally be available to the public. Public disclosure, it is argued, encourages vigilantism and may discourage offenders from registering, thus driving them underground. It may also encourage changes of name and the giving of false information. Public disclosure may also have an adverse effect on the welfare of the child or other family members, in cases where sexual abuse has occurred within the family. Even where it does not have that effect, public disclosure may 'undermine the struggle of the family to rebuild their lives at a time when what they most need is support'.[2] On the other hand, there may be an important public interest in such information being shared with other public bodies, such as local authorities, education departments and other relevant authorities.

---

1 See, eg, the *Observer*, 15 December 1996, which records that an offender, L, was 'driven-out' of his flat following disclosure of his identity by a national tabloid newspaper. See now *Devon County Council, ex parte L* (1997) unreported (DC). Note also the threats offered against another offender, a self-confessed predatory paedophile: see (1997) *The Times*, 5 July.
2 See, in particular, the National Society for Prevention of Cruelty to Children, and Children's Charities Consortium, conveniently cited by Mr Eddie O'Hara, MP, HC Deb, col 745, 7 July 1997. General public disclosure is also opposed by the Police Superintendents' Association and the Association of Chief Police Officers.

5.44 Nothing in the 1997 Act deals with the question as to the use to which information acquired by the police as a result of the notification requirement, or for that matter, in any other way, is to be put. During the passage of the 1997 Act there was recognition of the need for some further provision to deal with the question. The Government believed that guidance in the form of a Home Office Circular might be appropriate[1] resisting opposition amendments[2] which would have required both the making of regulations and the issue of a Code of Practice, which could also have dealt with the interrelation between the register under the 1997 Act and other registers containing details of sex offenders, whether convicted or suspected, such as the paedophile intelligence database held by the National Criminal Intelligence Service, the Department of Health's consultancy service index or the Department of Education's list 99 M.

---

1 Mr Timothy Kirkhope, Parliamentary Under Secretary, Home Office, HC Report, vol 578, no 63, col 226.
2 Mr Alan Michael, ibid, col 214.

5.45 The legal position of the police in respect of information in their possession is not beyond doubt, although authority suggests that, at any rate in some circumstances, disclosure can be justified.[1] Information in the hands of the police is not governed by the Official Secrets Act 1989, the information not being information held by or on behalf of the Crown. However, even if the 1989 Act did extend that far, it would not cover cases of authorised disclosure, and the main issue is the extent to which disclosure is, in fact, authorised in law.

The relevant legal provisions which govern the question of disclosure of information held by the police are piecemeal, and must be viewed in the context of the basic right to respect for private and family life contained in art 8 of the European Convention on Human Rights. That right is not absolute, and is subject to limits necessary for the protection of public safety or public health. If, therefore, disclosure is necessary for the purposes of such public protection it would not necessarily contravene art 8, although the action taken would need to be proportionate to the harm feared.[1] There might well be cases where the degree of risk posed by an offender was low, and the effects of public notification totally disproportionate to that risk.

Within that context, a variety of rules apply. In some circumstances the police owe those about whom they hold information a duty of care in respect of that information.[2] The law of defamation also applies. However, it is difficult to conceive of many cases where, provided disclosure was made properly and in good faith, and with a lack of negligence in the acquisition and verification of information held, that potential action in negligence would arise. So, too, with defamation: communication considered necessary for the protection of the public would surely be covered by the doctrine of qualified privilege.

---

1 See *Chief Constable of North Wales Police and Others, ex parte AB and Another* (1997) *The Times*, 14 July (DC).
2 *Swinney v Chief Constable of the Northumbria Police* [1996] 2 All ER 449 (CA); cf *Hill v Chief Constable of West Yorkshire* [1988] 2 All ER 238.

5.46 More difficult issues arise in the context of general issues of confidentiality. The equitable doctrine of breach of confidence does not provide absolute protection for information, even if that information is, presumptively, covered by confidence. Lord Bingham CJ in *Chief Constable of North Wales Police and Others, ex parte AB and Another*[1] doubted whether the doctrine of confidentiality extended to cover previous convictions, the applicants in that case having accepted that their convictions and sentences were announced in open court and thus in the public domain. This view is consistent with that expressed by the Queen's Bench Division in *Elliott v Chief Constable of Wiltshire*[2] where, in a case where a police officer disclosed to a journalist, for improper motives, information about criminal convictions, the judge held that there was no general duty attaching to convictions pronounced in open court. The police owed no duty of confidentiality to offenders, although on the facts of the case the police officer was liable in tort for misfeasance in a public office. The applicants in AB and CD, having made that concession, it was clear that, in that case, they were not subject to a duty of confidence in the hands of the police.

Arguably, the position is not as clear-cut as this might suggest, for it may well be that the concession by the applicants in *ex parte AB* was too wide. The fact that

AB and CD were convicted on a given date of specified offences is, of course, a fact in the public domain, and the factual conclusion in *AB* may well be correct. It does not follow from that, however, that information supplied to the police pursuant to a statutory requirement is likewise in the public domain. If it were, there would be no need for statute to require it to be given. Arguably, the register is governed by a duty of confidence. However, the point is probably academic, and of limited practical significance, because the issue is whether information, even if within an obligation of confidence, can be communicated to others. In *Hellewell v Chief Constable of Derbyshire*,[3] it was held that the police had a good defence to an action for breach of confidence. The police had circulated a photograph of a recidivist shoplifter to shopkeepers in the area, the photograph having been taken while the suspect was in police custody. It was held that, on the facts, the police had acted in good faith for the prevention or detection of crime and had distributed the photograph only to those who had reasonable need to make use of it. Even confidential information may be communicated to others if the confidence is outweighed by a greater public interest in disclosure.[4] This can only be judged on an individualised case-by-case basis, and a blanket approach would, arguably, be unlawful as would disclosure by individual officers on an ad hoc, unstructured basis.

Further, the impact of the Data Protection Act 1984 should be noted. This Act makes it an offence to disclose data beyond the categories of people or organisations listed in the data user's register entry. There are exceptions where failure to disclose would be likely to prejudice the prevention or detection of crime or where disclosure is urgently required to prevent injury or other damage to the health of any person. Again, these matters will need to be judged on a case-by-case basis.[5]

---

1 See (1997) *The Times*, 14 July.
2 (1995) Unreported (QBD).
3 [1995] 1 WLR 804 (QBD).
4 *Lion Laboratories v Evans* [1984] 2 All ER 417 (CA).
5 For the importance of this approach, see draft Home Office Circular 'Managing Information Acquired under the Provisions of the Sex Offenders Act 1997', also para **5.50**.

5.47 The question of disclosure of information has 'far reaching impli-cations',[1] and was considered by the Divisional Court in *Chief Constable of North Wales Police and Others, ex parte AB and Another*.[2] In that case the court dismissed a challenge by a married couple to a decision of the North Wales Police to notify the owner of a mobile home site when the couple, who had convictions for paedophile offences of rape and indecent assault, moved into the home on that site. The police had considerable concerns that during the Easter holidays many children would be staying at the caravan site where the applicants resided and, after consultation with social services and probation services, decided to inform the owner of the caravan site of the background of the applicants. It was that action that was the subject of challenge in the judicial review proceedings.

Lord Bingham CJ observed that although the identity of a sex offender should be protected, it was not an absolute right. He concluded that the policy and conduct of the police 'fell well within the bounds of legality'. Although it was true that the offender had served his sentence, and paid his debt, and was entitled to reintegrate himself into a normal life, some who committed sex offences have an incurable propensity to act in this way. The pattern of offending might well be repeated or even more serious offences committed. For these reasons it was in the interests of the community that those who might be the victims of such offences should be protected. Lord Bingham CJ accepted the submission of the Home Secretary that any policy adopted by the police should operate within a general presumption that information should not be disclosed. Where in the course of performing its duties, a public body such as the police comes into possession of information relating to a member of the public, being information not generally available and potentially damaging to that member of the public if disclosed, that body ought not to disclose it save for the purpose of and to the extent necessary for performance of its public duty. The police have an obligation to take all steps necessary to keep the peace, prevent and detect crime and to bring an offender to justice.[3] Although the police are entitled to make factual statements concerning police operations, even if they involve a report that an individual had been arrested or charged, there should not be disclosure of damaging information about individuals acquired by the police in the course of their operations unless there was a specific public justification for such disclosure. In a case such as that before the court, where the potential damage to the individual and potential harm to members of the community were so great and obvious, it could never be acceptable if decisions were made without close regard to the particular facts of the case, preferably in consultation with other agencies.

---

1 Per Lord Bingham CJ in *Chief Constable of North Wales Police and Others, ex parte AB and Another* (1997) *The Times*, 14 July.
2 See (1997) 147 NLJ 1061.
3 See *Glassbrook Brothers Ltd v Glamorgan County Council* [1925] AC 270 (HL); *Rice v Connolly* [1966] 2 QB 414; *Brown (Gregory)* [1994] QB 547 (CA); *Hellewell v Chief Constable of Derbyshire* [1995] 1 WLR 804.

5.48   The decision in this case naturally turns on its own facts, and beyond the principles set out in para **5.45**, there is no specific guidance as to how the disclosure power should be used. Lord Bingham CJ himself was concerned to stress the rights of the offender as well as the wider interests of the community. It was not acceptable, he said, that those who had undergone the lawful punishment imposed by the courts should be the subject of intimidation and private vengeance, harried from parish to parish like paupers under the old Poor Law. Whilst the risk of repeated offending might in some circumstances justify a *limited* measure of official disclosure, a general policy of disclosure could never be justified and the media should be slow to obstruct the rehabilitation of former offenders who had not offended again and who were seriously bent on reform.

However, these principles will not be easy to apply given the risks of repeat offending by those with a propensity for such conduct. Nor is the scope of appropriate disclosure clear. There is no doubt that the sharing of information between interested child protection agencies is justified, even on a confidential basis. The question is: how much further should disclosure go? The caravan site owner did not have child protection responsibilities, direct or indirect. Arguably, similar arguments could be put to justify disclosure to any person who might have contact with children as part of their business. Would disclosure to the owner of a sweetshop, children's bookshop, or manager of a local burger bar be appropriate if a known recidivist and predatory paedophile were known to be in the locality? The answer to each of those questions appears, potentially and subject to a sufficient degree of risk arising, to be 'yes'.

5.49 Questions arise as to the extent to which information is shared. In relation to agencies working in the area of child protection, the principle enshrined in *Working Together*[1] remains valid. At para 3.10 of that document, it is stated:

> 'Arrangements for the protection of children from abuse, and in particular child protection conferences, can only be successful if the professional staff concerned do all they can to work in partnership and share and exchange relevant information, in particular with Social Services departments (or the NSPCC) and the police.'[2]

---

1 (1989) Home Office/Dept of Health. Home Office Circular 54/1991, which deals with the duties and powers of the police under the Children Act 1989 remains valid: see also Home Office Circular 84/1991.
2 For the position in respect of the sharing of information relating to patients who are the subject of hospital orders, see *The Protection and Use of Patient Information* (Department of Health, 1996).

5.50 In an effort to provide guidance on these difficult issues, the Home Office has issued interim guidance. This guidance[1] places emphasis on the need for disclosure to be dealt with on an individual, case-by-case basis, judged on the basis of the likelihood of harm that might otherwise result. Disclosure should be seen as part of an overall plan for managing the risk posed by the offender and vulnerability of an individual child, group of children or other persons. Decisions should be guided by the assessment of the seriousness of risk, displacement of offending, the visibility of the offender and any operational considerations in respect of the management of risk posed by the offender. The Guidance is intended to be in respect of disclosure to third parties, because arrangements already exist for disclosure between statutory and voluntary agencies responsible for child protection.

Disclosure should be based on risk assessment of the individual committing an offence, taking account of the nature and pattern of previous offending, the probability that a further offence will be committed, the harm that such behaviour would cause, and any predatory behaviour which may indicate a likelihood that he will reoffend and the potential objects of the harm (and whether they are children or otherwise especially vulnerable). Also to be taken into account are the potential consequences of disclosure to the offender, his family and neighbours, and the potential consequences of disclosure in the wider context of law and order.

If disclosure is considered to be justified, the information that is to be disclosed and the person to whom disclosure is made should be carefully considered. It should normally be to an identified individual or individuals directly affected by the risk of harm or with the responsibilities towards others for the prevention of harm. A full record of the circumstances and grounds of disclosure must be kept.

Specific issues arise in the context of the workplace where care needs to be taken as to the extent and process of disclosure, communication to the local education authority in respect of known offenders seen in the vicinity of schools, with youth groups where an offender may have a role, official or unofficial, in the work of that organisation, in respect of the attendance of the offender at an education establishment such as a school, further education college or university.

---

1 Managing information acquired under the provisions of the Sex Offender Act 1997 (Home Office, 1997).

Offences

5.51 By s 3(1), if a person:

(a)   fails, without reasonable excuse, to comply with s 2(1) or (2); or

(b)   notifies to the police, in purported compliance with s 2(1) or (2), any information which he knows to be false,

he shall be liable on summary conviction to a fine not exceeding level 5 on the standard scale,[1] or to imprisonment for a term not exceeding six months, or to both.

A person commits an offence under s 3(1)(a) on the day on which he first fails, without reasonable excuse, to comply with s 2(1) or (2) and continues to commit it throughout any period during which the failure continues; but a person shall not be prosecuted under that provision more than once in respect of the same failure (s 3(2)).

Proceedings may be commenced in any court having jurisdiction in any place where the person charged with the offence resides or is found (s 3(3)).

---

1 See general annotations.

Proof of sexual offence

5.52   Proof of a conviction for a sexual offence, or the fact of caution, is dealt with by s 5 of the 1997 Act. By s 5(2), if the court by or before which the person is so convicted or so found:

(a)   states in open court:[1]

    (i)   that on the date he has been convicted, found not guilty by reason of insanity or found to be under a disability and to have done the act charged against him; and

    (ii)   that the offence in question is a sexual offence to which Pt I applies, and

(b)   certifies those facts (whether at that time or subsequently),

the certificate shall, for the purposes of Pt I, be evidence of those facts.

In respect of a caution by a constable in respect of a sexual offence to which Pt I applies and which at the time when the caution is given he has admitted:

(a)   if the constable informs the person that he has been cautioned on that date and that the offence in question is a sexual offence to which Pt I applies; and

(b)   certifies those facts (whether at the time or subsequently) in such form as the Secretary of State may by order prescribe,

the certificate shall, for the purposes of Pt I, be evidence of those facts (s 5(4)).

The Sex Offenders (Certificate of Caution) Order 1997[2] has now been made, which prescribes the form to be used by a constable to certify that a person has been cautioned for an offence to which Pt I of the 1997 Act applies and that the person has been so informed.

---

1 See annotations to s 11.
2 SI 1997/1921.

SEXUAL OFFENCES COMMITTED OUTSIDE THE UK – SEX TOURISM

5.53   Part II of the 1997 Act addresses the problem of 'sex tourism'. It extends the jurisdiction of the UK courts to allow trials in the UK of those who commit child sexual abuse abroad. This change is part of a strategy to take action against those who travel to countries where child prostitution is rife and sexually abuse young children there. The international organisation, UNICEF, estimates, for example, that some 60,000 children are abused in the Philippines.[1] An earlier legislative response was the passage of the Sexual Offences (Conspiracy and Incitement) Act 1996, which recognised the importance of extending the jurisdiction of the UK courts over acts of conspiracy or incitement in the UK to commit sexual offences against children abroad. More recently, the Home Office published a paper outlining the range of measures, actual and proposed, that could be deployed to curb the commercial sexual exploitation of children.[2]

---

1 (1997) *The Times*, 15 January.
2 *Action against the Commercial Sexual Exploitation of Children*, Home Office, August 1996, presented to the Stockholm World Congress on that subject, in 1996.

5.54 The intent of Pt II of the Sex Offenders Act 1997 is, within the principle of dual criminality, to bring certain conduct committed overseas within the jurisdiction of the UK courts. It is not the intention that the UK courts should be the primary forum for such matters. The Minister of State, Mr David Maclean, told Parliament[1] that 'we would look to the authorities concerned to prosecute [the alleged offender] under their own laws'. The requirements of oral testimony, and the difficulties of getting witnesses to testify in the UK provide practical constraints on prosecutors in the UK. Nevertheless, if for whatever reason extradition of alleged offenders is neither possible nor desirable, the new provisions will permit such an alleged offender to be tried in the UK.

---

1 Mr David Maclean, Minister of State, Home Office, Sex Offender Bill, Second Reading, HC Deb, vol 289, no 50, col 32, 27 January 1997.

5.55 The provisions will take effect from such date as may be specified by the Home Secretary by order. No such order had been made as at the date of going to press.

5.56 Section 7(1) provides that, subject to s 7(2), any act done by a person in a country or territory outside the UK which:

(a) constituted an offence under the law in force in that country or territory; and

(b) would constitute a sexual offence to which s 7 applies if it had been done in England and Wales, or in Northern Ireland,

shall constitute that sexual offence under the law of that part of the UK.

Section 7(1) is thus based on the principle of dual criminality. There is, on the one hand, no possibility of a foreign State forcing, unilaterally, its own standards or values on UK courts. Conversely, our own values are not being imposed on that foreign State.

5.57 The exception in s 7(2) provides that no proceedings shall be brought under s 7 unless he was at the commencement of s 7, or has subsequently become, a British citizen or resident in the UK.

5.58 The offences to which s 7 applies are identified by s 7(7) and Sch 1. They include the following offences under the Sexual Offences Act 1956:

(i) rape (s 1);

(ii) intercourse with a girl under 13 (s 5);

(iii) intercourse with a girl between 13 and 16 (s 6);

(iv) buggery (s 12);

(v) indecent assault on a woman (s 14);

(vi) indecent assault on a man (s 15);

(vii) assault with intent to commit buggery (s 16).

Other relevant offences include indecent conduct towards a young child (Indecency with Children Act 1960, s 1) and indecent photographs of children (Protection of Children Act 1978, s 1).

5.59 By s 7(3), an act punishable under the law in force in any country or territory constitutes an offence under that law for the purposes of s 7, however it is described in that law. The proof of that offence is governed by s 7(4), which provides that the condition in s 7(1)(a) shall be taken to be satisfied unless, not later than the rules of court may provide,[1] the defence serve on the prosecution a notice:

(a)   stating that, on the facts as alleged with respect to the act in question, the condition is not in their opinion satisfied;

(b)   showing their grounds for that opinion; and

(c)   requiring the prosecution to show that it is satisfied.

It is open to a court to waive the requirement for notice (s 7(6)). It should be remembered that the proof of the overseas offence lies, as is the case with the UK offence, on the prosecution.

---

1 No such rules had been made as at the date of going to press.

OTHER MEASURES RELATING TO SEX OFENDERS

5.60 A variety of other measures directly, or indirectly, relate to sex offenders, or alleged sex offenders, or their regulation. The first is the Criminal Evidence (Amendment) Act 1997. Section 1 of that Act amends s 63 of PACE, by inserting therein a new s 63(9A). This allows a non-intimate sample to be taken without consent from a person who has been convicted of a recordable offence, provided:

(a)   the offence is one listed in Sch 1 to the 1997 Act; and

(b)   at the time the sample is taken he is serving a sentence of imprisonment for that offence, or detained for that offence under the Mental Health Act 1983.

The offences specified in Sch 1 to that Act include the majority of offences under the Sexual Offences Act 1956, and offences under s 1 of the Indecency with Children Act 1960 and s 1 of the Protection of Children Act 1978. It also includes all the significant offences of violence under the Offences Against the Person Act 1861, burglary and aggravated burglary, and various offences involving explosives. The provision is clearly designed to assist in the acquisition of material which will provide information for the DNA database.

5.61 Secondly, the Sexual Offences (Protected Material) Act 1997 regulates access to materials which are disclosed by the prosecution or the Criminal Cases Review Commission, in connection with proceedings relating to certain sexual and other offences.

5.62 Thirdly, Pt V of the Police Act 1997 creates a scheme for the issue of criminal conviction certificates, criminal record certificates and enhanced criminal record certificates. This will facilitate to proof of good character in respect of criminal record checks that are likely, in due course, to provide added protection against sex offenders working with children or young persons.[1]

1 See (1997) *The Times*, 28 January. See Home Office Consultation Document, *Sex Offenders: A Ban on Working with Chlidren,* January 1997.

5.63 Finally, the provisions of the Protection from Harassment Act 1997 create new remedies, civil and criminal, in respect of those who engage in harassment. Such conduct is often, although not always, undertaken in the context of a sexual relationship. Pre-existing common law created the power for a court to issue an injunction to restrain a person from conduct where such injunctive relief was necessary to protect the plaintiff's legitimate interest.[1] Such injunctive relief can be used in some circumstances to prevent conduct amounting to harassment by an actual or potential sex offender. Other relevant provisions that could be deployed are the public order offences under s 4, s 4A and s 5 of the Public Order Act 1986, the common law powers of the police to prevent breaches of the peace from occurring or continuing and the offence created by s 1 of the Malicious Communications Act 1988.

1 See *Burris v Azadani* [1995] 1 WLR 1372 (CA); *Khorasandjian v Bush* [1993] QB 727 (CA).

5.64 Section 1(1) of the Protection from Harassment Act 1997 states that a person must not pursue a course of conduct:

(a)　which amounts to harassment of another; and
(b)　which he knows or ought to know amounts to harassment of the other.

It is an offence under s 2 of that Act to pursue a course of conduct in breach of the prohibition on harassment under s 1, punishable summarily with a term of imprisonment of up to six months and/or a fine not exceeding level 5 on the standard scale[1] (s 2(2)).

1 See general annotations.

Chapter 6

MENTALLY DISORDERED OFFENDERS

Introduction – Definition of mentally disordered offender – Existing powers – Reasons for extended powers – Miscellaneous changes

INTRODUCTION

6.1 Part II of the new Act contains consequential provisions that apply the framework of the new early release provisions, length of sentence provisions and supervision arrangements to those who suffer from mental disorder. However, Pt III of the new Act makes new provisions in respect of mentally disordered offenders. It gives to the courts the power when passing a prison sentence to attach a direction of immediate admission to hospital. Existing arrangements for the sentencing of disordered offenders require the courts to choose between punishment and treatment. A court may impose a hospital order instead of a prison sentence. The effect of this is that the offender will be discharged as soon as treatment is completed, regardless of how serious the offence was. The new Act introduces a new form of order, a hospital direction order and a hospital limitation direction.

The new hospital direction will provide a guarantee that a prisoner will receive treatment. It is intended that initially the hospital direction order and limitation direction will be available for offenders suffering from psychopathic disorders, but it is intended in due course to extend its operation for all mentally disordered offenders.[1] The new Act also contains provisions that modify the 1983 Act in small, but important, ways. In particular, the length of an interim hospital order, under s 38 of the 1983 Act, is increased from six to 12 months.[2]

---

1 Michael Howard, QC, MP, Home Secretary, 4 November 1996.
2 See para **6.17**.

Commencement

6.2 These new powers will come into force from such day as is appointed for that purpose by the Home Secretary, by statutory instrument (s 57(2)). No such day had been appointed as at the date of going to press.

The pre-existing law

6.3 Part III of the Mental Health Act 1983 deals with powers available to a court to deal with an offender who suffers from mental illness or mental disorder.[1] The general scheme of Pt III is to provide a range of powers and orders which form a basis for the treatment, rather than the punishment, of such offenders. Section 37 of the 1983 Act gives to a court the power to make a hospital order.[2] By such an order, a court can authorise the admission to, and detention within, a specified hospital, or within the guardianship of a local authority. The pre-conditions for the making of a hospital or guardianship order are set out in s 37(2) of the 1983 Act. These are that:

(a)   the court is satisfied, on the written or oral evidence of two registered medical practitioners, that the offender is suffering from mental illness, psychopathic disorder, severe mental impairment or mental impairment and that either:

    (i)   the mental disorder from which the offender is suffering is of a nature or degree which makes it appropriate for him to be detained in a hospital for medical treatment and, in the case of a psychopathic disorder or mental impairment, that such treatment is likely to alleviate or prevent a deterioration of his condition; or

    (ii)   in the case of an offender who has attained the age of 16 years, the mental disorder is of a nature or degree which warrants his reception into guardianship under (the 1983 Act);

(b)   the court is of the opinion, having regard to all the circumstances including the nature of the offence and the character and antecedents of the offender, and to the other available methods of dealing with him, that the most suitable method of disposing of the case is by means of an order under s 37.

As the Butler Report put it,[3] 'In making a hospital order, the court is placing the patient in the hands of the doctors, foregoing any question of punishment, and relinquishing from then onwards its own control over him'.

To prevent release from hospital in circumstances where the offender presents a risk of causing serious harm, the sentencing court may, in addition to making a hospital order, make a restriction order under s 41 of the 1983 Act.[4] This restricts the discharge of the patient from hospital for a specified or unlimited period if it considers it is necessary for the protection of the public. Clearly, the objective is to prevent the release of persons whilst they remain a risk of causing serious harm. A restriction order cannot, however, prevent the release of a person who has been made the subject of a hospital order, but who has ceased to be a risk to the public.[5]

---

1   Based in this respect on the recommendations of the Butler Committee, *The Report of the Committee on Mentally Abnormal Offenders* (HMSO, 1976) Cmnd 6244. See also *The Review of Mental Health Act 1959* (HMSO, 1976) Cmnd 7320. For the definitions of the expressions 'mental illness', 'mental impairment', psychopathic disorder' and 'any other disorder or disability of mind' see the Mental Health Act 1983, s 1, and annotations to s 46 and s 47.

2   See annotations to s 47.

3   Butler Committee, op cit, para 14.8.

4 See annotations to s 49.

5 For the release of persons who have been the subject of a restriction order, see s 42. The Home Secretary may direct that the order shall cease to have effect, discharge the patient unconditionally, or discharge the patient subject to conditions.

6.4 A sentencing court thus has a choice between punishment or treatment. The making of that choice can be informed by an interim assessment made during an interim hospital order under s 38(1).[1] This empowers a court to send a convicted person to hospital for a period not exceeding six months so that an assessment on him can be carried out as to whether he is a suitable person to be the subject of a hospital order. Further, s 47 of the 1983 Act[2] empowers the Home Secretary, where the pre-conditions are satisfied, to order the removal to hospital of a person serving a sentence of imprisonment.

1 See annotations to s 49.
2 See annotations to s 47.

6.5 The pre-condition for a transfer order under s 47 is that the Home Secretary has to be satisfied, by reports from at least two registered medical practitioners:

(a) that the said person is suffering from mental illness, psychopathic disorder, severe mental impairment or mental impairment; and

(b) that the mental disorder from which that person is suffering is of a nature or degree which makes it appropriate for him to be detained in a hospital for medical treatment and, in the case of psychopathic disorder or mental impairment, that such treatment is likely to alleviate or prevent a deterioration of his condition.

A restriction order may, and, in some cases, must be added to a transfer order under s 47. However, no power has existed to order the return to prison once a patient has been found not to require medical treatment. It is this gap that the new Act seeks to plug by the creation of new 'hospital' and 'limitation' directions.

Reasons for change

6.6 The Government in its White Paper[1] stated that it considered existing arrangements where the courts have to choose between punishment and treatment to be inadequate. In some cases, an offender requires treatment in hospital but the circumstances of the offence also require a fixed period to be served in detention because the offender is found to bear some significant responsibility for the offence notwithstanding his disorder, or because the link between the offending behaviour and the mental disorder is not clear at the time of sentencing.

The new hospital direction and limitation direction powers are intended to meet this difficulty in cases where, in respect of a serious offence, the court has heard evidence that the offender is mentally disordered, but is not satisfied that dealing with the mental disorder will prevent further serious offences after he is released.[2] Under the existing provisions of the 1983 Act the court must choose between a hospital order or a prison sentence. The former is likely to lead to the release of the offender as soon as his treatment is complete, or if the doctors consider that his condition is untreatable. Under the new proposals, if a doctor considers that the offender is untreatable he can recommend that the Home Office remit the offender to prison to serve the balance of his sentence. The new powers do not, and are not intended to, interfere with the existing power, or practice, of the courts in respect of the making of hospital orders.[3] The use of the power to make directions is expected to be limited, and most likely to be used in respect of those suffering from psychopathic disorder, where doubt exists as to whether the risk that psychopaths will re-offend can be influenced through clinical treatment.

---

1 (1997) op cit, para 8.14.
2 Baroness Blatch, Minister of State, Home Office, HL Catty, col 1359.
3 Ibid, col 1360. The new power is initially so limited, but can be extended by order: see para **6.12**.

6.7 Concerns have been realised about the new powers. The concept of a hybrid order, combining elements of a prison sentence and hospital order was originally recommended by an inter-departmental committee,[1] the Reid Committee, but the provisions of the new power have gone beyond the intent of those recommendations.[1] That Committee was considering the application of such an order solely in respect of those suffering from psychopathic disorder, or other mental illnesses, such as schizophrenia. The new power may be extended beyond the former, to include the latter.[2] Secondly, the Reid Committee did not envisage that when an offender has been successfully treated he be returned to prison, but rather that persons who are found not to be capable of responding to treatment should be so transferred. The dilemma a psychiatrist may face is that a break in the continuity of care may result, harming the benefits of the work undertaken in hospital. An offender might serve the first three years of an eight-year sentence in a secure unit,[2] respond to treatment effectively and then be transferred to prison. Concern has also been expressed that the nature of the powers is such as to make doctors reluctant to return the patient to prison, with the psychiatrist effectively, albeit indirectly, performing the role of gaoler,[3] having the obligation to determine at what stage the patient, having been cured of his illness, is sent to prison.

---

1 Inter-Departmental Committee on Psychopathic Disorder, established by Home Office and Department of Health, Chaired by Dr John Reid, 1994.
2 For extension and modification of the powers to make an order under the 1983 Act to a secure unit within a hospital, see para **6.12**.
3 See, eg, Lord Alderdice, HL Committee, col 1356.

The new powers

6.8 The power to make either a 'hospital direction' or a 'limitation direction' is introduced by a new s 45A of the Mental Health Act 1983, inserted into the

1983 Act by s 46 of the new Act. Section 46 comes into effect on such day as may be appointed by statutory instrument. No such day had been appointed as at the date of going to press.

6.9 A hospital direction is defined by s 45A(3)(a) as a direction that, instead of being removed to or detained in a prison, the offender be removed to and detained in such hospital as may be specified in the direction. A limitation direction is a direction that the offender be subject to the special restrictions set out in s 41 of the 1983 Act.

Where such a direction is made, it applies not only in respect of the sentence in respect of which it is given, but also as regards any other sentence of imprisonment imposed on the same or a previous occasion (1983 Act, s 45A(9)). The effect of this provision appears to be that if, for example, an offender is serving a term of imprisonment for a pre-commencement offence, is then tried and sentenced, post-commencement, for a different offence, and that court on that latter occasion making a direction, the direction made on that latter occasion applies in respect of both the earlier term and the latter term.

6.10 A pre-condition for the making of either of these directions is that s 45A should apply. The circumstances in which that section applies are specified by s 45A(1). By that subsection, s 45A applies where a person is convicted before the Crown Court of an offence for which the sentence is not fixed by law, and:

(a)   the conditions set out in s 45A(2) are satisfied; and
(b)   except where the sentence is one which falls to be imposed by virtue of s 2 of the 1997 Act (mandatory life sentence for second serious offence),[1] the court considers making a hospital order in respect of him before deciding to impose a sentence of imprisonment ('the relevant sentence') in respect of the offence.

The new powers are not available to a magistrates' court.

Thus, a court cannot impose a hospital or limitation direction unless it has first considered, and rejected, the making of a hospital order. This is intended to be a key safeguard so as to prevent the new powers being used to justify the imposition of a term of imprisonment where treatment, not punishment, is appropriate.[2]

---

1 See para **2.2**.
1 Baroness Blatch, Minister of State, Home Office, HL Committee, col 1360.

6.11 The pre-conditions contained in s 45A(2) are that the court is satisfied, on the written or oral evidence of two registered medical practitioners:

(a)   that the offender is suffering from psychopathic disorder;
(b)   that the mental disorder from which the offender is suffering is of a nature or degree which makes it appropriate for him to be detained in a hospital for medical treatment; and

(c)   that such treatment is likely to alleviate or prevent a deterioration of his condition.

A hospital direction and a limitation direction shall not be given in relation to an offender unless at least one of the medical practitioners whose evidence is taken into account by the court under s 45A(2) of the 1983 Act has given evidence orally before the court (1983 Act, s 45A(4)). Further, by s 45A(5), the court must be satisfied on the written or oral evidence of the registered medical practitioner who would be in charge of his treatment, or of some other person representing the managers of the hospital that arrangements have been made:

(a)   for his admission to that hospital; and
(b)   for his admission to it within the period of 28 days beginning with the day of the giving of such directions.

The position in respect of the availability of the hospital place under the new powers would appear to be the same as currently obtains in the context of hospital orders, namely, that it is for the hospital to determine whether a hospital place is available. If a hospital is unwilling to accept an individual, perhaps because he is known to misbehave or is considered to be dangerous, the court has no power of compulsion.

The court may, pending his admission within that 28-day period, give such directions as it thinks fit for his conveyance to and detention in a place of safety. If, within that period, it appears to the Secretary of State that by reason of an emergency or other special circumstances it is not practicable for the patient to be received into the hospital specified in the hospital direction, he may give instructions for the admission of the patient to such other hospital as appears to be appropriate instead of the hospital so specified (s 45A(6)). Unlike a court, the Secretary of State *does* have the power to require a hospital to take an offender. That does not have to be a special hospital. In such circumstances, the Secretary of State must cause the person having custody of the patient to be informed, and the hospital direction shall have effect as if the hospital specified in the instructions were substituted for the hospital specified in the hospital direction (s 45A(7)).

6.12   The power to make a hospital direction or a limitation direction initially only applies to cases where the offender is suffering psychopathic disorder.[1] This limitation was the subject of criticism when the provisions of the new Act were debated during the passage of the Act through Parliament, but it is intended that this power should be broadened out. For that purpose, s 45A(10) grants power to the Secretary of State to provide by order that s 45A shall have effect as if the reference to psychopathic disorder included a reference to a mental disorder[1] of such other description as may be specified in the order (s 45A(10)). Such an order may apply generally, or to certain classes of offenders or offences, may refer to custodial sentences or institutions of such decryption as may be specified, and contain such other supplementary, incidental or consequential matters as appear necessary or expedient to the Secretary of State (s 45A(11)).

1 See annotations to s 46.

6.13 The new powers may be made even though there is no causal connection between the offender's disorder and the offence for which he is being sentenced. That has been the position in respect to the making of hospital orders,[1] and nothing in the new Act appears to change that. Likewise, the gravity of the offence for which the offender is being sentenced is not decisive as to whether a hospital or limitation direction should be made.[2] The making of the order is a matter for the judge, who does not need for there to be a positive recommendation in favour of such a direction, or agreement to such a direction, by medical witnesses, provided he considers it to be 'appropriate' for an offender to be so detained.[3] Clearly, however, the attitude of the medical witnesses will be an important factor in determining whether such a direction should be made.

1 *McBride* [1972] Crim LR 332 (CA); *Hatt* [1962] Crim LR 647.
2 *Eaton* [1976] Crim LR 390 (CA).
3 *Royce* (1981) 3 Cr App R (S) 58 (CA).

6.14 It was noted earlier,[1] that a court could make an interim hospital order under s 38[2] to facilitate the making of an assessment. That power to make an interim order extends to the making of an interim hospital order for the purposes of determining whether the making of a hospital direction or a limitation direction is appropriate (1983 Act, s 45A(8)).

1 See para **6.3**.
2 See annotations to s 46.

6.15 The making of a hospital direction entitled a constable or other authorised person to convey the patient to the hospital specified in the direction within a period of 28 days, and for the managers of that hospital to admit him at any time within that period and thereafter detain him in accordance with the provisions of the 1983 Act (1983 Act, s 45B(1)(a)).[1] There would appear to be no power to so convey or detain outside that period of 28 days, with the result that the offender would be required to be detained in custody within the normal prison regime. The direction has the effect of a transfer direction, under s 47 of the 1983 Act.[1] It thus has the effect of a hospital order made without restrictions.

If a transfer direction is made, the Home Secretary may impose restrictions. A limitation direction is to be treated as a restriction order (1983 Act, s 45B(2)(b)). The effect of this is that the patient cannot be released from hospital without the consent of the Secretary of State (1983 Act, ss 41(3), 49(2)), and, because the patient has been made the subject of a term of imprisonment, may be returned to serve his custodial sentence once his release from hospital is justified on medical grounds.

1 See annotations to s 46.

6.16 Section 47 of the new Act includes powers which, in the detailed circumstances set out in s 47(2), entitles the maker of a hospital order subject to a restriction order under ss 37 and 41 of the 1983 Act, the maker of a hospital and limitation directions (1983 Act, s 45A), transfer directions subject to restriction directions (1983 Act, ss 47 and 49) or orders for admission to hospital subject to a direction (Criminal Procedure (Insanity and Unfitness to Plead) Act 1991, Sch 1, para 1, para 2(1)(b))[1] in each case to specify a particular hospital unit, within a hospital.

1 See annotations to s 47 of the new Act.

Other changes

6.17 The new Act makes a range of other changes to the 1983 Act. These are made by s 49 of the new Act. The effect of these changes is as follows:

(a) Section 49(1) amends s 38(1) of the 1983 Act.[1] The effect of this is that an interim hospital order may continue in force for up to 12 months, instead of the six-month period that has subsisted hitherto.

(b) Section 49(2) amends s 41(3) so as to make it clear that any transfer of a patient under s 19(3) of the 1983 Act[1] also requires the consent of the Home Secretary.

(c) Section 47(1) of the 1983 Act prohibits the making of a transfer direction for the purposes of detention in a mental nursing home.[1] Section 49(3) removes that restriction.

(d) Section 49(4) makes a complex amendment to Sch 1 to the 1983 Act, which in turn amended various provisions of the 1983 Act for certain purposes in connection with patients subject to hospital and guardianship orders. The effect of the amendment is to require the consent of the Home Secretary to a transfer of a patient by a hospital to another hospital managed by the same Health Authority (1983 Act, s 19(3), as amended by 1993 Act, Sch 1, Pt II, para 5 (as amended)).

The purpose of each of these changes is to increase the flexibility of existing arrangements for dealing with mentally disordered offenders at all stages of the process from remand through to the rehabilitation process.[2]

1 See annotations to s 49.
2 White Paper, op cit, para 8.12.

6.18 Section 48 of, and Sch 3 to, the new Act, introduced modified provisions relating to the transfer within the British Islands[1] of responsibility for offenders conditionally discharged from hospital. It does so by introducing new ss 80A, 81A, 82A, 83A, and 85A into the 1983 Act and making reciprocal changes to

Scottish legislation. The broad effect is that if it appears that a transfer of responsibility of a patient from England and Wales to Scotland or Northern Ireland would be in the interests of the patient, the Home Secretary may make it. The changes apply to persons who have been the subject of a restriction order (and in respect of transfers to Northern Ireland, a restriction direction), and who have been conditionally discharged.

---

1 See general annotations.

6.19 Section 5 of, and Sch 4 to, the new Act also makes minor amendments to various provisions in the 1983 Act. The new Act makes various other amendments to the 1983 Act. In each case these are minor, consequential changes, the need for which arises because of the changes made by the new Act itself.

Chapter 7

MISCELLANEOUS CHANGES

Disclosure of pre-sentence reports – Committals for sentence – Penalty for indecent assault – Young offenders – Abolition of consent for community orders – Attendance centre orders – Persistent petty offenders – Driving disqualification – Transfer within UK

7.1 The new Act makes a variety of other changes affecting criminal procedure or powers relating to sentence. These changes will come into effect on such days as may be appointed for the purpose by order made by the Home Secretary. One such order has been made as at the date of going to press. That is the Crime (Sentences) Act 1997 (Commencement) (No 1) Order 1997.[1] That brings into effect paras 14 and 19 of Sch 1 to the new Act, as from 25 June 1997.[2]

---

1 SI 1997/1581.
2 See para **7.41**.

DISCLOSURE OF PRE-SENTENCE REPORTS

7.2 Section 50 of the new Act deals with the availability and disclosure of pre-sentence reports (PSR).[1] For the first time it imposes a duty on the court to disclose a PSR to a prosecutor, subject to the limited exceptions contained in s 50(4).

---

1 For the definition of a PSR, see Criminal Justice Act 1991, s 3(5) and annotations to s 50 of the new Act.

7.3 Section 3 of the Criminal Justice Act 1991, as amended,[1] imposes a duty on a court sentencing an adult offender to obtain and consider a PSR before forming an opinion that only a custodial sentence can be justified, unless it is of the opinion that such a report is unnecessary. Nor need a court consider a PSR prior to the making of a community order if it considers such a report unnecessary (1991 Act, s 7). Different rules apply in respect of an offender aged under 18.[2] In respect of such an offender the power to dispense with a PSR only exists where the offence is triable only on indictment, unless there is a pre-existing PSR and the court relies on that PSR.[3] Those requirements remain unchanged.

However, the new Act does change the law relating to the availability of such reports. Section 46 of the Powers of Criminal Courts Act 1973 required copies of a PSR to be given by the court to the offender or his solicitor. It did not require a copy to be given to the prosecutor.

---

1 Amended by the Criminal Justice and Public Order Act 1994, s 168(1), Sch 9, para 40. See, generally, Card and Ward, *The Criminal Justice and Public Order Act 1994* (Jordans, 1994), paras 9.2–9.11.
2 See general annotations.
3 1991 Act, s 3(2A) and s 7.

7.4   Section 50(2) of the new Act provides that, subject to subsections (3) and (4), the court shall give a copy of the report to:

(a)   the offender or his counsel or solicitor; and

(b)   the prosecutor, that is to say, the person having the conduct of the proceedings in respect of the offence.

The first exception to this general rule is contained in subsection (3) which provides that if the offender is under 17[1] and is not represented by solicitor or counsel, a copy of the report need not be given to him but shall be given instead to his parent or guardian if present in court. The wording of this subsection is not entirely clear, but appears to justify the withholding of the report from the offender even if a copy cannot be given to the parent or guardian because neither of them is in fact present.

The second exception, in subsection (4), states that if the prosecutor is not of a description prescribed by order made by the Home Secretary, a copy of the PSR need not be given to the prosecutor if the court considers that it would be inappropriate for him to be given it. No such order has been made as at the date of going to press, but, clearly, the intent is that there be no automatic right to a PSR on the part of a private prosecutor.

---

1 See general annotations.

7.5   The purpose of the change is to ensure that the prosecutor is in possession of all relevant material in respect of sentence. Although the prosecution has no direct interest in the sentence imposed, the prosecutor is under a positive duty to assist the court, by bringing to the attention of the court relevant sentencing provisions and principles, and to correct errors where these are apparent.[1] It may also be the case that a prosecutor is under a duty to bring to the attention of the court matters put forward, in a PSR or in mitigation, and which he knows to be untrue or misleading. As the Government stated in its White Paper,[2] the non disclosure of a PSR to the prosecution 'can hamper the ability of the prosecution to assist the court by providing an informed response where conflicting information from the defence and the probation service is received'.

However, this might be perceived, by an offender, as a factor inhibiting full and frank disclosure of relevant facts to a report writer. These matters may be of a sensitive or embarrassing nature, or may even indicate matters that might be of interest to the police or to a prosecutor in another case. The courts have long recognised the importance of frankness in reports, by not allowing their use for other, unconnected, purposes.[3] This principle is preserved by s 50(5). That subsection states that no information obtained by virtue of subsection (2)(b) shall be used or disclosed otherwise than for the purpose of:

(a) determining whether representations as to matters contained in the report need to be made to the court; or

(b) making such representations to the court.

1 See *Richards* (1993) *The Times*, 1 April (CA); *Hartrey* [1993] Crim LR 230 (CA); *Johnstone (Darren)* (1996) *The Times*, 18 June (CA).
2 Op cit, para 5.25.
3 *Lenihan v West Yorkshire Metropolitan Police* (1981) 3 Cr App R (S) 42 (DC).

7.6 The precise effect of s 50 remains to be seen. Nothing in the new Act requires such a report to be supplied by the probation service or by the accused, and there appears no right to see a copy of the report in advance of the formal sentencing hearing.[1] Nor are the terms of s 50(5) entirely clear. Obviously, a prosecutor cannot use the PSR directly as evidence in another case, nor for the purposes of cross-examining an offender in another case. However, interesting problems will arise if a PSR discloses information, say as to the actions of an accused which are at variance with what is being said in evidence. Clearly, the report itself cannot be used, but, arguably, there is nothing in such circumstances to prevent a prosecutor from asking questions as to such matters, or, presumably, asking investigators to investigate certain matters, provided the course of the information directing the inquiry is not made clear.

Problems may also arise if a *Newton* hearing is held in the instant case. The terms of s 50(5) confine the use of information to the making of representations. Arguably, such a hearing might be held to determine whether those representations are in fact correct, and, in such a case, a literal reading of s 50(5) might preclude the use of such a report. Such a conclusion would, of course, have the desirable effect of maintaining the restrictions on use of such a report but, none the less, be an odd conclusion. It is submitted that the use of the report ought, at any rate, to extend to all sentencing matters in the instant case.

1 The view to the contrary expressed in Samuels, *Pre-Sentence Report Disclosure to the Prosecution – Objections and Justifications* (1997) 161 JP 550 appears to represent desirable practice but not the position under s 50.

COMMITTALS FOR SENTENCE

7.7 Section 49 of the Criminal Procedure and Investigations Act 1996[1] will, if implemented, invite defendants to state their plea before a decision on mode of trial is taken, and require a magistrates' court either to sentence or commit for sentence a defendant in the event of a guilty plea. However, the defendant may have been committed for trial on other offences. The effect of that may be that the offender is sentenced by different courts in respect of related offences.

1 See Card and Ward, *The Criminal Procedure and Investigations Act 1996* (Jordans, 1996).

7.8   To avoid this undesirable conclusion, s 51 of the new Act creates a new s 38A of the Magistrates' Courts Act 1980 which, in effect, provides that the offender may be committed to be dealt with in respect of those offences. The power applies equally where a magistrates' court has yet to commence proceedings into related offences as examining justices.

7.9   The new s 38A applies where:

'(i)   a person who is 18 or over[1] appears or is brought before a magistrates' court ('the court') on an information charging him with an offence triable either way ('the offence');

(j)   he or his representative indicates that he would plead guilty if the offence were to proceed to trial; and

(k)   proceeding as if s 9(1) above was complied with and he pleaded guilty under it, the court convicts him of the offence.'

1 See general annotations.

7.10   In cases where the court has committed the offender to the Crown Court for trial for one or more related offences, that is to say, one or more offences which, in its opinion, are related to the offence, it may, in accordance with s 56 of the Criminal Justice Act 1967 commit him in custody or on bail to be dealt with in respect of the offence in accordance with the provisions of s 42 of the Powers of Criminal Courts Act 1973[1] (1980 Act, s 38A(2)).

An offence is related to another for this purpose if, were they both to be tried on indictment, they could be joined in the same indictment.[1]

If the magistrates' court is committing pursuant to that power in s 38A(2), it should say so. If it does not state that, in its opinion, it also has the power to commit him under s 38(2) of the 1980 Act,[1] which deals with committals for sentence in respect of an either-way offence, then s 42 of the 1973 Act does not apply unless the person is convicted before the Crown Court of one or more of the related offences (1980 Act, s 38A(4)). If s 42 does not in fact apply, then the Crown Court can deal with the offender in any manner the magistrates' court might have dealt with him (1980 Act, s 38A(5)).

1 See annotations to s 51 of the new Act.

7.11   If, by contrast, s 38A(2) does not apply, because the court is still to inquire as examining justices into one or more of the related offences:

(a)   it shall adjourn the proceedings relating to the offence until after the conclusion of its inquiries; and

(b)   if it commits the offender to the Crown Court for trial for one or more related offences (as to which, see s 38A(6))[1] it may then exercise that power.

---

1 See annotations to s 51 of the new Act.

PENALTY FOR INDECENT ASSAULT ON A CHILD

7.12   The maximum penalty for the offence of indecency conduct towards a young child, contrary to the Indecency with Children Act 1960, s 1(1), is increased from two to 10 years by s 52 of the new Act. This is a change designed to remove an anomaly and to bring this offence into line with other offences of like seriousness, such as indecent assault upon a woman.[1]

---

1 See Baroness Blatch, Minister of State, Home Office, HL Second Reading, col 974.

YOUNG OFFENDERS

Publication of reports

7.13   A new s 49 of the Children and Young Persons Act 1933 was introduced by the Criminal Justice and Public Order Act 1994, s 49. The new s 49 of the 1933 Act[1] contains restrictions on publication of reports in young offender cases. The effect of the changes made by the 1994 Act was to restrict the power to dispense with the restrictions to a court, and then only within the terms of the 'new' s 49(5) of the 1933 Act. That 'new' provision provides that:

> '... a court may ... dispense to any specified extent with the requirements of this section ... if it is satisfied—
> (a)   that it is appropriate to do so for the purpose of avoiding injustice to the child or young person; or
> (b)   as respects a child or young person to whom this paragraph applies who is unlawfully at large, it is necessary to dispense with these requirements for the purpose of apprehending him and bringing him before a court or returning him to the place in which he was in custody.'[2]

The power to make a dispensation only exists under the 'new' s 49(5) if an application for the court to make such a dispensation has been made by or on behalf of the Director of Public Prosecutions, and notice of that application has been given by the DPP to any legal representative of the child or young person (1933 Act, s 49(7)).

---

1 See annotations to s 45.
2 Section 49(5)(b) only applied to a child charged with or convicted of a violent or sexual offence (as defined by the Criminal Justice Act 1991, s 31) or an offence punishable in the case of a person aged 21 or over with 14 years' or more imprisonment (1933 Act, s 49(6)).

7.14 Young offenders are 'no longer to be able to hide behind a cloak on anonymity'.[1] Section 49 is further amended by s 45 of the new Act, which introduces a new s 49(4A) into the 1933 Act. The effect of the new subsection is that a court, or a court dealing with an appeal from a youth court may dispense with the restrictions imposed by s 49 where it is satisfied that it is in the public interest to do so. No application by the Director of Public Prosecutions is required, and the restrictive pre-conditions in s 49(5)(a) and (b) no longer apply. The power in the new s 49(4A) only applies where the offence was committed on or after the date of commencement of s 45 of the new Act (s 45(2)).

---

1 Baroness Blatch, Minister of State, Home Office, HL Second Reading, col 974.

7.15 The proceedings to which the new s 49(4A) apply are:

(a) the prosecution or conviction of the offender for the offence;

(b) the manner in which he, or his parent or guardian, should be dealt with in respect of the offence;

(c) the enforcement, amendment, variation, revocation or discharge of any order made in respect of the offence;

(d) where an attendance centre order is made in respect of the offence, the enforcement of any rules made under s 16(3) of the Criminal Justice Act 1982; or

(e) where a secure training order is so made, the enforcement of any requirements imposed under s 3(7) of the Criminal Justice and Public Order Act 1994.

7.16 The object of the new provision is to remove some of the restrictive conditions that attached to s 49 and which prevented the shaming of young offenders by publicity as to what they had done. However, such a direction cannot be made without the opportunity to make representations. Section 49(4B) of the 1933 Act now states that a court shall not exercise its power under subsection (4A) without:

(a) affording the parties to the proceedings an opportunity to make representations; and

(b) taking into account any representations which are duly made.

Long-term detention of young offenders – indecent assault

7.17 By s 53(3) of the Children and Young Persons Act 1933,[1] if the court is of the opinion than none of the other methods in which the case may legally be dealt with is suitable, the court may sentence the offender to be detained for such period not exceeding the maximum term of imprisonment with which the offence is punishable in the case of an adult as may be specified in the sentence; and where such a sentence has been passed the child or young person shall, during that period, be liable to be detained in such place and on such conditions:

(a)   as the Secretary of State may direct; or

(b)   as the Secretary of State may arrange with any person.

---

1 As amended by the Criminal Justice and Public Order Act 1994, s 16.

7.18 Section 53(3) has hitherto applied in the cases identified by s 53(2) of the 1933 Act. This states that s 53(3) is to apply:

(a)   where a person of at least 10 but not more than 17 years[1] is convicted on indictment of:

    (i)   any offence punishable in the case of an adult with imprisonment for 14 years or more, not being an offence the sentence for which is fixed by law; or

    (ii)   an offence under s 14 of the Sexual Offences Act 1956 (indecent assault on a woman);

(b)   where a young person is convicted of:

    (i)   an offence under s 1 of the Road Traffic Act 1988 (causing death by dangerous driving); or

    (ii)   an offence under s 3A of the Road Traffic Act 1988 (causing death by careless driving while under the influence of drink and drugs.

---

1 See general annotations.

7.19 It is clearly anomalous to include a s 14 indecent assault on a woman but not a s 15 indecent assault on a man. That anomaly is rectified by the amendment made by s 44 of the new Act.

Curfew orders on young offenders

7.20 The Criminal Justice Act 1991 introduced powers to impose curfew orders, supported by electronic monitoring ('tagging'). Since then, trials have occurred through pilot schemes in Reading, Manchester and Norwich. These schemes have been regarded by Government as a success.[1] For this reason the new Act widens the scope of such powers, by amending the 1991 Act provisions. Courts will, when s 43 of the new Act is brought into force, be able to impose a curfew order, supported by electronic tagging, on 10- to 15-year-olds.[2]

---

1 See Baroness Blatch, Minister of State, Home Office, HL Second Reading, col 974; Mr Jack Straw, Home Secretary, *Sunday Times*, 20 July 1997.

7.21 Section 12 of the Criminal Justice Act 1991 permits a curfew order to be made in respect of any person aged 16 or over who is convicted of an offence, other than one which carries a mandatory sentence. Section 43 of the new Act removes that age restriction. Henceforth, a curfew order may be made in respect of any offender, of whatever age.

The order made under s 12 can require the offender to remain at the place or places named for a specified period. No such curfew restriction may extend beyond six months after the date of making the order. Section 43(2) introduces a new s 12(2A) into the 1991 Act, the effect of which is, in respect of an offender aged under 16, to limit the maximum duration of a curfew order on such a person to a period of three months. Further, a new s 12(6A), introduced by s 43(3) of the new Act, provides that before making a curfew order in respect of an offender who is under the age of 16, the court shall obtain and consider information about his family circumstances and the likely effect of such an order on those circumstances. In short, a court will need to look at the home and family environment, and consider both the effect of that on the offender, and of the offender on that environment.

7.22 Section 43 also amends the relevant provisions of the 1991 Act relating to enforcement, contained in Sch 2 to the 1991 Act. Paragraph 3(2) of Sch 2 permits a magistrates' court to require an offender found, without reasonable excuse, to be in breach of a probation order to be sentenced to a period at an attendance centre. Section 43(4) of the new Act amends para 3(2) but adding a curfew order to its terms. A young offender found to be in breach of a curfew order may, therefore, be required to attend at an attendance centre. The aggregate number of hours of attendance which can be ordered is that which generally applies in respect of such orders. The total number of hours at the attendance centre must not be less than 12, except where the offender is aged under 14 and the court considers that 12 hours would be excessive having regard to age or other circumstances (Criminal Justice Act 1982, s 17(4)). The maximum number of hours will not exceed 12, unless the court considers that 12 would be an inadequate total, in which case the hours shall not exceed 24 where the offender is under 16.

COMMUNITY ORDERS

Abolition or modification of certain consents

7.23 Section 38 modifies the requirements for consents in respect of supervision orders, certain probation orders, or community service orders. In respect of each of these types of orders, the law has hitherto required consent to be given, either for the making of the order itself, or for the imposition within the order of a particular requirement or condition. The willingness to undergo the period of supervision, or comply with the requirement or condition, has always been seen as a key characteristic of community sentences. The changes made by s 38 of the new Act therefore mark a departure of principle from what has gone before, based on the philosophy that 'it is quite wrong that offenders should be allowed to dictate their sentence to the court'. Whether the result will be an increase in the number of breach proceedings before the courts is, of course, yet to be seen.

---

1 Baroness Blatch, Minister of State, Home Office, HL Second Reading, col 974.

Supervision orders

7.24   A supervision order can be made on any young offender (ie under 18 years) (Children and Young Persons Act 1969, s 7). Such an order may be made without the consent of the offender, but s 12A(6) states that certain requirements, identified by s 12A(3)[1] shall not be imposed, inter alia, without the consent of the supervised person, or, if he is a child, his parent or guardian. The obligation that there should be consent to those requirements, contained in s 12A(6), is removed. Instead, a new s 12A(6) provides that if the supervised person is under the age of 16[2] the court cannot impose any such requirements unless it has obtained and considered information about the supervised person's family circumstances and the likely effect of the requirements on those circumstances. Given that the requirements in question in s 12A(3) relate to remaining in a particular place, or refraining from participating in specified activities, and are, in one sense, analogous to a curfew order, it is not inappropriate that a like requirement to that applicable to curfew orders should now be introduced in the new s 12A(6).

1 See annotations to s 38.
2 See general annotations.

Probation orders

7.25   Section 2(3) of the Powers of Criminal Courts Act 1973 states that a court shall not make a probation order unless the offender expresses his willingness to comply with its requirements. That requirement for consent is repealed by s 38(2)(a) of the new Act. Consequential amendments are made to the wording of s 14(2) of the 1973 Act.

By contrast, requirements for the offender's consent are introduced, or preserved, by s 38(3) and (4) of the new Act. The former modifies para 5(4) of Sch 1A to the 1973 Act. That paragraph deals with requirements in a probation order as to treatment for medical condition. The pre-existing para 5(4) states that a court shall not include in a probation order a requirement that the offender shall submit to treatment for his medical condition unless it is satisfied that arrangements have been made for the treatment intended to be specified in the order (including arrangements for the reception of the offender where he is to be required to submit to treatment as a resident patient). Section 38(3) amends this by adding the words '(b) the offender has expressed his willingness to comply with such a requirement'. This change is clearly confirmation that such treatment can only be properly, and effectively, undertaken with consent. The concept of medical treatment without consent is clearly one the law generally rejects.

A similar amendment is made to para 6(4), which contains like provisions relating to treatment for drug or alcohol dependency, and which is amended by s 38(4) of the new Act.

Curfew orders

7.26   It has already been noted that s 12 of the Criminal Justice Act 1991 introduced the concept of a curfew order.[1] Section 12(5) of the 1991 Act states, inter alia, that a court shall not make the order unless the offender expresses his willingness to comply with its requirements. Those words are repealed by s 38(2) of the new Act. In respect of orders made after the commencement of s 38, no such consent will be necessary, although, as already noted, the court will, in the case of an offender aged under 16, have to have regard to family circumstances.[2]

---

1 See para **7.20**.
2 See para **7.24**.

Community service order for fine defaulters

7.27 The Government has been concerned to seek to improve the effectiveness of fine enforcement with over three-quarters of all sentences imposed by the courts each year being fines.[1] The successful enforcement of financial penalties, without recourse to imprisonment, was seen by the Government in its White Paper as extremely important, not least because imprisonment expunges the fine and thus frustrates the intention of the sentencing court. During 1995, some 20,000 people were committed to prison for non-payment of fines,[2] a figure that fell in 1996 to some 8806, largely, it is believed, because of the Divisional Court decision in *Oldham Justices and another, ex parte Cawley*,[3] where, in the context of offenders under 21,[4] Simon Brown LJ observed:

> 'In respect of each apparent [enforcement] option there must be such a reason, for it is imperative that justices rigorously examine each, and only discard it for good reason ... The reasoning process must be clearly capable of articulation. They must indeed be articulated in open court.'

Different considerations appear to apply in respect of offenders aged 21 or over.[5]

---

1 White Paper, op cit, para 5.31.
2 See Baroness Blatch, Minister of State, Home Office, HL Committee, col 834.
3 [1996] 1 All ER 464.
4 See general annotations.
5 See *Stockport Justices, ex parte Conloan* (1996) (DC); *Newcastle Justices, ex parte Keenaghan* (1996) (DC).

7.28 The response of the Government to this problem is to extend the power to make a community service order or, in respect of those aged at least 16 (s 35(10)), a curfew order. Subject to the detailed limitation, either of these orders may be made in respect of a person who is in default of paying a sum of money adjudged to be paid by a conviction in a magistrates' court (s 35(1)). This is intended to include not only unpaid fines but unpaid compensation orders.[1] Section 35(2) empowers a magistrates' court to make a community service order, or (in the case of a person aged at least 16) a curfew order, in any case where, under Pt III of the Magistrates' Courts Act 1980,[2] it has power to issue a warrant of commitment for default in paying a sum adjudged to be paid by a magistrates' court, and in place of issuing such a warrant of commitment or, in the case of young offenders, proceedings under s 81 of the Magistrates'

Courts Act 1980.[2] The magistrates' court must have been notified that arrangements for implementing such orders are available in the relevant area and have not been withdrawn (s 35(11)).

It is intended to introduce this power by way of different pilot studies for different types of offender.[3]

---

1 Baroness Blatch, Minister of State, Home Office, HL Committee, col 872.
2 See annotations to s 35.
3 Ibid, col 841.

7.29 The making of such an order can be postponed until such time or on such conditions if any as the court thinks just (s 35(3)).

7.30 The two exceptions to the power to make a community service or curfew order in respect of financial penalty default are in respect of sums adjudged to be paid under the Criminal Justice Act 1988, s 71 or the Drug Trafficking Act 1994, s 2.[1] This is because community service orders are not considered appropriate sentences for default in respect of financial penalties imposed on persons considered to have profited from their criminal activities.

Community service

7.31 Where a community service order is made, it has the same meaning as in the Powers of Criminal Courts Act 1973 (s 35(4)). The effect of that is that the requirement contained in s 14(2) of the 1973 Act that the offender should consent to the making of the order and that the court, after hearing (if the court thinks it appropriate) from a probation officer or social worker from a local authority social services department, be satisfied that the offender is a suitable person to perform work under such an order, applies equally to an order made for fine default (s 34(4)(b)). Other provisions of the 1973 Act and of the Criminal Justice Act 1991 apply equally, subject to two important exceptions. First, the minimum number of hours, stated in s 14(1A) of the 1973 Act, to be 40 hours, is, by s 35(5)(a) of the new Act, reduced for this purpose (but for no other) to 20 hours. Secondly, the effect of s 35(5)(b) in disapplying s 14(3) of the 1973 Act is that no question of concurrent service of hours for fine default arises.

Curfew orders

7.32 A curfew order has, for this purpose, the same meaning as in Pt I of the Criminal Justice Act 1991. In particular, s 12(5) of the 1991 Act applies (s 35(7)). This requires a court to explain in ordinary language:

(a) the effect of the order (including any additional requirements proposed to be included in the order in accordance with s 13 of the 1991 Act);

(b) the consequences which may follow under Sch 2 to the 1991 Act if he fails to comply with any of the requirements of the order; and

(c) that the court has under that Schedule power to review the order on the application of either the offender or the supervising officer.

However, in the light of the changes made by the new Act to s 12(5), the consent of the offender is not required. In addition, certain provisions of Sch 2 to the 1991 Act, which normally apply to curfew orders, are disapplied by s 35(8) of the new Act. These are discussed below at para **7.34**.

The period to be served

7.33   The period of community service, or the number of days for which a curfew order applies, is determined by the amount of the default (s 35(6), (9)). The *maximum* periods of service are shown in Table 4 below.

Table 4: Periods to be served

Amount in default	Hours of community service	Days for curfew order
Not exceeding £200	40	20
Exceeding £200 but not exceeding £500	60	30
Exceeding £500 but not exceeding £1000	100	60
Exceeding £1000 but not exceeding £2500	100	90
Exceeding £2500	100	180

These periods may be varied by order (s 35(14)).

7.34   As already noted, the general provisions relating to community service orders are subject to the modifications contained in s 35(5) and (8). In particular, the powers to deal with the offender for breach of the community service or curfew orders, contained in Sch 2 to the 1991 Act, remain. Where there is breach of the community service or curfew order the court may revoke the order, and may deal with the offender for the failure to pay the fine (1991 Act, Sch 3(1) (d), as modified by s 35(5) (d) and (8) (a) of the new Act). There is no question of resentencing the offender for the original offence.

The following sanctions apply for failure to comply with the order:

–   fine not exceeding £1000 (1991 Act, Sch 2, para 3(1)(a));
–   community service order (1991 Act, Sch 2, para 3(1)(b));
–   revocation of the order and deal with offender for the default in paying sum in question (1991 Act, Sch 2, para 3(1)(d), as modified by s 35(5)(d) and (8)(a) of the new Act).

The effect of s 35(13) is that payment of the whole sum in respect of which the offender is in default causes the order made under s 35(2) to cease to have effect, with a partial payment reducing the period of community service or curfew proportionately. It is not possible to reduce the fine by partial compliance with the community service or curfew order. However, full service of the period or time specified by the order, or compliance with the order, has the effect of expunging the fine.

7.35 It should be borne in mind that these powers in s 35 to make a community service or curfew order are to be regarded as a last resort. Although the new Act does not expressly limit the power to make an order, the Magistrates' Courts Act 1980, s 82(4) makes it clear that a magistrates' court cannot issue a warrant of commitment unless it has tried and considered all other methods of enforcement and they have failed or the court has concluded that they are inappropriate. The power to make a community service or curfew order under s 35 is exercisable only where that power to issue a warrant of commitment has arisen (s 35(1)(a)). Indeed, there would be a real danger that the number of community service orders made will swamp the available resources and diminish the standing of community service as a substantial penalty for more serious offenders.[1] This criticism was emphatically rejected by the Government, who believed that the differences in seriousness levels is reflected in the lower minimum periods of time that can be ordered to be served.

1 Lord McIntosh, HL Committee, col 837.

Attendance centre order for fine defaulters under the age of 25

7.36 Section 36 amends the provisions of the Criminal Justice Act 1982, s 17 (attendance centre orders) by extending its terms to permit the making of an attendance centre order in respect of a person aged 21 or more, but under 25, and who is in default of payment of any sum of money.

This new power extends attendance centre orders for the first time to persons aged over 21, albeit only for this purpose. All of the other provisions relating to attendance centres, and contained in s 17 of the Criminal Justice Act 1982, remain unchanged. This includes the number of hours to be served, which, somewhat oddly, are not amended by the new Act. The relevant number of hours will be not less than 12, and not more than 36, if the offender is aged 16 or over.

Persistent petty offenders

7.37 The powers to make community orders are further extended by s 37(3). Section 37(3) provides that, where s 37 applies, a court may:

(a) make a community service order; or
(b) make a curfew order.

The intention is to provide the courts with an alternative non-financial penalty for a minor offence that would not have the sufficient level of seriousness to justify the imposition of a community sentence. Section 6 of the Criminal

Justice Act 1991 contains restrictions on the imposition of a community sentence. In particular, such a sentence is not to be imposed on an offender unless the court is of the opinion that the offence, or the combination of the offence and one other offence associated with it, was serious enough to warrant such a sentence. Those restrictions clearly prevent the imposition of a community order in cases which are of themselves relatively non serious, but where a community sentence is the appropriate or, in the light of absence of financial means, only realistic disposal. For that reason, in the case of persistent offenders, where the offender's circumstances make the imposition of a fine inappropriate, the making of a community service order or curfew order may be appropriate and is now permitted by s 37(3).

7.38 Section 37(3) applies where:

(a)   a person is convicted of an offence by a magistrates' court or before the Crown Court;

(b)   the court is satisfied that each of the conditions specified in s 37(2) is fulfilled; and

(c)   if it were not so satisfied, the court would be minded to impose a fine in respect of the offence.

The conditions set out in s 37(2) are:

(a)   that one or more fines imposed on the offender in respect of one or more previous offences have not been paid; and

(b)   if a fine was imposed in an amount which was commensurate with the seriousness of the offence, the offender would not have sufficient means to pay it.

The appropriate provisions of the 1973 Act and 1991 Act apply equally to a s 37 order as to orders made under s 35. In other words, the sanctions for failure to comply with the relevant order are the same as discussed earlier in respect of breach of community service or curfew orders imposed for fine default (s 37(4), (5)).[1]

---

1 See para 7.34.

DRIVING DISQUALIFICATIONS

7.39 Section 39 introduces a new power which entitles a court, in addition or (unless a sentence is mandatory) instead of dealing with an offender in any other way, disqualify him for such period as it thinks fit, from holding or obtaining a driving licence. There is no limit to the period of disqualification that may be imposed.

Driving disqualification is to be seen as a punishment in its own right, not simply a way of dealing with offences involving motor vehicles. For that reason, the last Government considered that disqualification could be an effective punishment in respect of a wider range of offences, and one which might have a significant impact on some offenders.

The rationale for the new provision was explained by Baroness Blatch, Minister of State at the Home Office, as follows:

> 'The [section] allows for the introduction of the provision on a pilot basis in courts specified by the Secretary of State. It is a punishment and another disposal which is available to the court. It would be dispensed as a punishment. Taking away the freedom to drive is already an effective penalty for a range of road traffic offences and other offences where a vehicle is involved – for example, theft of a car. We believe that disqualification from driving can usefully be used more widely, and that its extended use will give the courts greater flexibility to deal with offenders in the most effective way. Disqualification from driving is not just another means of keeping bad drivers off the road .... It can be an effective punishment because it denies the offender the freedom to drive. Thus it restricts his liberty in the same way as a fine restricts his economic liberty and community service his liberty to determine how to spend his time. ... This is just another way to restrict liberty.'[1]

It remains to be seen how effective this particular restriction will prove, in this context. It is intended to pilot the disqualification provision to test its effect and impact.

---

1 Baroness Blatch, Minister of State, Home Office, HL Committee, col 889.

7.40 Under s 40, disqualification for holding or obtaining a driving licence may also be ordered for fine default. The period of disqualification shall not exceed 12 months (s 40(2)).

The detailed provisions of s 40 are similar in construction and content to those in s 35 and which relate to the making of community service or curfew orders for fine default, discussed earlier.[1] In particular, the power to issue a warrant of commitment under Pt III of the Magistrates' Courts Act 1980 must exist. Likewise, the period of disqualification may be reduced proportionately by the payment of part of the fine (s 40(4)(b)).

---

1 See para **7.27**.

TRANSFER OF PRISONERS WITHIN THE UK AND REPATRIATION OF PRISONERS TO THE UK

7.41 Schedules 1 and 2 of the new Act contain detailed provisions regulating the treatment of such prisoners. The changes made by these provisions, which will supersede equivalent provisions in the Criminal Justice Act 1991 are intended to reflect the detailed changes as to sentencing, sentence length and release introduced by the new Act and discussed by this book.

APPENDIX

Crime (Sentences) Act 1997
(1997 c. 43)

ARRANGEMENT OF SECTIONS

PART I
MANDATORY AND MINIMUM CUSTODIAL SENTENCES

PART II
EFFECT OF CUSTODIAL SENTENCES

CHAPTER I
DETERMINATE SENTENCES

General

Early release

Additional days

CHAPTER II
LIFE SENTENCES

PART III
MISCELLANEOUS AND SUPPLEMENTAL

SCHEDULES

An Act to make further provision with respect to the treatment of offenders; and for connected purposes.

[21st March 1997]

GENERAL ANNOTATIONS

Certain frequently recurring terms are annotated here, and cross-reference is made to these annotations at the appropriate place.

Commencement—See s 57(2), and para **1.5**.

Age—A person reaches a particular age at the commencement of the relevant anniversary of the birth (Family Law Reform Act 1969, s 9).

England and Wales—'England and Wales' means, subject to any alteration of boundaries under Pt IV of the Local Government Act 1972, the area consisting of the counties established by s 1 and (as originally enacted) s 20 of that Act (subject, in the case of Wales, to any alteration made under s 73 of that Act), Greater London and the Isles of Scilly (Interpretation Act 1978, s 5 and Sch 1).

'Wales' means the combined area of the counties created by the Local Government Act 1972, as originally enacted, but subject to any alteration made under the 1972 Act, s 73 (consequential alteration of boundary following alteration of watercourse).

United Kingdom—'United Kingdom' means Great Britain and Northern Ireland (Interpretation Act 1978, s 5 and Sch 1). 'Great Britain' means England, Scotland and Wales (Union with Scotland Act 1706, preamble, art 1; Wales and Berwick Act 1746, s 3).

Standard scale—The 'standard scale' of fines applies only to offences which are only triable summarily. The meaning of the standard scale is that given by the Criminal Justice Act 1982, s 37. When this book went to press the standard scale was as follows:

level 1	£200
level 2	£500
level 3	£1,000
level 4	£2,500
level 5	£5,000

Summary offence, indictable offence—'Summary offence' means an offence which, if committed by an adult is triable only (Interpretation Act 1978, s 5 and Sch 1). 'Indictable offence' means an offence which, if committed by an adult, is triable on indictment, whether it is exclusively so triable or triable either way (Interpretation Act 1978, s 5 and Sch 1).

Day—The term 'day' is, like the terms 'year' and 'month', used in more senses than one. A day is strictly the period of time which begins with one midnight and ends with the next. It may also denote the period of 24 hours and again it may denote the period of time between sunrise and sunset (45 *Halsbury's Laws* 4th edn, revised, para 1113). Only the first of these three meanings is appropriate to the use, in this context, of the word 'day'.

PART I
MANDATORY AND MINIMUM CUSTODIAL SENTENCES

1   Conditions relating to mandatory and minimum custodial sentences

(1) This section has effect for the purposes of setting out the basis on which the court shall carry out its sentencing functions under this Part.

(2) Under section 2 below, when determining whether it would be appropriate not to impose a life sentence the court shall have regard to the circumstances relating to either of the offences or to the offender.

(3) Under sections 3 and 4 below, when determining whether it would be appropriate not to impose a custodial sentence of at least seven years under section 3(2) or, as the

case may be, of at least three years under section 4(2) the court shall have regard to the specific circumstances which—

(a) relate to any of the offences or to the offender; and

(b) would make the prescribed custodial sentence unjust in all the circumstances.

Explanatory text—See para **2.25**.

Custodial sentence (subss (3))—A 'custodial sentence' is defined by the Criminal Justice Act 1991, s 31(1)) as, in respect of a person aged 21 or over, a sentence of imprisonment, and, in relation to a person under that age, a sentence of detention in a young offenders' institution or under s 53 of the Children and Young Persons Act 1933, or a sentence of custody for life under s 8(2) of the Criminal Justice Act 1982. This is wider than the definition adopted for the specific purposes of Pt I of the new Act (see s 2(2) and s 3(6)).

By the Supreme Court Act 1981, s 47, a sentence imposed, or other order made, by the Crown Court when dealing with an offender shall take effect from the beginning of the day on which it is imposed, unless the court otherwise directs.

2   Mandatory life sentence for second serious offence

(1) This section applies where—

(a) a person is convicted of a serious offence committed after the commencement of this section; and

(b) at the time when that offence was committed, he was 18 or over and had been convicted in any part of the United Kingdom of another serious offence.

(2) The court shall impose a life sentence, that is to say—

(a) where the person is 21 or over, a sentence of imprisonment for life;

(b) where he is under 21, a sentence of custody for life under section 8(2) of the Criminal Justice Act 1982 ('the 1982 Act'),

unless the court is of the opinion that there are exceptional circumstances relating to either of the offences or to the offender which justify its not doing so.

(3) Where the court does not impose a life sentence, it shall state in open court that it is of that opinion and what the exceptional circumstances are.

(4) An offence the sentence for which is imposed under subsection (2) above shall not be regarded as an offence the sentence for which is fixed by law.

(5) An offence committed in England and Wales is a serious offence for the purposes of this section if it is any of the following, namely—

(a) an attempt to commit murder, a conspiracy to commit murder or an incitement to murder;

(b) an offence under section 4 of the Offences Against the Person Act 1861 (soliciting murder);

(c) manslaughter;

(d) an offence under section 18 of the Offences Against the Person Act 1861 (wounding, or causing grievous bodily harm, with intent);

(e) rape or an attempt to commit rape;

(f) an offence under section 5 of the Sexual Offences Act 1956 (intercourse with a girl under 13);

(g) an offence under section 16 (possession of a firearm with intent to injure), section 17 (use of a firearm to resist arrest) or section 18 (carrying a firearm with criminal intent) of the Firearms Act 1968; and

(h) robbery where, at some time during the commission of the offence, the offender had in his possession a firearm or imitation firearm within the meaning of that Act.

(6) An offence committed in Scotland is a serious offence for the purposes of this section if the conviction for it was obtained on indictment in the High Court of Justiciary and it is any of the following, namely—

(a) culpable homicide;
(b) attempted murder, incitement to commit murder or conspiracy to commit murder;
(c) rape or attempted rape;
(d) clandestine injury to women or an attempt to cause such injury;
(e) sodomy, or an attempt to commit sodomy, where the complainer, that is to say, the person against whom the offence was committed, did not consent;
(f) assault where the assault—
    (i) is aggravated because it was carried out to the victim's severe injury or the danger of the victim's life; or
    (ii) was carried out with an intention to rape or to ravish the victim;
(g) robbery where, at some time during the commission of the offence, the offender had in his possession a firearm or imitation firearm within the meaning of the Firearms Act 1968;
(h) an offence under section 16 (possession of a firearm with intent to injure), section 17 (use of a firearm to resist arrest) or section 18 (carrying a firearm with criminal intent) of that Act;
(i) lewd, libidinous or indecent behaviour or practices; and
(j) an offence under section 5(1) of the Criminal Law (Consolidation) (Scotland) Act 1995 (unlawful intercourse with a girl under 13).

(7) An offence committed in Northern Ireland is a serious offence for the purposes of this section if it is any of the following, namely—

(a) an offence falling within any of paragraphs (a) to (e) of subsection (5) above;
(b) an offence under section 4 of the Criminal Law Amendment Act 1885 (intercourse with a girl under 14);
(c) an offence under Article 17 (possession of a firearm with intent to injure), Article 18(1) (use of a firearm to resist arrest) or Article 19 (carrying a firearm with criminal intent) of the Firearms (Northern Ireland) Order 1981; and
(d) robbery where, at some time during the commission of the offence, the offender had in his possession a firearm or imitation firearm within the meaning of that Order.

Explanatory text—See para **2.2**.

Age (subss (1), (2))—See general annotations.

United Kingdom (sub (1))—See general annotations.

Section 8(2) of the Criminal Justice Act 1982 (sub (2))—This subsection provides that where a person aged 18 or over but under the age of 21 is convicted of any offence other than murder for which a person aged 21 years or over would be liable to imprisonment for life, the court shall, if it considers that a custodial sentence for life would be appropriate, sentence him to custody for life.

Not regarded as an offence the sentence for which is fixed by law (subs (4))—The effect of s 2(4) is that the life sentence imposed by virtue of s 2 will not be a life sentence to which s 28 of the new Act applies. Instead, the early release arrangements in s 29 apply. See para **4.15**.

England and Wales (subs (5))—See general annotations.

Section 4 of the Offences Against the Person Act 1861 (subs (5))—Section 4 provides:

'Whosoever shall solicit, encourage, persuade, or endeavour to persuade, or shall propose to any person, to murder any other person, whether he be a subject of Her majesty or not, and whether he be within the Queen's dominions or not, shall be guilty of a misdemeanour, and on being convicted thereof shall be liable to imprisonment for life.'

Section 18 of the Offences Against the Person Act 1861 (subs (5))—Section 18 provides:

'Whosoever shall unlawfully and maliciously by any means wound or cause any grievous bodily harm to any person ... with intent ... to do some ... grievous bodily harm to any person, or with intent to resist or prevent the lawful apprehension or detainer of any person, shall be guilty of an offence, and being convicted thereof shall be liable ... to imprisonment for life.'

Section 5 of the Sexual Offences Act 1956 (subs (5))—'It is an offence for a man to have unlawful sexual intercourse with a girl under the age of thirteen.' The offence is punishable with life imprisonment (1956 Act, s 37(3) and Sch 2, para 2(a)).

Sections 16, 17 and 18 of the Firearms Act 1968 (subs (5))—Section 16 provides:

'It is an offence for a person to have in his possession any firearm or ammunition with intent by means thereof to endanger life ... or to enable another person by means thereof to endanger life ... whether any injury ... has been caused or not.'

The offence is punishable with life imprisonment or a fine, or both.

Section 17 states:

'(1) It is an offence for a person to make or attempt to make any use whatsoever of a firearm or imitation firearm with intent to resist or prevent the lawful arrest or detention of himself or another person.

(2) If a person, at the time of his committing or being arrested for an offence specified in Schedule 1 to this Act has in his possession a firearm or imitation firearm, he shall be guilty of an offence under this subsection unless he shows that he had it in his possession for a lawful object ...'.

Both offences are triable on indictment and punishable with life imprisonment or a fine or both. It is unclear whether s 2(5) of the 1997 Act is intended to refer to both offences or merely that under s 17(1) of the 1968 Act. The words of the subsection place 'use of a firearm to resist arrest' in parenthesis, but use is only an element in a s 17(1) offence, whereas s 17(2) is a possession offence. However, the subsection refers to 'section 17' without qualification. Logically both should be included within the scope of s 2(5): they each carry a maximum punishment of life imprisonment.

Section 18(1) states:

'It is an offence for a person to have with him a firearm or imitation firearm with intent to commit an indictable offence, or to resist arrest or prevent the arrest of another, in either case while he has the firearm or imitation firearm with him.'

The offence is punishable with life imprisonment or a fine, or both.

Robbery (subs (5))—Section 8(1) of the Theft Act 1968 provides that a person is guilty of robbery if he steals and immediately before or at the time of doing so and in order to do so, he uses force on any person or puts or seeks to put any person in fear of then and there being subjected to force. The maximum punishment is imprisonment for life. The offence clearly overlaps with those in s 2(5)(g).

Firearm/imitation firearm (subs (5))—A firearm is defined by the Firearms Act 1968, s 57(1) as meaning:

'a lethal barrelled weapon of any description from which any shot, bullet or other missile can be discharged and includes—

(a) any prohibited weapon, whether it such a lethal weapon as aforesaid or not; and

(b) any component part of such a lethal or prohibited weapon; and

(c) any accessory to such weapon designed or adapted to diminish the noise or flash caused by firing the weapon;

and so much of section 1 of this Act as excludes any description of firearm from the category of firearms to which that section applies shall be construed as also excluding component parts of, and accessories to, firearms of that description.'

A 'lethal weapon' is one which, when misused, is capable of causing injury from which death may result: *Moore v Gooderham* [1960] 3 All ER 575 (DC). See, generally, Card, Cross and Jones *Criminal Law* 13th edn (Butterworths, 1995), at para 19.1.

A 'prohibited weapon' is, by s 5(1) of the 1968 Act:

'(a) any firearm which is so designed or adapted that, if pressure is applied to the trigger, missiles continue to be discharged until pressure is removed from the trigger or the magazine containing the missiles is empty;

(b) any weapon of whatever description designed or adapted for the discharge of any noxious liquid, gas or other thing.'

An 'imitation firearm' means 'any thing which has the appearance of being a firearm (other than such a weapon as is mentioned in section 5(1)(b) of this Act) whether or not it is capable of discharging any shot, bullet or other missile' (1968 Act, s 57(4)).

Culpable homicide (subs (6))—In Scots law, every charge of murder impliedly includes the lesser charge of culpable homicide (*HM Advocate v Robertson and Donoghue* (1945) Unreported). The distinguishing feature is the question of intent. Culpable homicide is established by the proof of gross negligence, of something akin to indifference: *Paten v HM Advocate* [1935] JC 19, or by the commission of an unlawful act (such as an assault) with death resulting: *Bird v HM Advocate* [1952] JC 23.

Clandestine injury to women (subs (6))—See, eg, *HM Advocate v Grainger and Rae* [1932] JC 40, where sexual intercourse with a woman whilst she was in a state of insensibility or unconsciousness from the effects of alcohol was not raped, but would amount, if charged, to the crime of the common law crime of clandestine injury to women.

Lewd, libidinous or indecent behaviour or practices (subs (6))—It is a crime at common law to indulge in indecent practices towards children under the age of puberty, with or without their consent. Such practices may include the performance of sexual acts in the presence of a child. A woman may be convicted of using lewd practices towards a girl, and, perhaps, also to a boy.

Section 5(1) of the Criminal Law (Consolidation) (Scotland) Act 1995 (subs (6))—This provides:

'Any person who uses towards a girl of or above the age of 12 years and under the age of 16 years, any lewd, indecent or libidinous practice or behaviour which, if used towards a girl under the age of 12 years, would have constituted an offence at common law shall, whether the girl consented ... or not be guilty of an offence.'

3 Minimum of seven years for third class A drug trafficking offence

(1) This section applies where—

(a) a person is convicted of a class A drug trafficking offence committed after the commencement of this section;

(b) at the time when that offence was committed, he was 18 or over and had been convicted in any part of the United Kingdom of two other class A drug trafficking offences; and

(c) one of those other offences was committed after he had been convicted of the other.

(2) The court shall impose a custodial sentence for a term of at least seven years except where the court is of the opinion that there are specific circumstances which—

    (a) relate to any of the offences or to the offender; and

    (b) would make the prescribed custodial sentence unjust in all the circumstances.

(3) Where the court does not impose such a sentence, it shall state in open court that it is of that opinion and what the specific circumstances are.

(4) Where—

    (a) a person is charged with a class A drug trafficking offence (which, apart from this subsection, would be triable either way); and

    (b) the circumstances are such that, if he were convicted of the offence, he could be sentenced for it under subsection (2) above,

the offence shall be triable only on indictment.

(5) In this section 'class A drug trafficking offence' means a drug trafficking offence committed in respect of a class A drug; and for this purpose—

    'class A drug' has the same meaning as in the Misuse of Drugs Act 1971;

    'drug trafficking offence' means a drug trafficking offence within the meaning of the Drug Trafficking Act 1994, the Proceeds of Crime (Scotland) Act 1995 or the Proceeds of Crime (Northern Ireland) Order 1996.

(6) In this section and section 4 below 'custodial sentence' means—

    (a) in relation to a person who is 21 or over, a sentence of imprisonment;

    (b) in relation to a person who is under 21, a sentence of detention in a young offender institution.

Explanatory text—See para **2.33**.

Class A drug trafficking offence (subss (1), (4), (5))—The Misuse of Drugs Act 1971, s 2 and Sch 2, Pt I, define, inter alia, Class A drugs as any of the substances and products for the time being specified in Pt I of that Schedule. Among the common drugs falling to be regarded as Class A drugs are cocaine, ecstasy (methylenedioxymethylamphetamine – MDMA) (which is a prohibited compound), and morphine.

The Drug Trafficking Act 1994, s 1(3) provides:

'In this Act "drug trafficking offence" means any of the following—

    (a) an offence under section 4(2) or (3) or 5(3) of the Misuse of Drugs Act 1971 (production, supply and possession for supply of controlled drugs);

    (b) in connection with a prohibition or restriction on importation and exportation having effect by virtue of section 3 of the 1971 Act;

    (c) an offence under (i) section 50(2) or (3) of the Customs and Excise Management Act 1979 (improper importation); (ii) section 68(2) of that Act (exportation) or (iii) section 170 of that Act (fraudulent evasion).

    In connection with a prohibition or restriction on importation or exportation having effect by virtue of section 3 of the Misuse of Drugs Act 1971:

    (d) an offence under section 12 of the Criminal Justice (International Co-operation) Act 1990 (manufacture or supply of substance specified in Schedule 2 to that Act);

    (e) an offence under section 19 of that Act (using ship for illicit trafficking of controlled drugs);

    (f) an offence under section 49, 50 or 51 of this Act or section 14 of the Criminal Justice (International Co-operation) Act 1990 (which makes, in relation to Scotland and Northern Ireland, provision corresponding to section 49 of this Act);

    (g) an offence under section 1 of the Criminal Law Act 1977 of conspiracy to commit any of the offences in paragraphs (a) to (f) above;

(h) an offence under section 1 of the Criminal Attempts Act 1981 of attempting to commit any of those offences; and

(i) an offence of inciting another person to commit any of those offences whether under section 19 of the Misuse of Drugs Act 1971 or at common law;

and includes aiding, abetting, counselling or procuring the commission of any of the offences in paragraphs (a) to (f) above.'

The Proceeds of Crime (Scotland) Act 1995, s 49, and the Proceeds of Crime (Northern Ireland (Order) 1996 contain equivalent provisions relating to the substantive Scottish and Northern Ireland legislation.

Age (subss (1), (6))—See general annotations.

United Kingdom (subs (1))—See general annotations.

Custodial sentence (subs (2))—See s 3(6) and annotations to s 2.

Open court (subs (3))—In *Denbeigh Justices, ex parte Williams* [1974] QB 759, Lord Widgery CJ stated as follows, in the context of a submission that a hearing had not been in open court:

'The trial should be "public" in the ordinary common-sense acceptation of that term. The doors of the courtroom are expected to be kept open, the public are entitled to be admitted, and the trial is to be public in all respects ... with due regard to the size of the courtroom, the conveniences of the court, the right to exclude objectionable characters and youth of tender years, and to do other things which may facilitate the proper conduct of the trial.'

A trial is conducted in open court even if reporting restrictions under the Contempt of Court Act 1981, s 4 or s 11, or under other enactments, are in force.

United Kingdom (subs (1))—See general annotations.

4   Minimum of three years for third domestic burglary

(1) This section applies where—

(a) a person is convicted of a domestic burglary committed after the commencement of this section;

(b) at the time when that burglary was committed, he was 18 or over and had been convicted in England and Wales of two other domestic burglaries; and

(c) one of those other burglaries was committed after he had been convicted of the other, and both of them were committed after the commencement of this section.

(2) The court shall impose a custodial sentence for a term of at least three years except where the court is of the opinion that there are specific circumstances which—

(a) relate to any of the offences or to the offender; and

(b) would make the prescribed custodial sentence unjust in all the circumstances.

(3) Where the court does not impose such a sentence, it shall state in open court that it is of that opinion and what the specific circumstances are.

(4) Where—

(a) a person is charged with a domestic burglary which, apart from this subsection, would be triable either way; and

(b) the circumstances are such that, if he were convicted of the burglary, he could be sentenced for it under subsection (2) above,

the burglary shall be triable only on indictment.

(5) In this section 'domestic burglary' means a burglary committed in respect of a building or part of a building which is a dwelling.

Explanatory text—See para **2.47**.

Age; England and Wales (subs (1))—See general annotations.

Burglary/domestic burglary (subss (1), (4))—By Theft Act 1968, s 9(1), a person is guilty of burglary if:

> '(a) he enters any building or part of a building as a trespasser and with intent to commit any such offence as is mentioned in subsection (2) below; or
>
> (b) having entered any building or part of a building as a trespasser he steals or attempts to steal anything in the building or that part of it or inflicts or attempts to inflict on any person therein any grievous bodily harm.
>
> (2) The offences referred to in subsection (1)(a) are offences of stealing anything in the building or part of a building in question, of inflicting on any person therein any grievous bodily harm or raping any person therein, and of doing unlawful damage to the building or anything therein.'

The maximum term for burglary on conviction on indictment is, in respect of a dwelling, 14 years and , in respect of any other building, 10 years.

'Domestic burglary' is defined by s 4(5) in terms of burglaries committed in respect of buildings, or part of buildings, which is a dwelling. A 'dwelling' for this purpose is not defined. A definition of 'dwelling' is to be found in the Public Order Act 1986, s 8 which states that:

> ' "dwelling" means any structure or part of a structure occupied as a person's home or as other living accommodation (whether the occupation is separate or shared with others) but does not include any part not so occupied, and for this purpose "structure" includes a tent, caravan, vehicle, vessel or other temporary moveable structure.'

Custodial sentence (subs (2))—See s 3(6) and annotations to s 2.

5 Appeals where previous convictions set aside

(1) This section applies where—

> (a) a sentence has been imposed on any person under subsection (2) of section 2, 3 or 4 above; and
>
> (b) any previous conviction of his without which that section would not have applied has been subsequently set aside on appeal.

(2) Notwithstanding anything in section 18 of the Criminal Appeal Act 1968, notice of appeal against the sentence may be given at any time within 28 days from the date on which the previous conviction was set aside.

Explanatory text—See para **2.15**.

Section 18 of the Criminal Appeal Act 1968 (subs (2))—This states:

> '(1) A person who wishes to appeal under this Part of this Act to the Court of Appeal, or to obtain the leave of the court to appeal, shall give notice of appeal, or, as the case may be, notice of application for leave to appeal, in such manner as may be directed by rules of court.
>
> (2) Notice of appeal, or of application for leave to appeal, shall be given within twenty-eight days from the date of conviction, verdict or finding appealed against, or in the case of appeal against sentence, from the date on which sentence was passed or, in the case of an order made or treated as made on conviction, from the date of making of the order.

(3) The time for giving notice under this section may be extended, either before or after it expires, by the Court of Appeal.'

6 Certificates of convictions for purposes of Part I

(1) Where—

(a) on any date after the commencement of this section a person is convicted in England and Wales of a serious offence, a class A drug trafficking offence or a domestic burglary; and

(b) the court by or before which he is so convicted states in open court that he has been convicted of such an offence on that date; and

(c) that court subsequently certifies that fact,

the certificate shall be evidence, for the purposes of the relevant section, that he was convicted of such an offence on that date.

(2) Where—

(a) after the commencement of this section a person is convicted in England and Wales of a class A drug trafficking offence or a domestic burglary; and

(b) the court by or before which he is so convicted states in open court that the offence was committed on a particular day or over, or at some time during, a particular period; and

(c) that court subsequently certifies that fact,

the certificate shall be evidence, for the purposes of the relevant section, that the offence was committed on that day or over, or at some time during, that period.

(3) In this section—

'serious offence', 'class A drug trafficking offence' and 'domestic burglary' have the same meanings as in sections 2, 3 and 4 respectively; and

'the relevant section', in relation to any such offence, shall be construed accordingly.

Explanatory text—See para **2.24**, **2.41** and **2.55**.

Commencement; England and Wales (subss (1),(2))—See general annotations.

Serious offence (subss (1), (2), (3))—see s 2(5)–(7).

Domestic burglary (subss (1), (2), (3))—See s 6(1) and annotations to s 4.

Open court (subs (2))—See annotations to s 3.

Class A drug trafficking offence (subss (1), (2))—See s 6(3), s 2(5) and annotations to s 2.

7 Offences under service law

(1) Where—

(a) a person has at any time been convicted of an offence under section 70 of the Army Act 1955 or the Air Force Act 1955 or section 42 of the Naval Discipline Act 1957; and

(b) the corresponding civil offence (within the meaning of that Act) was a serious offence, a class A drug trafficking offence or a domestic burglary,

the relevant section shall have effect as if he had at that time been convicted in England and Wales of the corresponding civil offence.

(2) Subsection (3) of section 6 above applies for the purposes of this section as it applies for the purposes of that section.

Explanatory text—See para **2.16**, **2.38** and **2.54**.

Army Act 1956, s 70 (as amended)—This provides:

'(1) Any person subject to military law who commits a civil offence, whether in the United Kingdom or elsewhere, shall be guilty of an offence under this section.

(2) In this Act the expression "civil offence" means any act or omission punishable by the law of England or which, if committed in England, would be punishable by that law; and in this Act the "the corresponding civil offence" means the civil offence the commission of which constitutes the offence against this section.

(2A) For the purposes of determining under this section whether an attempt to commit an offence is a civil offence, subsection (4) of section (1) of the Criminal Attempts Act 1981 (which relates to the offence of attempt) shall have effect as if for the words "offence, if it were completed, would be triable in England and Wales as an indictable offence" there were substituted the words "civil offence consisting of an act punishable by the law of England and Wales as an indictable offence or an act which, if committed in England and Wales, would be so punishable by that law".

(3) Subject to section 71A below, a person convicted by court-martial of an offence against this section shall—

  (a) if the corresponding civil offence is treason ... be liable to suffer death;

  (aa) if the corresponding civil offence is murder, be liable to imprisonment for life;

  (ab) if the corresponding civil offence is an offence of genocide consisting of the killing of any person, be liable to imprisonment for life;

  (b) in any other case, be liable to suffer any punishment or punishments which a civil court could award for the corresponding civil offence, if committed in England, being a punishment or punishments provided by this Act, or such punishment, less than the maximum punishment which a civil court could so award, as is so provided.

(4) A person shall not be charged with an offence against this section committed in the United Kingdom if the corresponding civil offence is treason, murder, manslaughter, treason, felony or rape or an offence of genocide or an offence under section 1 of the Biological Weapons Act 1974.

In this and the following subsection the references to murder shall apply also to aiding, abetting, counselling or procuring suicide.

(5) Where the corresponding civil offence is murder or manslaughter, or an offence of genocide consisting of the killing of any person, an offence against this section shall be deemed, for the purposes of the last foregoing subsection, to have been committed at the place of the commission of the act or occurrence of the neglect which caused the death, irrespective of the place of the death.

(6) A person subject to military law may be charged with an offence against this section notwithstanding that he could on the same facts be charged with an offence against any other provision of this part of this Act.'

Air Force Act 1955, s 70 (subs (1))—This provision is in like terms to that of the Army Act 1955, save for the substitution of 'air-force law' for the expression 'military law'.

Section 42 of the Naval Discipline Act 1957 (subs (1))—As amended, this provides:

'(1) Every person subject to this Act who is guilty of any civil offence (that is to say, any act or omission punishable by the law of England or would be so punishable if committed in England) shall subject to section 43A below, be liable on conviction under this Act—

  (a) in the case of an offence of treason ... to death;

  (b) in the case of ... any ... offence of murder, or of genocide consisting of the killing of any person, to imprisonment for life;

  (c) in the case of any other offence to such punishment or punishments (being a punishment or punishments authorised by this Act) as could be imposed on the offender on conviction by a civil court of a like offence committed in England, or to any punishment so authorised which is less than the maximum punishment which could be so imposed.

(2) A person subject to this Act may be charged with an offence under this section notwithstanding that he could on the same facts be charged with an offence under any other provision of this Part of this Act.

(2A) For the purposes of determining under this section whether an attempt to commit an offence is a civil offence, subsection (4) of section (1) of the Criminal Attempts Act 1981 (which relates to the offence of attempt) shall have effect as if for the words "offence, if it were completed, would be triable in England and Wales as an indictable offence" there were substituted the words "civil offence consisting of an act punishable by the law of England and Wales as an indictable offence or an act which, if committed in England and Wales, would be so punishable by that law".'

Serious offence (subs (1))—See s 2(5)–(7).

Class A drug trafficking offence (subs (1))—See s 3(5) and annotations to s 3.

Domestic burglary (subs (1))—See annotations to s 4.

England and Wales (subs (1))—See general annotations.

PART II
EFFECT OF CUSTODIAL SENTENCES

CHAPTER I
DETERMINATE SENTENCES

General

8   Time to be served

(1) Subject to the following provisions of this Chapter, a prisoner shall be released when he has served his sentence.

(2) In this Chapter 'prisoner' means any person who is sentenced to imprisonment for a term in respect of an offence committed after the commencement of this Chapter.

Explanatory text—See para **3.17**.

Sentence of imprisonment (subs (2))—See s 27(1).

Commencement of this Chapter—See general annotations and para **3.2**.

9   Crediting of periods of remand in custody

(1) This section applies where—

(a) a court sentences an offender to imprisonment for a term in respect of an offence committed after the commencement of this section; and
(b) the offender has been remanded in custody in connection with the offence or a related offence, that is to say, any other offence the charge for which was founded on the same facts or evidence.

(2) It is immaterial for that purpose whether the offender—

(a) has also been remanded in custody in connection with other offences; or
(b) has also been detained in connection with other matters.

(3) Subject to subsection (4) below, the court shall direct that the number of days for which the offender was remanded in custody in connection with the offence or a related offence shall count as time served by him as part of the sentence.

(4) Subsection (3) above shall not apply if and to the extent that—

  (a) rules made by the Secretary of State so provide in the case of—

    (i) a remand in custody which is wholly or partly concurrent with a sentence of imprisonment; or

    (ii) sentences of imprisonment for consecutive terms or for terms which are wholly or partly concurrent; or

  (b) it is in the opinion of the court just in all the circumstances not to give a direction under that subsection.

(5) Where the court gives a direction under subsection (3) above, it shall state in open court—

  (a) the number of days for which the offender was remanded in custody; and

  (b) the number of days in relation to which the direction is given.

(6) Where the court does not give a direction under subsection (3) above, or gives such a direction in relation to a number of days less than that for which the offender was remanded in custody, it shall state in open court—

  (a) that its decision is in accordance with rules made under paragraph (a) of subsection (4) above; or

  (b) that it is of the opinion mentioned in paragraph (b) of that subsection and what the circumstances are.

(7) The power to make rules under subsection (4)(a) above shall be exercisable by statutory instrument; but no such rules shall be made unless a draft of the rules has been laid before and approved by a resolution of each House of Parliament.

(8) For the purposes of this section a suspended sentence shall be treated as a sentence of imprisonment when it takes effect under section 23 of the Powers of Criminal Courts Act 1973 ('the 1973 Act') and as being imposed by the order under which it takes effect.

(9) References in this section to an offender being remanded in custody are references to his being—

  (a) held in police detention; or

  (b) remanded in or committed to custody by an order of a court.

(10) A person is in police detention for the purposes of this section—

  (a) at any time when he is in police detention for the purposes of the Police and Criminal Evidence Act 1984; and

  (b) at any time when he is detained under section 14 of the Prevention of Terrorism (Temporary Provisions) Act 1989.

Explanatory text—See para **3.18**.

Court (subss (1), (3), (5), (6))—See s 27(1).

Imprisonment (subss (1), (4), (8))—See s 27(1).

Commencement of this section (subs (1))—See general annotations and para **3.xx**.

Section 23 of the Powers of Criminal Courts Act 1973 (subs (8))—Section 23 of the 1973 Act provides:

  '(1) Where an offender is convicted of an offence punishable with imprisonment committed during the operational period of a suspended sentence and either he is so convicted by or before a court having power under section 24 of this Act to deal with him in respect of the suspended sentence or he subsequently appears or is brought before such a court, then, unless the sentence has already taken effect, that court shall consider his case and deal with him by one of the following methods—

(a) the court may order that the suspended sentence shall take effect with the original term unaltered;

(b) it may order that the sentence shall take effect with the substitution of a lesser term for the original term;

(c) it may by order vary the original order under section 22(1) of this Act by substituting for the period specified therein a period expiring not later than two years from the date of the variation; or

(d) it may make no order with respect to the suspended sentence;

and a court shall make an order under paragraph (a) of this subsection unless the court is of opinion that it would be unjust to do so in view of all the circumstances including the facts of the subsequent offence, and where it is of that opinion the court shall state its reasons.

(2) Where a court orders that a suspended sentence shall take effect, with or without any variation of the original term, the court may order that the sentence shall take effect immediately or that the term thereof shall commence on the expiration of another term of imprisonment passed on the offender by that or another court.

(3)–(5) [repealed]

(6) In proceedings for dealing with an offender in respect of a suspended sentence which take place before a Crown Court any question whether the offender has been convicted of an offence punishable with imprisonment committed during the operational period of the suspended sentence shall be determined by the court and not by the verdict of a jury.

(7) Where a court deals with an offender under this section in respect of a suspended sentence the appropriate officer of the court shall notify the appropriate officer of the court which passed the sentence of the method adopted.

(8) Where on consideration of the case of an offender a court makes no order with respect to a suspended sentence, the appropriate officer of the court shall record that fact.

(9) For the purposes of any enactment conferring rights of appeal in criminal cases any order made by a court with respect to a suspended sentence shall be treated as a sentence passed on the offender by that court for the offence for which the suspended sentence was passed.'

Section 23 deals with the question of the bringing into effect of a suspended sentence passed pursuant to s 22. That section provides:

'(1) Subject to subsection (2) below, a court which passes a sentence of imprisonment for a term of not more than two years for an offence may order that the sentence shall not take effect unless, during a period specified in the order, being not less than one year or more than two years from the date of the order, the offender commits in Great Britain another offence punishable with imprisonment and thereafter a court having power to do so orders under section 23 of this Act that the original sentence shall take effect; and in this part of the Act "operational period", in relation to a suspended sentence, means the period so specified.

(2) A court shall not deal with an offender by means of a suspended sentence unless it is of the opinion—

(a) that the case is one in which a sentence of imprisonment would have been appropriate even without the power to suspend the sentence; and

(b) that the exercise of that power can be justified by the exceptional circumstances of the case.

(2A) A court which passes a suspended sentence on any person for an offence shall consider whether the circumstances of the case are such as to warrant in addition the imposition of a fine or the making of a compensation order.

(3) A court which passes a suspended sentence on any person for an offence shall not make a probation order in his case in respect of another offence of which he is convicted by or before the court or for which he is dealt with by the court.

(4) On passing a suspended sentence the court shall explain to the offender in ordinary language his liability under section 23 of this Act if during the operational period he commits an offence punishable with imprisonment.

(5) [repealed].'

Police detention (subss (9), (10))—'Police detention' comes within the meaning of s 118(2) of PACE 1984. For this purpose, a person is in police detention if:

(a) he has been taken to the police station after being arrested for an offence or after being arrested under s 14 of the Prevention of Terrorism (Temporary Provisions) Act 1989 or under para 6 of Sch 5 to that Act by an examining officer who is a constable; or

(b) he is arrested at a police station after attending voluntarily at the police station or accompanying a constable to it,

and is detained there or is detained elsewhere in the charge of a constable, except that a person who is at a court after being charged is not in police detention for these purposes.

A person who is voluntarily at the police station is not in police detention for this purpose, although he is entitled to the protection of Code C relating to the treatment of suspects, made pursuant to s 66 of PACE.

Section 14 of the Prevention of Terrorism (Temporary Provisions) Act 1989 (sub (10))—This provides as follows:

'(1) Subject to subsection (2) below, a constable may arrest without warrant a person whom he has reasonable grounds for suspecting to be—

(a) a person guilty of an offence under section 2, 8, 9, 10 or 11 above,

(b) a person who is or has been concerned in commission, preparation or instigation of acts of terrorism to which this section applies, or

(c) a person subject to an exclusion order.

(2) The acts of terrorism to which this section applies are—

(b) acts of terrorism connected with the affairs of Northern Ireland; and

(c) acts of terrorism of any other description except acts connected solely with the affairs of the United Kingdom or any part of the United Kingdom other than Northern Ireland.

(3) ...

(4) Subject to subsection (5) below, a person arrested under this section shall not be detained in right of the arrest for more than forty-eight hours after his arrest.

(5) The Secretary of State may, in any particular case, extend the period of forty-eight hours mentioned in subsection (4) above by a period or periods specified by him, but any such period or further periods shall not exceed five days in all and if an application for such an extension is made the person detained shall as soon as practicable be given written notice of that fact and of the time when the application was made ...'.

Related offence (subs (1))—Comparison should be made between the formulation in s 9(1)(b) ('charge founded on the same facts or evidence') and that in s 38A of the Magistrates' Courts Act 1980 (as substituted by s 51 of the new Act) ('if the charges could be joined in the same indictment'.) Rule 9 of the Indictment Rules 1971 states: 'Charges for any offences may be joined in the same indictment if those charges are founded on the same facts, or form or a part of a series of offences of the same or a similar character.' The definition in s 9(1)(b) is therefore narrower than that in s 38A of the 1980 Act.

Whether charges are 'founded on the same facts' turns on whether a common factual origin exists. If the 'subsidiary' charge could not be alleged but for the facts that give rise to the primary charge, joinder may legitimately occur: *Barrall and Wilson* (1979) 68 Cr App R 250 (CA); *Barnes* (1986) Cr App R 38 (CA). In *Conti* (1974) 58 Cr App R 387 (CA), C was charged with assault occasioning actual bodily harm, possession of an offensive weapon and possession of a prohibited drug. This last count was held to be properly joined, the prosecution case being that the drug was taken for the purposes of achieving a state of mind which would facilitate the commission of the assault. See also: *Clayton-Wright* (1954) 33 Cr App R 22 (CA); *Williams* [1993] Crim LR 533 (CA).

Early release

10 Early release on compassionate grounds

(1) The Secretary of State may at any time release a prisoner if he is satisfied that exceptional circumstances exist which justify the prisoner's release on compassionate grounds.

(2) Before releasing under subsection (1) above a prisoner who is serving a sentence of imprisonment for a term of three years or more, the Secretary of State shall consult the Parole Board, unless the circumstances are such as to render such consultation impracticable.

Explanatory text—See para **3.26**.

Prisoner (subss (1), (2))—See s 27(1).

Sentence of imprisonment (sub (2))—See s 27(1) and s 8(2).

11 Award of early release days for good behaviour

(1) This section applies where a prisoner is serving a sentence of imprisonment for a term of more than two months and less than three years.

(2) For each initial assessment period, the prescribed person may award the prisoner such number of early release days, not exceeding twelve, as he may determine having regard to the extent to which the prisoner's behaviour during the period has attained the prescribed minimum standard.

(3) For each subsequent assessment period, the prescribed person may award the prisoner—

    (a) such number of early release days, not exceeding six, as he may determine having regard to the extent to which the prisoner's behaviour during the period has attained the prescribed minimum standard; and

    (b) such number of such days, not exceeding six, as he may determine having regard to the extent to which the prisoner's behaviour during the period has exceeded that standard.

(4) Where at any time this section applies in place of section 12, 28 or 29 below because a sentence is set aside or varied on appeal, then, for each assessment period for the purposes of this section beginning before that time, the prescribed person shall assume, for the purposes of subsection (2) or (3) above, that the prisoner's behaviour was such as to entitle him to the maximum number of early release days available under that subsection.

(5) Where any early release days are awarded to a prisoner, any period which he must serve before becoming entitled to be released shall be reduced by the aggregate of those days; but nothing in this subsection shall entitle a prisoner to be released on the basis of an award before the day after that on which the award is made.

(6) Prison rules may—

    (a) require determinations under this section to be made at prescribed times, and to be notified to the prisoners concerned in the prescribed manner; and

    (b) make provision for enabling prisoners to appeal against such determinations to prescribed persons.

(7) The Secretary of State may by order provide that subsections (2) and (3) above shall have effect subject to such amendments as may be specified in the order; but no amendment so specified shall reduce—

(a) the number of days specified in subsection (2) or (3)(a); or

(b) the total number of days specified in subsection (3).

(8) The power to make an order under this section shall be exercisable by statutory instrument which shall be subject to annulment in pursuance of a resolution of either House of Parliament.

(9) In this section, in relation to a prisoner—

'assessment period' means—

(a) the period of two months beginning with the day on which he was sentenced; and

(b) each successive period of two months ending before his release;

'initial assessment period' means an assessment period beginning less than twelve months after the day on which he was sentenced and 'subsequent assessment period' shall be construed accordingly.

Explanatory text—See para **3.27**.

Sentence of imprisonment (subs (1))—See s 27(1).

Prisoner (subss (1), (3), (4), (5), (6))—See s 27(1) and s 8(2).

Prescribed/prescribed period/prescribed minimum standard (subss (2), (3), (4), (6))—See s 27(1).

Prison rules (subs (6))—See s 27(1).

12 Early release on Parole Board recommendation

(1) This section applies where a prisoner is serving a sentence of imprisonment for a term of three years or more.

(2) As soon as the prisoner has served five-sixths of his sentence, the Secretary of State shall, if recommended to do so by the Parole Board, release him.

Explanatory text—See para **3.34**.

Sentence of imprisonment (subs (1))—See s 27(1).

13 Provisional early release days for remand prisoners

(1) This section applies where an accused is remanded in custody in connection with one or more offences—

(a) which are alleged to have been committed after the commencement of this Chapter; and

(b) in respect of which he would be liable, if convicted, to a life sentence or to imprisonment for a term of more than two months.

(2) For the purpose of enabling early release days to be awarded on a provisional basis, subsections (2) and (3) of section 11 above shall have effect as if—

(a) the accused had been convicted of, or of an offence related to, the offence or any of the offences, and had been sentenced to imprisonment for a term of more than two months and less than three years, on the day on which he was remanded in custody;

(b) any days falling after that day for which he is not remanded in custody were disregarded; and

(c) references in that section to periods of two months were references to periods of 60 days.

(3) Subsections (4) to (6) below shall apply if, and only if, each of the following conditions is fulfilled, namely—

    (a) the accused is convicted of, or of an offence related to, the offence or any of the offences;

    (b) he is sentenced to imprisonment for a term of more than two months and less than three years; and

    (c) a direction is given under section 9 above.

(4) For the purposes of section 11(5) above, any early release days provisionally awarded under subsection (2) above shall be treated as early release days awarded on the day on which the direction under section 9 above is given.

(5) For the purpose of securing that any days for which the accused was remanded in custody are taken into account in determining assessment periods for the purposes of section 11 above, that section shall have effect as if—

    (a) the accused had been convicted and sentenced on the day on which he was remanded in custody;

    (b) any days which fell before the day on which he was sentenced, and for which he was not remanded in custody, were disregarded; and

    (c) references to periods of two months, in their application to periods beginning before that day, were references to periods of 60 days.

(6) If the direction under section 9 above is given in relation to a number of days less than that for which the accused was remanded in custody—

    (a) subsection (4) above shall have effect as if the reference to any early release days provisionally awarded under subsection (2) above were a reference to the appropriate proportion of those days (rounded up to the nearest whole day); and

    (b) subsection (5) above shall have effect as if the reference to days for which he was not remanded in custody included a reference to the complementary proportion of the days for which he was so remanded (rounded down to the nearest whole day).

(7) Where for any period the accused has been held in police detention, the prescribed person shall assume, for the purposes of section 11(2) and (3) above as modified by subsection (2) above, that during that period—

    (a) the prisoner had been in prison; and

    (b) his behaviour had attained, but not exceeded, the prescribed minimum standard for the purposes of that section.

(8) In this section—

    'the appropriate proportion' means the proportion which the number of days in relation to which the direction under section 9 above is given bears to the number of days for which the accused was remanded in custody, and 'the complementary proportion' shall be construed accordingly;

    'life sentence' has the same meaning as in section 34 below;

    'related', in relation to an offence, has the same meaning as in section 9 above;

and subsections (2), (9) and (10) of section 9 above shall apply for the purposes of this section as they apply for the purposes of that section.

Explanatory text—See para **3.32**.

Commencement of this Chapter (subs (1))—See para **3.2** and general annotations.

Related to the offence (subss (2), (3))—See s 9.

Life sentence (subs (1))—See s 34.

Police detention (subs (7))—See annotations to s 9.

Additional days

14 Award of additional days for disciplinary offences

(1) Prison rules may include provision for the award of additional days to prisoners who are guilty of disciplinary offences.

(2) Subject to subsection (3) below, where any additional days are awarded to a prisoner, and are not remitted in accordance with prison rules, any period which he must serve before becoming—

(a) entitled to be released under section 11 above; or
(b) eligible to be released under section 12 above,

shall be extended by the aggregate of those days.

(3) Nothing in subsection (2) above shall have the effect of extending any such period beyond the end of the prisoner's sentence, taking into account for this purpose any days directed by the court to count as time served as part of that sentence.

Explanatory text—See para **3.36**.

Prison rules (subs (1))—Made pursuant to the Prison Act 1952.

15 Provisional additional days for remand prisoners

(1) This section applies where an accused is remanded in custody in connection with one or more offences—

(a) which are alleged to have been committed after the commencement of this Chapter; and
(b) in respect of which he would be liable, if convicted, to a life sentence or to imprisonment for a term of more than two months.

(2) For the purpose of enabling additional days to be awarded on a provisional basis, prison rules made by virtue of section 14(1) above shall have effect as if the accused—

(a) had been convicted of, or of an offence related to, the offence or any of the offences; and
(b) had been sentenced to imprisonment for a term of more than two months, on the day on which he was remanded in custody.

(3) Subsections (4) and (5) below shall apply if, and only if, each of the following conditions is fulfilled, namely—

(a) the accused is convicted of, or of an offence related to, the offence or any of the offences;
(b) he is sentenced to imprisonment for a term of more than two months; and
(c) a direction is given under section 9 above.

(4) For the purposes of section 14(2) and (3) above, any additional days provisionally awarded under subsection (2) above shall be treated as additional days awarded on the day on which the direction under section 9 above is given.

(5) If the direction under section 9 above is given in relation to a number of days less than that for which the accused was remanded in custody, subsection (4) above shall have effect as if the reference to any additional days provisionally awarded under subsection (2) above were a reference to the appropriate proportion of those days (rounded up to the nearest whole day).

(6) In this section—

> 'the appropriate proportion' has the same meaning as in section 13 above;

> 'life sentence' has the same meaning as in section 34 below;

> 'related', in relation to an offence, has the same meaning as in section 9 above;

and subsections (2), (9) and (10) of section 9 above shall apply for the purposes of this section as they apply for the purposes of that section.

Explanatory text—See para **3.37**.

Commencement (subs (1))—See general annotations and para **3.20**.

Life sentence (subs (1))—See s 34.

Prison rules (subs (2))—See annotations to s 14.

Related offence (subs (3))—See annotations to s 9.

Appropriate proportion (subs (5))—See s 13.

Supervision after release

16   Release supervision orders

(1) This section applies where—

(a) an offender who has been sentenced to imprisonment for a term of twelve months or more in respect of an offence committed after the commencement of this Chapter is released otherwise than under section 10 above;

(b) an offender who has been so sentenced is released under that section; or

(c) an offender who has been sentenced to imprisonment for a term of less than twelve months in respect of an offence committed after that commencement is released under that section.

(2) On his release, the offender shall be subject to a release supervision order—

(a) in a case falling within subsection (1)(a) above, for a period equal to 25 per cent of his term of imprisonment (rounded up to the nearest whole day) or a period of three months, whichever is the greater;

(b) in a case falling within subsection (1)(b) above, for a period equal to the aggregate of the period mentioned in paragraph (a) above and the period mentioned in paragraph (c) below;

(c) in a case falling within subsection (1)(c) above, for a period equal to so much of the remainder of his term as he would have been liable to serve but for his release under section 10 above;

and in applying paragraphs (b) and (c) above account shall be taken of any early release or additional days awarded to the offender before his release.

(3) The release supervision order, which shall be made by the Secretary of State, shall provide that, throughout the period for which the order is in force ('the release supervision period'), the offender, so long as he is at large—

(a) shall be under the supervision of a probation officer; and

(b) shall comply with such conditions as are for the time being specified in the order.

(4) The Secretary of State—

(a) shall not specify any condition which—

    (i) requires the offender to live in an approved probation hostel; or

    (ii) makes such provision as is made by a curfew order,

except in accordance with recommendations of the Parole Board made after an oral hearing at which the offender had the opportunity to be heard or represented; and

(b) in the case of an offender who has been sentenced to imprisonment for a term of three years or more, shall not specify any other condition except in accordance with recommendations of that Board.

(5) The Secretary of State may make rules for regulating the supervision under this section of any description of offenders.

(6) The power to make rules under this section shall be exercisable by statutory instrument which shall be subject to annulment in pursuance of a resolution of either House of Parliament.

(7) In this section—

'approved probation hostel' has the same meaning as in the Probation Service Act 1993;

'curfew order' has the same meaning as in the Criminal Justice Act 1991 ('the 1991 Act').

Explanatory text—See para **3.38**.

Commencement of this section (subs (1))—See general annotations and para **3.2**.

Day (subs (2))—See general annotations.

Probation officer (subs (3))—See s 1 of the Probation Service Act 1993. The duties of probation officers are defined by s 14 of the 1993 Act.

Approved probation hostel (subss (4), (7))—Defined by Probation Service Act 1993.

Curfew order (subs (4))—Section 12 of the Criminal Justice Act 1991 provides as follows, as amended by the new Act:

'(1) Where a person of or over the age of 16 years is convicted of an offence (not being an offence for which the sentence is fixed by law), the court by or before he is convicted may make a curfew order, that is to say, an order requiring him to remain, for periods specified in the order, at a place so specified.

(2) A curfew order may specify different places or different periods for different days, but shall not specify—

    (a) periods which fall outside the period of six months beginning with the day on which it is made; or

    (b) periods which amount to less than two hours or more than 12 hours in any one day.

(3) The requirements in a curfew order shall, as far as practicable, be such as to avoid—

    (a) any conflict with the offender's religious beliefs or with the requirements of any other community order to which he may be subject; and

    (b) any interference with the times, at any, at which he normally works or attends school or other educational establishment.

(4) A curfew order shall include provision for making a person responsible for monitoring the offender's whereabouts during the curfew periods specified in the order, and a person who is made so responsible shall be of a description specified in an order made by the Secretary of State.

(5) Before making a curfew order, the court shall explain to the offender in ordinary language—

(a) the effect of the order (including any additional requirements proposed to be included in the order in accordance with section 13 below);

(b) the consequences which may follow under Schedule 2 to this Act if he fails to comply with any of the requirements of the order; and

(c) that the court has under that Schedule power to review the order on the application either of the offender or of the supervising officer.

(6) Before making a curfew order the court shall obtain and consider information about the place proposed to be specified in the order (including information as to the attitude of person likely to be affected by the enforced presence there of the offender).

(7) The Secretary of State may by order direct—

(a) that subsection (2) above shall have effect with the substitution, for any period there specified, of such period as may be specified in the order; or

(b) that subsection (3) above shall have effect with such additional restrictions as may be so specified.'

See also paras **7.26** and **7.32**.

17 Breach of conditions of release supervision order

(1) If any offender in respect of whom a release supervision order is in force fails without reasonable excuse to comply with any of the conditions of the order, he shall be liable—

(a) on conviction on indictment, to imprisonment for a term not exceeding the relevant period or a fine or both;

(b) on summary conviction, to imprisonment for a term not exceeding the relevant period or a fine not exceeding level 3 on the standard scale or both.

(2) An offence under subsection (1) above shall not be triable on indictment unless—

(a) the relevant period would be longer than six months; or

(b) the act or omission in question constitutes another offence which is punishable with imprisonment and is triable on indictment.

(3) A magistrates' court by which an offender is convicted of an offence under subsection (1) above which could have been tried on indictment may commit him in custody or on bail to the Crown Court for sentence; and the Crown Court to which he has been so committed may impose on him such a sentence as is mentioned in subsection (1)(a) above.

(4) A court shall not impose a sentence of imprisonment under subsection (1) above unless—

(a) it considers it expedient to do so in the interests of protecting the public from serious harm from the offender; or

(b) the offender's failure to comply with the condition in question consisted of the commission of an offence punishable with imprisonment.

(5) Nothing in section 1 or 2 of the 1991 Act shall apply in relation to such a sentence; and nothing in section 6 of that Act shall prevent a court from dealing with the offender in respect of an offence under subsection (1) above in any one of the following ways, namely—

(a) where the offender is 16 or over—
  (i)   by making a community service order, probation order or combination order in respect of him; or
  (ii) by making a curfew order in respect of him; or
  (iii) by doing both of those things;
(b) where the offender is under 18—
  (i)   by making a supervision order in respect of him; or
  (ii) by making both such an order and a curfew order in respect of him; and
(c) where the case is one to which section 17 of the 1982 Act applies—
  (i)   by making an order under that section requiring the offender to attend at an attendance centre; or
  (ii) by making both such an order and a curfew order in respect of him.

(6) In this section—

'combination order' and 'curfew order' have the same meanings as in the 1991 Act;

'community service order' and 'probation order' have the same meanings as in the 1973 Act;

'supervision order' means a supervision order under the Children and Young Persons Act 1969 ('the 1969 Act');

'the relevant period' means—

  (a) on conviction on indictment, so much of the release supervision period as falls after the day on which the offender failed to comply with the condition;
  (b) on summary conviction, so much of that period as so falls or six months, whichever is the shorter.

Explanatory text—See para **3.49**.

Level 3 on the standard scale (subs (1))—See general annotations.

Reasonable excuse (subs (1))—In other contexts it has been held that whether there is a reasonable excuse depends on whether a reasonable man would think the excuse reasonable in all the circumstances (*Bryan v Mott* (1975) 62 Cr App R 71 (DC)), but that as a matter of law there are limitations (imposed by the courts) as to what a reasonable man thinks (*Bryan v Mott; Evans v Hughes* [1972] 3 All ER 412 (DC)). This is likely to be the approach taken by the courts in relation to the instant provision.

Sentence of imprisonment (subs (4))—See s 27.

Age (subs (5))—See general annotations.

Combination order (subs (6))—Section 11 of the Criminal Justice Act 1991 provides:

'(1) Where a court by or before which a person of or over the age of 16 years is convicted of an offence punishable with imprisonment (not being an offence for which the sentence is fixed by law) is of the opinion mentioned in subsection (2) below, the court may make a combination order, that is to say, an order requiring him both—

  (a) to be under the supervision of a probation officer for a period specified in the order, being not less than 12 months nor more than three years; and
  (b) to perform unpaid work for a number of hours to be specified, being in the aggregate not less than 40 nor more than 100.

(2) The opinion referred to in subsection (1) above is that the making of a combination order is desirable in the interests of—

  (a) securing the rehabilitation of the offender; or
  (b) protecting the public from harm from him or preventing the commission by him of further offences.

(3) Subject to subsection (1) above, Pt I of the 1973 Act shall apply in relation to combination orders—

    (a) insofar as they impose such a requirement as is mentioned in paragraph (a) of that subsection, as if they were probation orders; and

    (b) insofar as they impose such a requirement as is mentioned in paragraph (b) of that subsection, as if they were community service orders.'

Curfew order (subss (5), (6))—See annotations to s 16.

Community service order (subss (5), (6))—Section 14 of the Powers of Criminal Courts Act 1973 (as amended) provides:

'(1) Where a person of or over 16 years of age is convicted of an offence punishable with imprisonment, the court by or before which he is convicted may (but subject to subsection (2) below) make an order (in this Act referred to as a 'community service order') requiring him to perform unpaid work in accordance with the subsequent provisions of this Act.

The reference in this subsection to an offence punishable with imprisonment shall be construed without regard to any prohibition or restriction imposed by or under any enactment on the imprisonment of young offenders.

(1A) The number of hours which a person may be required to work under a community service order shall be specified in the order and shall be in the aggregate—
    (a) not less than 40; and
    (b) not more than 240 ...'.

[subsections (2)–(8) specify the procedural requirements]

Section 15(1) of the 1973 Act provides:

'An offender in respect of whom a community service order is in force shall—

    (a) keep in touch with the relevant officer in accordance with such instructions as he may from time to time be given by that officer and notify him of any change of address;

    (b) perform for the number of hours specified in the order such work at such times as he may be instructed by the relevant officer.'

Probation order (subss (5), (6))—Section 2(1) of the Powers of Criminal Courts Act 1973 states:

'Where a court by or before which a person of or over the age of 16 years is convicted of an offence (not being an offence for which the sentence is fixed by law) is of the opinion that the supervision of the offender by a probation officer is desirable in the interests of—

    (a) securing the rehabilitation of the offender; or

    (b) protecting the public from harm from him or preventing the commission by him of further offences,

the court may make a probation order, that is to say, an order requiring him to be under the supervision of a probation officer for a period specified in the order of not less than six months nor more than three years ...'.

Supervision order (subss (5), (6))—A 'supervision order' is defined by s 11 of the Children and Young Persons Act 1969 as an order placing any person under the supervision of a local authority designated by the order or of a probation officer. For the powers of a court to deal with breaches of such orders, see s 15.

18   Powers of arrest and search warrants

(1) A constable may arrest without warrant any person whom he has reasonable grounds for suspecting to have committed an offence under section 17 above.

(2) If a justice of the peace is by written information on oath satisfied that there is reasonable ground for suspecting that a person who is liable to be arrested under

subsection (1) above is to be found on any premises, he may grant a warrant authorising any constable to enter, if need be by force, the premises named in the warrant for the purposes of searching for and arresting that person.

(3) Section 8 of the Police and Criminal Evidence Act 1984 (power of justice to authorise entry and search of premises) shall have effect as if the reference in subsection (1) of that section to a serious arrestable offence included a reference to an offence under section 17 above.

Explanatory text—See para **3.51**.

Constable (subs (1))—This expression includes all those who hold the office of constable pursuant to the Police Act 1964, s 19, including special constables and those who hold office as police officers under police forces established for specific purposes. See, eg, British Transport police (Transport Act 1962, s 69), Civil Aviation police (Civil Aviation Act 1982, s 57), Ministry of Defence Police (Ministry of Defence Act 1987). It will include those whose geographical jurisdiction is limited (eg Port of London Act 1968, s 2(1)), which limits jurisdiction of officers to the docks, landing places and land vested in, belonging to or administered by the Port of London Authority). It does not extend to persons who have, for limited purposes, powers of constables (see, eg, water bailiffs, pursuant to the Salmon and Fisheries Act 1975, s 36).

Section 8(1) of the Police and Criminal Evidence Act 1984 (subs (3))—As amended, s 8(1) of PACE reads:

'If on an application made by a constable a justice of the peace is satisfied that there are reasonable grounds for believing—

   (a) that a serious arrestable offence or an offence under s 17 of the Crime (Sentences) Act 1997 has been committed;

   (b) that there is material on premises specified in the application which is likely to be of substantial value (whether by itself or together with other material) to the investigation of the offence;

   (c) that the material is likely to be relevant evidence; and

   (d) that it does not consist of or include items subject to legal privilege, excluded material or special procedure material; and

   (e) that any of the conditions specified in subsection (3) below applies,

he may issue a warrant authorising a constable to enter and search the premises.'

Special cases

19 Young offenders

(1) Subject to the provisions of this section, this Chapter applies to—

   (a) a sentence of detention in a young offender institution; and

   (b) a determinate sentence of detention under section 53 of the Children and Young Persons Act 1933 ('the 1933 Act'),

as it applies to an equivalent sentence of imprisonment.

(2) References in this Chapter to prisoners, or to prison or imprisonment, shall be construed in accordance with subsection (1) above.

(3) Section 9 above applies to periods of detention which offenders are liable to serve under secure training orders as it applies to sentences of imprisonment; and sections 9, 13 and 15 above apply to persons—

   (a) remanded or committed to local authority accommodation under section 23 of the 1969 Act or section 37 of the Magistrates' Courts Act 1980 ('the 1980 Act'); and

   (b) placed and kept in secure accommodation,

as they apply to persons remanded in or committed to custody by an order of a court.

(4) For each assessment period for the purposes of section 11 above during the whole or part of which the prisoner—

(a) is under 16; or

(b) is detained in local authority accommodation, or a home provided by the Secretary of State under section 82(5) of the Children Act 1989,

the prescribed person shall assume, for the purposes of subsection (2) or (3) of that section, that the prisoner's behaviour had been such as to entitle him to the maximum number of early release days available under that subsection.

(5) For each assessment period for the purposes of section 13 above during the whole or part of which the accused—

(a) is under 16; or

(b) is a person to whom section 9 applies by virtue of subsection (3) above,

the prescribed person shall assume, for the purposes of subsection (2) or (3) of section 11 above as modified by section 13(2) above, that the accused's behaviour had been such as to entitle him to the maximum number of early release days available under that subsection.

(6) In relation to a released offender who is under 22, section 16 above shall have effect as if—

(a) in subsection (1), paragraph (c) and, in paragraph (a), the words 'of twelve months or more' were omitted; and

(b) in subsection (3)(a), the reference to supervision by a probation officer included a reference to supervision by a social worker of a local authority social services department.

(7) Where a released offender who is under 18 and whose sentence was a determinate sentence of detention under section 53 of the 1933 Act commits an offence under section 17 above, the court may deal with him as if subsection (3) of section 53 applied; but no sentence of detention imposed by virtue of this subsection shall be for a term exceeding the relevant period within the meaning of section 17 above.

(8) In relation to a released offender who is under 22 and whose sentence—

(a) was a sentence of detention in a young offender institution, or a sentence of detention under section 53 of the 1933 Act, for a term of less than 12 months; and

(b) was not imposed in respect of a sexual offence committed after the commencement of this Chapter,

section 17 above shall have effect as if the relevant period for the purposes of that section were a period of 30 days.

(9) Where an offender is released from a sentence of detention imposed under section 17 above as modified by subsection (8) above, he shall not be liable to a release supervision order in consequence of his conviction under that section.

(10) In this section 'secure accommodation' has the same meaning as in section 23 of the 1969 Act, and—

(a) any reference to a sentence of detention in a young offender institution includes a reference to a sentence under a custodial order within the meaning of section 71AA of the Army Act 1955 or the Air Force Act 1955 or section 43AA of the Naval Discipline Act 1957; and

(b) any reference (however expressed) to a determinate sentence of detention under section 53 of the 1933 Act includes a reference to a sentence of detention under subsection (4) of section 71A of the Army Act 1955 or the Air Force Act 1955 or section 43A of the Naval Discipline Act 1957.

Explanatory text—See generally, Ch 3 and annotations to s 33.

Section 53 of the Children and Young Persons Act 1933 (subss (1), (7))—See para **3.43**.

Section 23 of the Children and Young Persons Act 1969 (sub (3))—As substituted by Criminal Justice Act 1991, s 60, s 23(1) provides that where: (a) a court remands a child or young person charged with or convicted of one or more offences or commits him for trial or sentence; and (b) he is not released on bail, the remand or committal shall be to local authority accommodation and, in this section a reference (however expressed) to a remand shall be construed as including a reference to a committal. Section 23(4) states that a court remanding a person to local authority accommodation may, after consultation with the designated authority, require that authority to comply with a security requirement, that is to say, a requirement that the person in question be placed and kept in secure accommodation. By s 23(5), a court shall not impose security requirement except in respect of a young person who has attained the age of [15] and then only if:

(a) he is charged with or has been convicted of a violent or sexual offence, or an offence punishable with imprisonment for a term of 14 years or more; or
(b) he has a recent history of absconding while remanded to local authority accommodation, and is charged with or has been convicted of an imprisonable offence alleged or found to have been committed while he was so remanded.

The age in square brackets is amended prospectively by s 20 of the Criminal Justice and Public Order Act 1994. That amendment has not yet been brought into force.

Section 37 of the Magistrates' Courts Act 1980 (subs (3))—Section 37 states:

'(1) Where a person who is not less than 15 but under 18 years old is convicted by a magistrates' court of an offence punishable on conviction on indictment with a term of imprisonment exceeding six months, then, if the court is of opinion that he should be sentenced to a greater term of detention in a young offenders institution than it has the power to impose, the court may, subject to s 25 of the Criminal Justice and Public Order Act 1994, commit him in custody or on bail to the Crown Court for sentence.

(2) When a person is committed in custody under subsection (1) above is not less than 17 years old, he shall be committed—

(a) if the court has been notified by the Secretary of State that a remand centre is available for the reception, from that court, of persons of the class or description of the person committed, to a remand centre;
(b) if the court has not been so notified, to a prison.

(3) Where a person is committed in custody under subsection (1) is less than 17 years old—

(a) he shall be committed to accommodation provided by or on behalf of a local authority (within the meaning of the Children Act 1989); and
(b) the court by which he is so committed shall impose a security requirement within the meaning of s 23 of the Children and Young Persons Act 1969.'

Age (subss (5), (6), (7), (8))—See general annotations.

Section 71AA of the Army Act 1955 (subs (10))—Section s 71AA(1) provides that where a person who has attained 17 years of age but is under 21 years of age is found guilty by a court martial of an offence punishable under this Act with imprisonment, the court shall have the power . . . to make an order (a 'custodial order') committing him to be detained under s 71AA for a period to be specified in the order not exceeding the maximum period for which he could have been sentenced to imprisonment if he had attained the age of 21 years.

Section 71AA of the Air Force Act 1955 or s 43AA of the Naval Discipline Act 1957 (subs (10))—These provisions contain equivalent and similar provisions to that contained in s 71AA of the Army Act 1955.

Section 71(4) of the Army Act 1955 (subs (10))—This provides that a person under 17 years of age found guilty of a civil offence (other than one the sentence for which is fixed) which is punishable by a civil court in England and Wales on indictment by, in the case of an adult, a term of imprisonment for 14 years or more, may be sentenced by the court, if it is of opinion that none of the methods in which the case may legally be dealt with is suitable, to be detained for such period, not exceeding the statutory maximum term of imprisonment with which the offence is punishable by such a civil court in the case of an adult, as may be specified in the sentence; and where such a sentence has been passed, the person on whom it is passed shall during that period be liable to be detained in such place and on such conditions as the Secretary of State may direct.

Section 71A of the Air Force Act 1955 or s 43A of the Naval Discipline Act 1957 (subs (10))—These provisions contain equivalent and similar provisions to that contained in s 71A of the Army Act 1955.

20 Sexual offenders

(1) Subsection (2) below applies where—

(a) there is released under this Chapter an offender who has been sentenced to imprisonment for a term in respect of a sexual offence committed after the commencement of this Chapter; and

(b) the court by which he was so sentenced gave a direction under subsection (3) below.

(2) Section 16 above shall have effect in relation to the offender as if—

(a) in subsection (1), paragraph (c) and, in paragraph (a), the words 'of twelve months or more' were omitted; and

(b) for subsection (2) there were substituted the following subsection—

'(2) On his release, the offender shall be subject to a release supervision order—

(a) where he is released otherwise than under section 10 above, for such period as is specified in the direction under section 20(3) below;

(b) where he is released under section 10 above, for a period equal to the aggregate of—

(i) the period mentioned in paragraph (a) above; and

(ii) a period equal to so much of the remainder of his term as he would have been liable to serve but for his release under section 10 above; and in applying paragraph (b) above account shall be taken of any early release or additional days awarded to the offender before his release.'

(3) Where a court sentences an offender to imprisonment for a term in respect of a sexual offence committed after the commencement of this Chapter, it shall give a direction under this subsection unless it is of the opinion that there are exceptional circumstances which justify its not doing so.

(4) Where the court does not give a direction under subsection (3) above, it shall state in open court that it is of that opinion and what the exceptional circumstances are.

(5) A direction under subsection (3) above shall direct that the offender's release supervision period shall be such period as is specified in the direction.

(6) The period so specified shall be—

(a) a period equal to 50 per cent of the offender's term of imprisonment (rounded up to the nearest whole day) or a period of twelve months, whichever is the longer; or

(b) if the court considers a longer period necessary for the purpose of preventing the commission by the offender of further offences and of securing his rehabilitation, such longer period, not exceeding ten years, as it may determine.

Explanatory text—See para **3.44** and paras **5.5–5.13**.

Sexual offence (subss (1), (3))—See s 27.

Commencement of this Chapter (subs (3))—See para **3.2**.

Open court (subs (4))—See annotations to s 2.

Day (subs (6))—See general annotations.

21 Violent offenders

(1) Subsection (2) below applies where—

(a) there is released under this Chapter an offender who has been sentenced to imprisonment for a term of three years or more in respect of a violent offence committed after the commencement of this Chapter; and

(b) the court by which he was so sentenced gave a direction under subsection (3) below.

(2) Section 16 above shall have effect in relation to the offender as if for subsection (2) there were substituted the following subsection—

'(2) On his release, the offender shall be subject to a release supervision order—

(a) where he is released otherwise than under section 10 above, for such period as is specified in the direction under section 21(3) below;

(b) where he is released under section 10 above, for a period equal to the aggregate of—

(i) the period mentioned in paragraph (a) above; and

(ii) a period equal to so much of the remainder of his term as he would have been liable to serve but for his release under section 10 above.'

(3) Where a court sentences an offender to imprisonment for a term of three years or more in respect of a violent offence committed after the commencement of this Chapter, it may give a direction under this subsection if it considers a longer release supervision period necessary for the purpose of preventing the commission by the offender of further offences and of securing his rehabilitation.

(4) A direction under subsection (3) above shall direct that the offender's release supervision period shall be such period, not more than 50 per cent of the offender's term of imprisonment, as is specified in the direction.

(5) In this section 'violent offence' has the same meaning as in Part I of the 1991 Act.

Explanatory text—See para **3.46**.

Violent offence (subss (1), (3), (5))—This bears the meaning ascribed to it by s 31(1) of the Criminal Justice Act 1991. This states that 'violent offence' means an offence which leads, or is intended or likely to lead, to a person's death or physical injury to a person, and includes an offence which is required to be charged as arson (whether or not it would otherwise fall within this definition).

Robbery, in which the victim is threatened with a knife is a violent offence: *Cochrane* (1994) 15 Cr App R (S) 708 (CA). So too is robbery with a firearm: *Touriq Khan* (1995) 16 Cr App R (S) 180. An offence of threatening to kill which does not involve the actual use of force will not normally be a violent offence: *Rickhart* (1995) 16 Cr App R (S) 977 (CA).

22   Mentally disordered offenders

(1) Subject to subsection (3) below, sections 9 and 13 above apply to persons—

(a) remanded to hospital under section 35 or 36 (remands to hospital) of the Mental Health Act 1983 ('the 1983 Act');

(b) admitted to hospital under section 38 of that Act (interim hospital orders); or

(c) removed to hospital under section 48 of that Act (removal to hospital),

as they apply to persons remanded in or committed to custody by an order of a court.

(2) In the case of a prisoner who for any period is detained in a hospital under section 45A of the 1983 Act (power of courts to direct hospital admission), or under section 47 (removal of prisoners to hospital) and section 49 (restriction on discharge of prisoners removed to hospital) of that Act—

(a) section 11 above shall apply as if references to the prescribed person in subsections (2) and (3) were references to the Secretary of State and subsection (6) were omitted; and

(b) the Secretary of State shall assume, for the purposes of subsection (2) or (3) of that section as so modified, that during that period—
  (i)   the prisoner had been in prison; and
  (ii) his behaviour had been such as to entitle him to the maximum number of early release days available under that subsection.

(3) In the case of an accused who for any period is a person to whom section 13 above applies by virtue of subsection (1) above—

(a) that section shall apply as if references to the prescribed person in section 11(2) and (3) above as modified by section 13(2) above were references to the Secretary of State; and

(b) the Secretary of State shall assume, for the purposes of section 11(2) or (3) above as modified by section 13(2) above, that during that period—
  (i)   the accused had been in prison; and
  (ii) his behaviour had been such as to entitle him to the maximum number of early release days available under that subsection.

(4) Where, immediately before the expiration of his sentence, a prisoner is detained in a hospital under section 45A of the 1983 Act, or under section 47 and 49 of that Act, section 16 above shall have effect as if—

(a) the prisoner had been released on the expiration of his sentence;

(b) the reference in subsection (3)(a) to supervision by a probation officer included a reference to supervision by a social worker of a local authority social services department;

(c) the reference in subsection (4)(a) to an approved probation hostel included a reference to any hostel or home whose residents are subject to supervision; and

(d) subsection (4)(b) were omitted.

(5) In this section references to the expiration of the prisoner's sentence shall be construed in accordance with subsection (3) of section 50 of the 1983 Act (prisoners under sentence).

Explanatory text—See generally, Ch 3 and para **3.21**.

Section 35 or s 36 of the Mental Health Act 1983 (subs (1))—By s 35(1), the Crown Court or a magistrates' court may remand an accused person to a hospital specified by the court for a report on his mental condition. The prerequisite for the exercise of this power is contained in s 35(3). It may be exercised if:

(a) the court is satisfied, on the written or oral evidence of a registered medical practitioner, that there is reason to suspect that the accused person is suffering from mental illness, psychopathic disorder, severe mental impairment or mental impairment; and

(b) the court is of the opinion that it would be impracticable for a report on his mental condition to be made if he were remanded on bail. The power is not exercisable in respect of a person convicted of an offence in respect of which the sentence is fixed by law.

Section 35(4) provides that the court shall not remand an accused person to hospital under s 35 unless satisfied, on the written or oral evidence of the registered medical practitioner who would be responsible for making the report or for some other person representing the managers of the hospital, that arrangements have been made for his admission to the hospital and for his admission to it within the period of seven days beginning with the date of remand; and if the court is so satisfied it may, pending his admission, give directions for his conveyance to and detention in a place of safety.

Section 36(1) of the 1983 Act states that a Crown Court may, instead of remanding an accused person in custody remand him to a hospital specified by the court, if satisfied, on the written or oral evidence of two registered medical practitioners, that he is suffering from mental illness or severe mental impairment of a nature or degree which makes it appropriate for him to be detained in a hospital for medical treatment. The section contains similar procedural provisions as are contained in s 35.

Section 38 of the Mental Health Act 1983 (subs (1))—Section 38(1) states that where a person is convicted before the Crown Court of an offence punishable with imprisonment (other than an offence the sentence for which is fixed by law) or is convicted by a magistrates' court of an offence punishable with imprisonment and the court before or by which he is convicted is satisfied, on the written or oral evidence of two registered medical practitioners:

(a) that the offender is suffering from mental illness, psychopathic disorder, severe mental impairment or mental impairment; and

(b) that there is reason to suppose that the mental disorder from which the offender is suffering is such that it may be appropriate for a hospital order to be made in his case, the court may, before making a hospital order or dealing with him in some other way, make an order (an 'interim hospital order') authorising his admission to such hospital as may be specified in the order and his detention there.

Section 48 of the Mental Health Act 1983 (subs (1))—Section 48 provides that, in respect of the person to whom it applies, the Secretary of State may order detention in a hospital. The section applies to persons detained in a prison or remand centre, persons remanded in custody by a magistrates' court, civil prisoners and persons detained under the Immigration Act 1971.

Section 45A of the Mental Health Act 1983 (subss (2), (4))—See para **6.8**.

23 Fine defaulters and contemnors

This Chapter (except sections 16 to 18 above) applies to persons committed to prison or to be detained under section 9 of the 1982 Act—

(a) in default of payment of a sum adjudged to be paid by a conviction; or

(b) for contempt of court or any kindred offence,

as it applies to persons serving equivalent sentences of imprisonment; and references in this Chapter to prisoners, or to prison or imprisonment, shall be construed accordingly.

Explanatory text—See para **3.10**.

Sentence of imprisonment—See s 27.

24 Persons liable to removal from the United Kingdom

(1) In relation to an offender who is liable to removal from the United Kingdom—

(a) section 12 above shall have effect as if, in subsection (2), for the words 'shall, if recommended to do so by the Parole Board,' there were substituted the word 'may'; and (b)	section 16 above shall have effect as if, in subsection (2), for the words 'On his release, the offender shall' there were substituted the words 'If the Secretary of State thinks fit, the offender shall, on his release,'.

(2) An offender is liable to removal from the United Kingdom for the purposes of this section if—

(a)	he is liable to deportation under section 3(5) of the Immigration Act 1971 and has been notified of a decision to make a deportation order against him;
(b)	he is liable to deportation under section 3(6) of that Act;
(c)	he has been notified of a decision to refuse him leave to enter the United Kingdom; or
(d)	he is an illegal entrant within the meaning of section 33(1) of that Act.

Explanatory text—See para **3.58** and **3.39**.

United Kingdom (subs (1), (2))—See general annotations.

25   Persons extradited to the United Kingdom

(1) A prisoner is an extradited prisoner for the purposes of this section if—

(i)	he was tried for the offence in respect of which his sentence was imposed—
	(ii)	after having been extradited to the United Kingdom; and
	(ii)	without having first been restored or had an opportunity of leaving the United Kingdom; and
(b)	he was kept in custody while awaiting his extradition to the United Kingdom as mentioned in paragraph (a) above.

(2) If, in the case of an extradited prisoner, the court by which he was sentenced so ordered, this Chapter shall have effect in relation to him as if a number of days specified in the order were a number of days in relation to which a direction under section 9 above had been given.

(3) The number of days that may be so specified is such number as in the opinion of the court is just in all the circumstances and does not exceed the number of days for which he was kept in custody as mentioned in subsection (1)(b) above.

(4) In this section—

'extradited to the United Kingdom' means returned to the United Kingdom—

(i)	in pursuance of extradition arrangements;
(ii)	under any law of a designated Commonwealth country corresponding to the Extradition Act 1989;
(iii)	under that Act as extended to a colony or under any corresponding law of a colony;
(iv)	in pursuance of a warrant of arrest endorsed in the Republic of Ireland under the law of that country corresponding to the Backing of Warrants (Republic of Ireland) Act 1965; or
(v)	in pursuance of arrangements with a foreign state in respect of which an Order in Council under section 2 of the Extradition Act 1870 is in force;

'extradition arrangements' has the meaning given by section 3 of the Extradition Act 1989;

'designated Commonwealth country' has the meaning given by section 5(1) of that Act.

Explanatory text—See para **3.18**.

United Kingdom (subs (1), (3))—See general annotations.

Supplemental

26 Continuity of sentencing

(1) This section has effect for the purpose of securing that, where a person is sentenced to a term of imprisonment in respect of an offence—

(a) to which this section applies; and

(b) which is committed after the commencement of this Chapter,

he serves approximately the same time in prison as he would have served if the offence had been committed immediately before that commencement.

(2) Subject to sections 3(2) and 4(2) above, the court by which a person is so sentenced at any time shall impose a term which is equal to two-thirds of the term which, at that time, it would have considered to be appropriate if the offence had been so committed.

(3) This section applies to any offence other than one—

(a) which did not subsist, or was not punishable with imprisonment, immediately before the commencement of this Chapter; or

(b) for which the maximum sentence of imprisonment that may be imposed has been varied after that commencement.

Explanatory text—See para **3.7**.

Before ... commencement (subss (1), (2))—See para **3.2** and general annotations.

27 Interpretation of Chapter I

(1) In this Chapter—

'court', except in sections 9, 17 and 19 above, includes a court-martial and a Standing Civilian Court;

'prescribed' means prescribed by prison rules;

'prison rules' means rules made under section 47 of the Prison Act 1952;

'prisoner' has the meaning given by section 8(2) above;

'sentence of imprisonment' does not include a committal—

(a) in default of payment of any sum of money;

(b) for want of sufficient distress to satisfy any sum of money; or

(c) for failure to do or abstain from doing anything required to be done or left undone;

and cognate expressions shall be construed accordingly;

'sexual offence' has the same meaning as in Part I of the 1991 Act.

(2) Subject to subsections (3) and (4) below, for the purposes of any reference in this Chapter, however expressed, to the term of imprisonment to which a person has been or could be sentenced, consecutive terms and terms which are wholly or partly concurrent shall be treated as a single term.

(3) Subsection (4) below applies where—

(a) an offender sentenced to two or more concurrent or consecutive terms of imprisonment is released from prison; and

(b) a direction was given under section 20(3) or 21(3) above in respect of one or more of those terms.

(4) The offender's release supervision period shall be equal to the aggregate of the following, namely—

(a) the period which would be applicable if he had been sentenced only to the term or terms in respect of which such a direction was given; and

(b) the period which would be applicable if he had not been sentenced to the following, namely—

   (i) the term or terms mentioned in paragraph (a) above; and

   (ii) so much of any other term as was concurrent with, or with any part of, the term or any of the terms so mentioned.

(5) Any order, rules or prison rules made under or by virtue of this Chapter may make such incidental, supplemental and consequential provisions as may appear to the Secretary of State to be necessary or expedient.

Explanatory text—See generally, Ch 3.

Sexual offence (subs (1))—Section 31 of the Criminal Justice Act 1991, as amended states that the term 'Sexual offence' means:

> 'an offence under the Sexual Offences Act 1956 (other than an offence under section 30, 31 or 33 to 36 of that Act), an offence under s 128 of the Mental Health Act 1959, the Indecency with Children Act 1960, the Sexual Offences Act 1967, an offence of burglary with intent to commit rape, contrary to s 9 of the Theft Act 1968, section 54 of the Criminal Law Act 1977, under the Protection of Children Act 1978. In addition, conspiracies attempts and incitements to commit any of these offences amount to a sexual offence.'

CHAPTER II
LIFE SENTENCES

Release on licence

28 Duty to release certain life prisoners

(1) A life prisoner is one to whom this section applies if—

(a) the conditions mentioned in subsection (2) below are fulfilled; or

(b) he was under 18 at the time when he committed the offence for which his sentence was imposed.

(2) The conditions referred to in subsection (1)(a) above are—

(a) that the prisoner's sentence was imposed for an offence the sentence for which is not fixed by law; and

(b) that the court by which he was sentenced for that offence ordered that this section should apply to him as soon as he had served a part of his sentence specified in the order.

(3) A part of a sentence specified in an order under subsection (2)(b) above shall be such part as the court considers appropriate taking into account—

(a) the seriousness of the offence, or the combination of the offence and other offences associated with it; and

(b) the effect of any direction which it would have given under section 9 above if it had sentenced him to a term of imprisonment.

(4) Where in the case of a life prisoner to whom this section applies the conditions mentioned in subsection (2) above are not fulfilled, the Secretary of State shall direct that this section shall apply to him as soon as he has served a part of his sentence specified in the direction.

(5) As soon as, in the case of a life prisoner to whom this section applies—

   (a) he has served the part of his sentence specified in the order or direction ('the relevant part'); and

   (b) the Parole Board has directed his release under this section,

it shall be the duty of the Secretary of State to release him on licence.

(6) The Parole Board shall not give a direction under subsection (5) above with respect to a life prisoner to whom this section applies unless—

   (a) the Secretary of State has referred the prisoner's case to the Board; and

   (b) the Board is satisfied that it is no longer necessary for the protection of the public that the prisoner should be confined.

(7) A life prisoner to whom this section applies may require the Secretary of State to refer his case to the Parole Board at any time—

   (a) after he has served the relevant part of his sentence; and

   (b) where there has been a previous reference of his case to the Board, after the end of the period of two years beginning with the disposal of that reference; and

   (c) where he is also serving a sentence of imprisonment or detention for a term, after the time when, but for his life sentence, he would be entitled to be released;

and in this subsection 'previous reference' means a reference under subsection (6) above or section 32(4) below.

(8) In determining for the purpose of subsection (5) or (7) above whether a life prisoner to whom this section applies has served the relevant part of his sentence, no account shall be taken of any time during which he was unlawfully at large within the meaning of section 49 of the Prison Act 1952.

(9) An offence is associated with another for the purposes of this section if it is so associated for the purposes of Part I of the 1991 Act.

Explanatory text—See para **4.9**.

Age (subs (1))—See general annotations.

Associated offence (subss (3), (9))—By s 31(2) of the Criminal Justice Act 1991, an offence is associated with another if:

   (a) the offender is convicted of it in the proceedings in which he is convicted of the other offence, or (although convicted of it in earlier proceedings) is sentenced for it at the same time as he is sentenced for that offence; or

   (b) the offender admits the commission of it in the proceedings in which he is sentenced for the other offence and requests the court to take it into consideration in sentencing him for that offence.

Life prisoner (subss (1), (4), (5), (7), (8))—See s 34.

29   Power to release other life prisoners

(1) If recommended to do so by the Parole Board, the Secretary of State may, after consultation with the Lord Chief Justice together with the trial judge if available, release on licence a life prisoner who is not one to whom section 28 above applies.

(2) The Parole Board shall not make a recommendation under subsection (1) above unless the Secretary of State has referred the particular case, or the class of case to which that case belongs, to the Board for its advice.

Explanatory text—See para **4.15**.

Life prisoner (subs (1))—See s 34.

30   Power to release life prisoners on compassionate grounds

(1) The Secretary of State may at any time release a life prisoner on licence if he is satisfied that exceptional circumstances exist which justify the prisoner's release on compassionate grounds.

(2) Before releasing a life prisoner under subsection (1) above, the Secretary of State shall consult the Parole Board, unless the circumstances are such as to render such consultation impracticable.

Explanatory text—See para **4.16**.

Life prisoner (subss (1), (2))—See s 34.

Licences and recall

31   Duration and conditions of licences

(1) Where a life prisoner is released on licence, the licence shall, unless previously revoked under section 32(1) or (2) below, remain in force until his death.

(2) A life prisoner subject to a licence shall comply with such conditions (which shall include on his release conditions as to his supervision by a probation officer) as may for the time being be specified in the licence; and the Secretary of State may make rules for regulating the supervision of any description of such persons.

(3) The Secretary of State shall not include on release, or subsequently insert, a condition in the licence of a life prisoner, or vary or cancel any such condition, except—

   (a) in the case of the inclusion of a condition in the licence of a life prisoner to whom section 28 above applies, in accordance with recommendations of the Parole Board; and
   (b) in any other case, after consultation with the Board.

(4) For the purposes of subsection (3) above, the Secretary of State shall be treated as having consulted the Parole Board about a proposal to include, insert, vary or cancel a condition in any case if he has consulted the Board about the implementation of proposals of that description generally or in that class of case.

(5) The power to make rules under this section shall be exercisable by statutory instrument which shall be subject to annulment in pursuance of a resolution of either House of Parliament.

(6) In relation to a life prisoner who is liable to removal from the United Kingdom (within the meaning given by section 24(2) above), subsection (2) above shall have effect as if the words in parentheses were omitted.

Explanatory text—See para **4.18**.

United Kingdom (subs (5))—See general annotations.

Life prisoner (subss (1), (2), (3), (6))—See s 34.

32 Recall of life prisoners while on licence

(1) If recommended to do so by the Parole Board in the case of a life prisoner who has been released on licence under this Chapter, the Secretary of State may revoke his licence and recall him to prison.

(2) The Secretary of State may revoke the licence of any life prisoner and recall him to prison without a recommendation by the Parole Board, where it appears to him that it is expedient in the public interest to recall that person before such a recommendation is practicable.

(3) A life prisoner recalled to prison under subsection (1) or (2) above—

- (a) may make representations in writing with respect to his recall; and
- (b) on his return to prison, shall be informed of the reasons for his recall and of his right to make representations.

(4) The Secretary of State shall refer to the Parole Board—

- (a) the case of a life prisoner recalled under subsection (1) above who makes representations under subsection (3) above; and
- (b) the case of a life prisoner recalled under subsection (2) above.

(5) Where on a reference under subsection (4) above the Parole Board—

- (a) directs in the case of a life prisoner to whom section 28 above applies; or
- (b) recommends in the case of any other life prisoner,

his immediate release on licence under this section, the Secretary of State shall give effect to the direction or recommendation.

(6) On the revocation of the licence of any life prisoner under this section, he shall be liable to be detained in pursuance of his sentence and, if at large, shall be deemed to be unlawfully at large.

Explanatory text—See para **4.19**.

Life prisoner (subss (2), (3), (4), (5), (6))—See s 34.

Miscellaneous and supplemental

33 Life prisoners transferred to England and Wales

(1) This section applies where, in the case of a transferred life prisoner, the Secretary of State, after consultation with the Lord Chief Justice, certifies his opinion that, if—

- (a) the prisoner's offence had been committed after the commencement of this Chapter; and
- (b) he had been sentenced for it in England and Wales,

the court by which he was so sentenced would have ordered that section 28 above should apply to him as soon as he had served a part of his sentence specified in the certificate.

(2) This section also applies where, in the case of a transferred life prisoner, the Secretary of State certifies his opinion that, if—

- (a) the prisoner's offence had been committed after the commencement of this Chapter; and
- (b) he had been sentenced for it in England and Wales,

the Secretary of State would have directed that section 28 above should apply to him as soon as he had served a part of his sentence specified in the certificate.

(3) In a case to which this section applies, this Chapter except section 29(1) above shall apply as if—

(a) the transferred life prisoner were a life prisoner to whom section 28 above applies; and

(b) the relevant part of his sentence within the meaning of section 28 above were the part specified in the certificate.

(4) In this section 'transferred life prisoner' means a person—

(a) on whom a court in a country or territory outside England and Wales has imposed one or more sentences of imprisonment or detention for an indeterminate period; and

(b) who has been transferred to England and Wales, in pursuance of—

(i) an order made by the Secretary of State under paragraph 1 of Schedule 1 to this Act or section 2 of the Colonial Prisoners Removal Act 1884; or

(ii) a warrant issued by the Secretary of State under the Repatriation of Prisoners Act 1984,

there to serve his sentence or sentences or the remainder of his sentence or sentences.

(5) A person who is required so to serve the whole or part of two or more such sentences shall not be treated as a life prisoner to whom section 28 above applies unless the requirements of subsection (1) or (2) above are satisfied as respects each of those sentences; and subsections (5) and (7) of section 28 above shall not apply in relation to such a person until after he has served the relevant part of each of those sentences.

Explanatory text—See para **4.20**.

Life prisoner (subss (1), (2), (3), (4))—See s 34.

England and Wales (subss (1), (4))—See general annotations.

34 Interpretation of Chapter II

(1) In this Chapter 'life prisoner' means a person serving one or more life sentences; but—

(a) a person serving two or more such sentences shall not be treated as a life prisoner to whom section 28 above applies unless the requirements of section 28(1) above are satisfied as respects each of those sentences; and

(b) subsections (5) and (7) of that section shall not apply in relation to such a person until after he has served the relevant part of each of those sentences.

(2) In this section 'life sentence' means any of the following imposed for an offence, whether committed before or after the commencement of this Chapter, namely—

(a) a sentence of imprisonment for life;

(b) a sentence of detention during Her Majesty's pleasure or for life under section 53 of the 1933 Act; and

(c) a sentence of custody for life under section 8 of the 1982 Act.

(3) In this Chapter 'court' includes a court-martial and 'trial judge' includes a trial judge advocate; and in subsection (2) above—

(a) the reference to section 53 of the 1933 Act includes a reference to subsections (3) and (4) of section 71A of the Army Act 1955 and the Air Force Act 1955 and section 43A of the Naval Discipline Act 1957; and

(b) the reference to section 8 of the 1982 Act includes a reference to subsections (1A) and (1B) of those sections.

Explanatory text—See para **4.8**.

Section 53 of the Children and Young Persons Act 1933 (subs (1))—This provides:

'(1) A person convicted of an offence who appears to the court to have been under the age of eighteen years at the time the offence was committed shall not, if he is convicted of murder, be sentenced to imprisonment for life ... but in lieu thereof the court shall ... sentence him to be detained during Her Majesty's pleasure, and if so sentenced he shall be liable to be detained in such place and under such conditions as the Secretary of State may direct.

(2) Where (a) a young person is convicted on indictment of any offence punishable in the case of an adult with imprisonment for fourteen years or more, not being an offence the sentence for which is fixed by law; or (b) a child is convicted of manslaughter, and the court is of opinion that none of the other methods in which the case may legally be dealt with is suitable, the court may sentence the offender to be detained for such period (not exceeding the maximum term of imprisonment with which the offence is punishable in the case of an adult as may be specified in the sentence; and where such a sentence has been passed the child or young person shall ... during that period ... be liable to be detained in such place and on such conditions as the Secretary of State may direct.'

Sentence of custody for life under s 8 of the 1982 Act (subs (2))—See annotations to s 2.

Section 71A of the Army Act 1955, Air Force Act 1955 and s 43A of the Naval Discipline Act 1957 (subs (3))—See annotations to s 19.

PART III
MISCELLANEOUS AND SUPPLEMENTAL

Community sentences

35 Fine defaulters: general

(1) Subsection (2) below applies in any case where a magistrates' court—

(a) has power under Part III of the 1980 Act to issue a warrant of commitment for default in paying a sum adjudged to be paid by a conviction of a magistrates' court (other than a sum ordered to be paid under section 71 of the Criminal Justice Act 1988 or section 2 of the Drug Trafficking Act 1994); or

(b) would, but for section 1 of the 1982 Act (restrictions on custodial sentences for persons under 21), have power to issue such a warrant for such default.

(2) The magistrates' court may—

(a) subject to subsections (4) to (6) and (11) below, make a community service order; or

(b) subject to subsections (7) to (11) below, make a curfew order,

in respect of the person in default instead of issuing a warrant of commitment or, as the case may be, proceeding under section 81 of the 1980 Act (enforcement of fines imposed on young offenders).

(3) Where a magistrates' court has power to make an order under subsection (2)(a) or (b) above, it may, if it thinks it expedient to do so, postpone the making of the order until such time and on such conditions, if any, as it thinks just.

(4) In this section 'community service order' has the same meaning as in the 1973 Act and—

   (a)   section 14(2) of that Act; and
   (b)   so far as applicable, the other provisions of that Act relating to community service orders and the provisions of Part I of the 1991 Act so relating,

shall have effect in relation to an order under subsection (2)(a) above as they have effect in relation to an order in respect of an offender, but subject to the exceptions in subsection (5) below.

(5) The following are the exceptions, namely—

   (a)   the reference in section 14(1A)(a) of the 1973 Act to 40 hours shall be construed as a reference to 20 hours;
   (b)   section 14(3) of that Act shall not apply;
   (c)   the requirements in the order under subsection (2)(a) above shall, as far as practicable, be such as to avoid any interference with the times, if any, at which the offender normally works or attends school or other educational establishment;
   (d)   the power conferred by paragraph 3(1)(d) of Schedule 2 to the 1991 Act shall be construed as a power to revoke the order or deal with the person in respect of whom the order was made for his default in paying the sum in question or do both of those things; and
   (e)   paragraph 3(2)(a) of that Schedule shall not apply.

(6) In the case of an amount in default which is described in the first column of the following Table, the period of community service specified in an order under subsection (2)(a) above shall not exceed the number of hours set out opposite that amount in the second column of that Table.

TABLE

Amount	Number of hours
An amount not exceeding £200	40 hours
An amount exceeding £200 but not exceeding £500	60 hours
An amount exceeding £500	100 hours

(7) In this section 'curfew order' has the same meaning as in Part I of the 1991 Act and—

   (a)   section 12(5) of that Act; and
   (b)   so far as applicable, the other provisions of that Part relating to curfew orders,

shall have effect in relation to an order under subsection (2)(b) above as they have effect in relation to an order in respect of an offender, but subject to the exceptions in subsection (8) below.

(8) The following are the exceptions, namely—

   (a)   the power conferred by paragraph 3(1)(d) of Schedule 2 to the 1991 Act to revoke the order and deal with an offender for the offence in respect of which the order was made shall be construed as a power to revoke the order or deal with the person in respect of whom the order was made for his default in paying the sum in question or do both of those things; and
   (b)   paragraph 3(2)(a) of that Schedule shall not apply.

(9) In the case of an amount in default which is described in the first column of the following Table, the number of days to which an order under subsection (2)(b) above relates shall not exceed the number of days set out opposite that amount in the second column of that Table.

TABLE

Amount	Number of days
An amount not exceeding £200	20 days
An amount exceeding £200 but not exceeding £500	30 days
An amount exceeding £500 but not exceeding £1,000	60 days
An amount exceeding £1,000 but not exceeding £2,500	90 days
An amount exceeding £2,500	180 days

(10) A magistrates' court shall not make an order under subsection (2)(b) above in respect of a person who is under 16.

(11) A magistrates court shall not make an order under subsection (2)(a) or (b) above unless the court has been notified by the Secretary of State that arrangements for implementing such orders are available in the relevant area and the notice has not been withdrawn.

(12) In subsection (11) above 'the relevant area' means—

(a) in relation to an order under subsection (2)(a) above, the area proposed to be specified in the order;

(b) in relation to an order under subsection (2)(b) above, the area in which the place proposed to be specified in the order is situated.

(13) Where an order has been made under subsection (2)(a) or (b) above for default in paying any sum—

(a) on payment of the whole sum to any person authorised to receive it, the order shall cease to have effect;

(b) on payment of a part of that sum to any such person, the total number of hours or days to which the order relates shall be reduced proportionately;

and the total number is so reduced if it is reduced by such number of complete hours or days as bears to the total number the proportion most nearly approximating to, without exceeding, the proportion which the part paid bears to the whole sum.

(14) The Secretary of State may by order direct that subsection (5)(a), (6) or (9) above shall be amended by substituting for any number of hours or days there specified such number of hours or days as may be specified in the order.

(15) The power to make an order under this section shall be exercisable by statutory instrument; but no such order shall be made unless a draft of the order has been laid before and approved by a resolution of each House of Parliament.

Explanatory text—See para **7.27**.

Section 71 of the Criminal Justice Act 1988 (subs (1))—Section 71 empowers, and in some cases requires, a court to make a confiscation order where a person has benefited for relevant criminal conduct. If a court determines that the offender has so benefited, it shall determine the amount to be recovered by virtue of s 71, and make an order requiring the offender to pay that amount.

Section 2 of the Drug Trafficking Act 1994 (subs (1))—Under s 2, where a court considers that an offender has benefited from a drug trafficking offence (as to which, see annotations to s 2), it may make an order requiring the offender to pay the amount the court determined is to be recovered from him.

Community service order (subs (4))—See annotations to s 17.

Curfew order (subs (7))—See annotations to s 16.

36   Fine defaulters under 25

(1) In subsection (1) of section 17 of the 1982 Act (attendance centre orders), after paragraph (b) there shall be inserted the words 'or

> (c) has power to commit to prison for default in payment of any sum of money a person who is under 25 but is not less than 21 years of age,'.

(2) In subsection (5) of that section, after the words 'under 21' there shall be inserted the words 'or, as the case may be, 25'.

Explanatory text—See para **7.36**.

Attendance centre order (subs (1))—See para **7.36**.

37   Persistent petty offenders

(1) This section applies where—

    (a) a person is convicted of an offence by a magistrates' court or before the Crown Court;

    (b) the court is satisfied that each of the conditions mentioned in subsection (2) below is fulfilled; and

    (c) if it were not so satisfied, the court would be minded to impose a fine in respect of the offence.

(2) The conditions are—

    (a) that one or more fines imposed on the offender in respect of one or more previous offences have not been paid; and

    (b) if a fine were imposed in an amount which was commensurate with the seriousness of the offence, the offender would not have sufficient means to pay it.

(3) Notwithstanding anything in section 6 of the 1991 Act, the court may—

    (a) subject to subsections (4) and (6) below, make a community service order; or

    (b) subject to subsections (5) and (6) below, make a curfew order,

in respect of the offender instead of imposing a fine.

(4) Subsections (4) and (5) of section 35 above shall apply for the purposes of this section as they apply for the purposes of that section except that—

    (a) the reference in subsection (4) to subsection (2)(a) of that section shall be construed as a reference to subsection (3)(a) of this section;

    (b) paragraph (a) of subsection (5) shall not apply; and

    (c) the reference in paragraph (d) of that subsection to dealing with the person in respect of whom the order was made for his default in paying the sum in question shall be construed as a reference to dealing with the offender for the offence in respect of which the order was made.

(5) Subsections (7), (8) and (10) of section 35 above shall apply for the purposes of this section as they apply for the purposes of that section except that the references in subsections (7) and (10) to subsection (2)(b) of that section shall be construed as references to subsection (3)(b) of this section.

(6) A court shall not make an order under subsection (3)(a) or (b) above unless the court has been notified by the Secretary of State that arrangements for implementing such orders are available in the relevant area and the notice has not been withdrawn.

(7) In subsection (6) above 'the relevant area' means—

- (a) in relation to an order under subsection (3)(a) above, the area proposed to be specified in the order;
- (b) in relation to an order under subsection (3)(b) above, the area in which the place proposed to be specified in the order is situated.

Explanatory text—See para **7.37**.

Community service order (subs (3))—See annotations to s 17.

Curfew order (subs (3))—See annotations to s 16.

38 Abolition of certain consent etc. requirements

(1) In subsection (6) of section 12A of the 1969 Act (young offenders), for paragraph (c) there shall be substituted the following paragraph—

'(c) if the supervised person is under the age of sixteen, it has obtained and considered information about his family circumstances and the likely effect of the requirements on those circumstances.'

(2) The following provisions shall cease to have effect, namely—

- (a) in subsection (3) of section 2 of the 1973 Act (probation orders), the words from 'and the court' to the end;
- (b) in subsection (2) of section 14 of that Act (community service orders), the words 'the offender consents and'; and
- (c) in subsection (5) of section 12 of the 1991 Act (curfew orders), the words from 'and the court' to the end.

(3) For sub-paragraph (4) of paragraph 5 of Schedule 1A to the 1973 Act (requirements as to treatment for mental condition etc) there shall be substituted the following sub-paragraph—

'(4) A court shall not by virtue of this paragraph include in a probation order a requirement that the offender shall submit to treatment for his mental condition unless—

- (a) it is satisfied that arrangements have been made for the treatment intended to be specified in the order (including arrangements for the reception of the offender where he is to be required to submit to treatment as a resident patient); and
- (b) the offender has expressed his willingness to comply with such a requirement.'

(4) For sub-paragraph (4) of paragraph 6 of that Schedule (requirements as to treatment for drug or alcohol dependency) there shall be substituted the following sub-paragraph—

'(4) A court shall not by virtue of this paragraph include in a probation order a requirement that the offender shall submit to treatment for his dependency on drugs or alcohol unless—

- (a) it is satisfied that arrangements have been made for the treatment intended to be specified in the order (including arrangements for the reception of the offender where he is to be required to submit to treatment as a resident patient); and
- (b) the offender has expressed his willingness to comply with such a requirement.'

Explanatory text—See paras **7.23–7.26**.

Section 12A of the 1969 Act (subs (1))—See para **7.22**.

Driving disqualifications

39   Offenders

(1) Subject to subsections (2) and (3) below, the court by or before which a person is convicted of an offence may, in addition to or instead of dealing with him in any other way, order him to be disqualified, for such period as it thinks fit, for holding or obtaining a driving licence.

(2) Where the person is convicted of an offence the sentence for which is fixed by law or falls to be imposed under section 2(2), 3(2), or 4(2) above, subsection (1) above shall have effect as if the words 'or instead of' were omitted.

(3) A court shall not make an order under subsection (1) above unless the court has been notified by the Secretary of State that the power to make such orders is exercisable by the court and the notice has not been withdrawn.

(4) A court which makes an order under this section disqualifying a person for holding or obtaining a driving licence shall require him to produce any such licence held by him together with its counterpart.

(5) The following provisions, namely—

  (a)   section 164(5) of the Road Traffic Act 1988 (power of constables to require production of driving licence etc.); and
  (b)   section 27(3) of the Road Traffic Offenders Act 1988 (failure to produce driving licence),

shall have effect as if the reference to section 44 of the 1973 Act included a reference to this section.

(6) In this section—

  'counterpart', in relation to a driving licence, has the meaning given by section 108(1) of the Road Traffic Act 1988;

  'driving licence' means a licence to drive a motor vehicle granted under Part III of that Act.

Explanatory text—See para **7.39**.

40   Fine defaulters

(1) This section applies in any case where a magistrates' court—

  (a)   has power under Part III of the 1980 Act to issue a warrant of commitment for default in paying a sum adjudged to be paid by a conviction of a magistrates' court (other than a sum ordered to be paid under section 71 of the Criminal Justice Act 1988 or section 2 of the Drug Trafficking Act 1994); or
  (b)   would, but for section 1 of the 1982 Act (restrictions on custodial sentences for persons under 21), have power to issue such a warrant for such default.

(2) Subject to subsection (3) below, the magistrates' court may, instead of issuing a warrant of commitment or, as the case may be, proceeding under section 81 of the 1980 Act (enforcement of fines imposed on young offenders), order the person in default to be disqualified, for such period not exceeding twelve months as it thinks fit, for holding or obtaining a driving licence.

(3) A magistrates' court shall not make an order under subsection (2) above unless the court has been notified by the Secretary of State that the power to make such orders is exercisable by the court and the notice has not been withdrawn.

(4) Where an order has been made under subsection (2) above for default in paying any sum—

(a) on payment of the whole sum to any person authorised to receive it, the order shall cease to have effect;

(b) on payment of a part of that sum to any such person, the number of weeks or months to which the order relates shall be reduced proportionately;

and the total number is so reduced if it is reduced by such number of complete weeks or months as bears to the total number the proportion most nearly approximating to, without exceeding, the proportion which the part paid bears to the whole sum.

(5) The Secretary of State may by order made by statutory instrument vary the period specified in subsection (2) above; but no such order shall be made unless a draft of the order has been laid before and approved by a resolution of each House of Parliament.

(6) Subsections (4) to (6) of section 39 above shall apply for the purposes of this section as they apply for the purposes of that section.

Explanatory text—See para **7.27–7.29**.

Section 71 of the Criminal Justice Act 1988 or s 2 of the Drug Trafficking Act 1994 (subs (1))—See annotations to s 35.

Transfer and repatriation of prisoners

41 Transfer of prisoners within the British Islands

Schedule 1 to this Act (which makes provision with respect to the transfer of prisoners within the British Islands) shall have effect.

Explanatory text—See para **7.41**.

42 Repatriation of prisoners to the British Islands

Schedule 2 to this Act (which makes provision, including retrospective provision, with respect to prisoners repatriated to the British Islands) shall have effect.

Explanatory text—See para **7.41**.

Young offenders

43 Curfew orders

(1) In subsection (1) of section 12 of the 1991 Act (curfew orders), the words 'of or over the age of sixteen years' shall cease to have effect.

(2) After subsection (2) of that section there shall be inserted the following subsection—

'(2A) In relation to an offender who is under the age of sixteen years, subsection (2)(a) above shall have effect as if the reference to six months were a reference to three months.'

(3) After subsection (6) of that section there shall be inserted the following subsection—

'(6A) Before making a curfew order in respect of an offender who is under the age of sixteen years, the court shall obtain and consider information about his family circumstances and the likely effect of such an order on those circumstances.'

(4) In paragraph 3(1) of Schedule 2 to the 1991 Act (enforcement of community orders), for paragraph (c) there shall be substituted the following paragraph—

'(c) where—
    (i)   the relevant order is a probation order, or
    (ii) the relevant order is a curfew order and the offender is under the age of sixteen years,

and the case is one to which section 17 of the 1982 Act applies, it may make an order under that section requiring him to attend at an attendance centre; or'.

Explanatory text—See para **7.22**.

Age (subss (1), (2))—See general annotations.

Curfew order (subss (3),(4))—See annotations to s 16, and para **7.22**.

Probation order (subs (4))—See annotations to s 17 and para **7.22**.

44   Long term detention

In subsection (2)(a) of section 53 of the 1933 Act (long term detention of children and young persons for certain grave crimes), for sub-paragraph (ii) there shall be substituted the following sub-paragraph—

'(ii)   an offence under section 14 (indecent assault on a woman) or section 15 (indecent assault on a man) of the Sexual Offences Act 1956;'.

Explanatory text—See para **7.17**.

Section 53 of the 1933 Act—See annotations to s 34.

45   Publication of reports

(1) After subsection (4) of section 49 of the 1933 Act (restrictions on reports of proceedings in which children or young persons are concerned) there shall be inserted the following subsections—

'(4A) If a court is satisfied that it is in the public interest to do so, it may, in relation to a child or young person who has been convicted of an offence, by order dispense to any specified extent with the requirements of this section in relation to any proceedings before it to which this section applies by virtue of subsection (2)(a) or (b) above, being proceedings relating to—

(a) the prosecution or conviction of the offender for the offence;
(b) the manner in which he, or his parent or guardian, should be dealt with in respect of the offence;
(c) the enforcement, amendment, variation, revocation or discharge of any order made in respect of the offence;
(d) where an attendance centre order is made in respect of the offence, the enforcement of any rules made under section 16(3) of the Criminal Justice Act 1982; or
(e) where a secure training order is so made, the enforcement of any requirements imposed under section 3(7) of the Criminal Justice and Public Order Act 1994.

(4B) A court shall not exercise its power under subsection (4A) above without—

    (a) affording the parties to the proceedings an opportunity to make represen-
tations; and

    (b) taking into account any representations which are duly made.'

(2) Subsection (1) above shall not apply where the offence was committed before the commencement of this section.

Explanatory text—See para **7.13**.

Section 3(7) of the Criminal Justice and Public Order Act 1994 (subs (1))—A secure training order provision was introduced by s 1 of the 1994 Act, but is not yet in force. A secure training order is an order that the offender in respect of whom it is made shall be subject to a period of detention at a secure training centre, for a period not less than six months or more than two years. Section 3(7) of the 1994 Act entitles the Secretary of State to impose requirements on such an order.

Mentally disordered offenders

46   Power to make hospital and limitation directions

After section 45 of the 1983 Act there shall be inserted the following sections—

'Hospital and limitation directions

45A   Power of higher courts to direct hospital admission

(1) This section applies where, in the case of a person convicted before the Crown Court of an offence the sentence for which is not fixed by law—

    (a) the conditions mentioned in subsection (2) below are fulfilled; and

    (b) except where the offence is one the sentence for which falls to be imposed
under section 2 of the Crime (Sentences) Act 1997, the court considers
making a hospital order in respect of him before deciding to impose a
sentence of imprisonment ("the relevant sentence") in respect of the
offence.

(2) The conditions referred to in subsection (1) above are that the court is satisfied, on the written or oral evidence of two registered medical practitioners—

    (a) that the offender is suffering from psychopathic disorder;

    (b) that the mental disorder from which the offender is suffering is of a nature
or degree which makes it appropriate for him to be detained in a hospital for
medical treatment; and

    (c) that such treatment is likely to alleviate or prevent a deterioration of his
condition.

(3) The court may give both of the following directions, namely—

    (a) a direction that, instead of being removed to and detained in a prison, the
offender be removed to and detained in such hospital as may be specified in
the direction (in this Act referred to as a "hospital direction"); and

    (b) a direction that the offender be subject to the special restrictions set out in
section 41 above (in this Act referred to as a "limitation direction").

(4) A hospital direction and a limitation direction shall not be given in relation to an offender unless at least one of the medical practitioners whose evidence is taken into account by the court under subsection (2) above has given evidence orally before the court.

(5) A hospital direction and a limitation direction shall not be given in relation to an offender unless the court is satisfied on the written or oral evidence of the registered medical practitioner who would be in charge of his treatment, or of some other person representing the managers of the hospital that arrangements have been made—

  (a) for his admission to that hospital; and
  (b) for his admission to it within the period of 28 days beginning with the day of the giving of such directions;

and the court may, pending his admission within that period, give such directions as it thinks fit for his conveyance to and detention in a place of safety.

(6) If within the said period of 28 days it appears to the Secretary of State that by reason of an emergency or other special circumstances it is not practicable for the patient to be received into the hospital specified in the hospital direction, he may give instructions for the admission of the patient to such other hospital as appears to be appropriate instead of the hospital so specified.

(7) Where such instructions are given—

  (a) the Secretary of State shall cause the person having the custody of the patient to be informed, and
  (b) the hospital direction shall have effect as if the hospital specified in the instructions were substituted for the hospital specified in the hospital direction.

(8) Section 38(1) and (5) and section 39 above shall have effect as if any reference to the making of a hospital order included a reference to the giving of a hospital direction and a limitation direction.

(9) A hospital direction and a limitation direction given in relation to an offender shall have effect not only as regards the relevant sentence but also (so far as applicable) as regards any other sentence of imprisonment imposed on the same or a previous occasion.

(10) The Secretary of State may by order provide that this section shall have effect as if the reference in subsection (2) above to psychopathic disorder included a reference to a mental disorder of such other description as may be specified in the order.

(11) An order made under this section may—

  (a) apply generally, or in relation to such classes of offenders or offences as may be specified in the order;
  (b) provide that any reference in this section to a sentence of imprisonment, or to a prison, shall include a reference to a custodial sentence, or to an institution, of such description as may be so specified; and
  (c) include such supplementary, incidental or consequential provisions as appear to the Secretary of State to be necessary or expedient.

45B Effect of hospital and limitation directions

(1) A hospital direction and a limitation direction shall be sufficient authority—

  (a) for a constable or any other person directed to do so by the court to convey the patient to the hospital specified in the hospital direction within a period of 28 days; and

(b) for the managers of the hospital to admit him at any time within that period and thereafter detain him in accordance with the provisions of this Act.

(2) With respect to any person—

(a) a hospital direction shall have effect as a transfer direction; and
(b) a limitation direction shall have effect as a restriction direction.

(3) While a person is subject to a hospital direction and a limitation direction the responsible medical officer shall at such intervals (not exceeding one year) as the Secretary of State may direct examine and report to the Secretary of State on that person; and every report shall contain such particulars as the Secretary of State may require.'

Explanatory text—See para **6.8**.

Hospital order (1983 Act, s 45(1)(b))—See ss 37–38 of the 1983 Act, and para **6.3**.

Registered medical practitioners (1983 Act, s 45A(2))—Registered in accordance with the Medical Act 1983, s 2.

Psychopathic disorder (1983 Act, s 45A(2))—Defined by the 1983 Act, s 1, as a persistent disorder or disability of mind (whether or not including significant impairment of intelligence) with results in abnormally aggressive or seriously irresponsible conduct on the part of the person concerned.

For the compulsory detention in hospital for treatment of such patients, see 1983 Act, ss 3, 37 and 47, also see para **6.3**.

Mental disorder (1983 Act, s 45A(2))—This means mental illness, arrested or incomplete development of mind, psychopathic disorder and any other disorder or disability of mind, 'mental disorder' being construed accordingly (1983 Act, s 1(2)).

Medical treatment (1983 Act, s 45A(2))—Defined by 1983 Act, s 145(1) as including nursing, and also includes care habitation and rehabilitation under medical supervision. 'Habitation' is defined by the *Shorter Oxford Dictionary* as 'the action of enabling or endowing with ability or fitness, or capacitation, qualification'.

Managers of the hospital (1983 Act, s 45A(5))—Section 145(1) of the 1983 Act provides that 'the managers' means:

'(a) in relation to a hospital vested in the Secretary of State for the purposes of his functions under the National Health Service Act 1977, and in relation to any accommodation provided by a local authority and used as a hospital by or on behalf of the Secretary of State under that Act, the District Health Authority or special health authority responsible for the administration of the hospital;
(b) in relation to a special hospital, the Secretary of State;
(c) in relation to a mental nursing home registered in pursuance of the Nursing Homes Act 1975, the persons registered in respect of the home.'

Days (subs (1))—See general annotations.

47 Power to specify hospital units

(1) Subject to subsection (2) below, any power to specify a hospital which is conferred by—

(a) section 37 of the 1983 Act (hospital orders);
(b) section 45A of that Act (hospital and limitation directions);
(c) section 47 of that Act (transfer directions); or
(d) paragraph 1 of Schedule 1 to the Criminal Procedure (Insanity and Unfitness to Plead) Act 1991 (orders for admission to hospital),

includes power to specify a hospital unit; and where such a unit is specified in relation to any person in the exercise of such a power, any reference in any enactment (including one contained in this Act) to him being, or being liable to be, detained in a hospital shall be construed accordingly.

(2) In subsection (1) above—

(a) paragraph (a) shall not apply unless the court also makes an order under section 41 of the 1983 Act (restriction orders);

(b) paragraph (c) shall not apply unless the Secretary of State also gives a direction under section 49 of that Act (restriction directions); and

(c) paragraph (d) shall not apply unless the court has given a direction under paragraph 2(1)(b) of Schedule 1 to the Criminal Procedure (Insanity and Unfitness to Plead) Act 1991.

(3) In this section—

'hospital', in relation to any exercise of a power, has the same meaning as in the enactment which confers the power;

'hospital unit' means any part of a hospital which is treated as a separate unit.

(4) In this section—

(a) the reference to paragraph 1 of Schedule 1 to the Criminal Procedure (Insanity and Unfitness to Plead) Act 1991 includes a reference to subsection (1) of section 116B of the Army Act 1955 and the Air Force Act 1955 and section 63B of the Naval Discipline Act 1957; and

(b) the reference to paragraph 2(1)(b) of that Schedule includes a reference to subsection (2) of those sections.

Explanatory text—See para **6.11**.

Section 37 of the 1983 Act (subs (1))—As amended by s 55 of and Sch 4 to the new Act, this provides:

'(1) Where a person is convicted before the Crown Court of an offence punishable with imprisonment other than an offence the sentence for which is fixed by law or falls to be imposed under section 2(2) of the Crime (Sentences) Act 1997, or is convicted by a magistrates' court of an offence punishable on summary conviction with imprisonment, and the conditions mentioned in subsection (2) below are satisfied, the court may by order authorise his admission to and detention in such hospital as may be specified in the order or, as the case may be, place him under the guardianship of the local social services authority as may be so specified.

(2) The conditions referred to in subsection (1) above are that—

(a) the court is satisfied, on the written or oral evidence of two registered medical practitioners, that the offender is suffering from mental illness, psychopathic disorder, severe mental impairment or mental impairment and that either—

(i) the mental disorder from which the offender is suffering is of a nature or degree which makes it appropriate for him to be detained in a hospital for medical treatment and, in the case of a psychopathic disorder or mental impairment, that such treatment is likely to alleviate or prevent a deterioration of his condition; or

(ii) in the case of an offender who has attained the age of 16 years, the mental disorder is of a nature or degree which warrants his reception into guardianship under this Act;

(b) the court is of the opinion, having regard to all the circumstances including the nature of the offence and the character and antecedents of the offender, and to the other available methods of dealing with him, that the most suitable method of disposing of the case is by means of an order under this section.

48 Offenders conditionally discharged from hospital

(1) The 1983 Act and the 1984 Act shall have effect subject to the amendments specified in Schedule 3 to this Act, being amendments making provision with respect to transfers within the British Islands of responsibility for offenders conditionally discharged from hospital.

(2) In this section and that Schedule 'the 1984 Act' means the Mental Health (Scotland) Act 1984.

Explanatory text—See para **6.18**.

49 Other amendments of the 1983 Act

(1) In subsection (5) of section 38 of the 1983 Act (interim hospital orders), for the words 'six months' there shall be substituted the words 'twelve months'.

(2) In subsection (3) of section 41 of that Act (power of higher courts to restrict discharge from hospital), in paragraph (c) (ii), after the words 'section 19 above' there shall be inserted the words 'or in pursuance of subsection (3) of that section'.

(3) In subsection (1) of section 47 of that Act (removal to hospital of persons serving sentences of imprisonment etc.), the words '(not being a mental nursing home)' shall cease to have effect.

(4) In paragraph 5 of Part II of Schedule 1 to that Act (patients subject to hospital and guardianship orders)—

    (a) the word 'and' immediately following sub-paragraph (a) shall cease to have effect; and

    (b) after sub-paragraph (b) there shall be inserted the words 'and

        (c) in subsection (3) after the words "may at any time" there shall be inserted the words ", with the consent of the Secretary of State,".'

Explanatory text—See para **6.17**.

Miscellaneous

50 Disclosure of pre-sentence reports

(1) This section applies where a court obtains a pre-sentence report within the meaning of Part I of the 1991 Act.

(2) Subject to subsections (3) and (4) below, the court shall give a copy of the report—

    (a) to the offender or his counsel or solicitor; and

    (b) to the prosecutor, that is to say, the person having the conduct of the proceedings in respect of the offence.

(3) If the offender is under 17 and is not represented by counsel or a solicitor, a copy of the report need not be given to him but shall be given to his parent or guardian if present in court.

(4) If the prosecutor is not of a description prescribed by order made by the Secretary of State, a copy of the report need not be given to the prosecutor if the court considers that it would be inappropriate for him to be given it.

(5) No information obtained by virtue of subsection (2)(b) above shall be used or disclosed otherwise than for the purpose of—

(a) determining whether representations as to matters contained in the report need to be made to the court; or

(b) making such representations to the court.

(6) The power to make orders under this section shall be exercisable by statutory instrument which shall be subject to annulment in pursuance of a resolution of either House of Parliament.

Explanatory text—See para **7.2**.

Age (subs (3))—See general annotations.

Pre-sentence report (subss (1), (2))—Section 3(5) states that this expression means a report in writing which:

> (a) with a view to assisting the court in determining the most suitable method of dealing with an offender, is made or submitted by a probation officer or by a social worker of a local authority social services department; and
> (b) contains information as to such matters, presented in such manner as may be prescribed by rules made by the Secretary of State.

51 Committals for sentence

(1) After section 38 of the 1980 Act there shall be inserted the following section—

'38A Committal for sentence on indication of guilty plea to offence triable either way

(1) This section applies where—

(a) a person who is 18 or over appears or is brought before a magistrates' court ("the court") on an information charging him with an offence triable either way ("the offence");

(b) he or his representative indicates that he would plead guilty if the offence were to proceed to trial; and

(c) proceeding as if section 9(1) above was complied with and he pleaded guilty under it, the court convicts him of the offence.

(2) If the court has committed the offender to the Crown Court for trial for one or more related offences, that is to say, one or more offences which, in its opinion, are related to the offence, it may, in accordance with section 56 of the Criminal Justice Act 1967, commit him in custody or on bail to the Crown Court to be dealt with in respect of the offence in accordance with the provisions of section 42 of the Powers of Criminal Courts Act 1973.

(3) If the power conferred by subsection (2) above is not exercisable but the court is still to inquire, as examining justices, into one or more related offences—

(a) it shall adjourn the proceedings relating to the offence until after the conclusion of its inquiries; and

(b) if it commits the offender to the Crown Court for trial for one or more related offences, it may then exercise that power.

(4) Where the court—

(a) commits the offender to the Crown Court to be dealt with in respect of the offence; and

(b) does not state that, in its opinion, it also has power so to commit him under section 38(2) above, the provisions of section 42 of the Powers of Criminal Courts Act 1973 shall not apply unless he is convicted before the Crown Court of one or more of the related offences.

(5) Where those provisions of that section do not apply, the Crown Court shall have power to deal with the offender in respect of the offence in any manner in which the court might have dealt with him.

(6) For the purposes of this section one offence is related to another if, were they both to be prosecuted on indictment, the charges for them could be joined in the same indictment.'

Explanatory text—See para **7.7**.

Age (subs (1))—See general annotations.

52   Increased penalty for offence of indecency with children

In subsection (1) of section 1 of the Indecency with Children Act 1960 (indecent conduct towards young child), for the words 'two years' there shall be substituted the words 'ten years'.

Explanatory text—See para **7.12**.

Supplemental

53   Financial provisions

There shall be paid out of money provided by Parliament any increase attributable to this Act in the sums payable out of money so provided under any other Act.

54   General interpretation

(1) In this Act—

   'the 1933 Act' means the Children and Young Persons Act 1933;

   'the 1969 Act' means the Children and Young Persons Act 1969;

   'the 1973 Act' means the Powers of Criminal Courts Act 1973;

   'the 1980 Act' means the Magistrates' Courts Act 1980;

   'the 1982 Act' means the Criminal Justice Act 1982;

   'the 1983 Act' means the Mental Health Act 1983;

   'the 1991 Act' means the Criminal Justice Act 1991.

(2) Any reference in this Act to the commencement of Chapter I of Part II of this Act is a reference to the commencement of the provisions of that Chapter other than sections 9, 20 and 21 above.

(3) Where an offence is found to have been committed over a period of two or more days, or at some time during a period of two or more days, it shall be taken for the purposes of this Act to have been committed on the last of those days.

55   Minor and consequential amendments

(1) The enactments mentioned in Schedule 4 to this Act shall have effect subject to the amendments there specified, being minor amendments and amendments consequential on the provisions of this Act.

(2) For the purposes of any of those enactments as so amended—

(a) a sentence falls to be imposed under subsection (2) of section 2, 3 or 4 above if it is required by that subsection in any case where the court is not of the opinion there mentioned; and

(b) a sentence falls to be imposed under subsection (3A) of section 70 of the Army Act 1955 or the Air Force Act 1955 or subsection (1A) of section 42 of the Naval Discipline Act 1957 if it is required by that subsection in any case where the court-martial is not of the opinion there mentioned.

56 Transitional provisions, savings and repeals

(1) The transitional provisions and savings contained in Schedule 5 to this Act shall have effect; but nothing in this subsection shall be taken as prejudicing the operation of sections 16 and 17 of the Interpretation Act 1978 (which relate to the effect of repeals).

(2) The enactments specified in Schedule 6 to this Act are hereby repealed to the extent specified in the third column of that Schedule.

57 Short title, commencement and extent

(1) This Act may be cited as the Crime (Sentences) Act 1997.

(2) This Act shall come into force on such day as the Secretary of State may by order made by statutory instrument appoint; and different days may be appointed for different purposes.

(3) Without prejudice to the provisions of Schedule 5 to this Act, an order under subsection (2) above may make such transitional provisions and savings as appear to the Secretary of State necessary or expedient in connection with any provision brought into force by the order.

(4) Subject to subsections (5) to (8) below, this Act extends to England and Wales only.

(5) The following provisions of this Act extend to Scotland, Northern Ireland and the Channel Islands, namely—

(a) section 41 and Schedule 1; and

(b) section 56(2) and Schedule 6 so far as relating to the repeal of Part III of the Criminal Justice Act 1961.

(6) The following provisions of this Act extend to Scotland, namely—

(a) section 45;

(b) paragraphs 1 and 5 to 8 of Schedule 2 and section 42 so far as relating to those paragraphs;

(c) paragraphs 1 and 6 to 10 of Schedule 3 and section 48 so far as relating to those paragraphs;

(d) paragraph 16 of Schedule 4 to this Act and section 55 so far as relating to that paragraph; and

(e) paragraphs 9, 11 and 12 of Schedule 5 and section 56(1) so far as relating to those paragraphs.

(7) The following provisions of this Act extend to Northern Ireland, namely—

(a) paragraphs 1, 9 and 10 of Schedule 2 and section 42 so far as relating to those paragraphs;

(b) paragraphs 2, 3, 7 and 8 of Schedule 3 and section 48 so far as relating to those paragraphs; and

(c) paragraphs 10 and 12 of Schedule 5 and section 56(1) so far as relating to those paragraphs.

(8) Nothing in subsection (4) above affects the extent of this Act in so far as it—

(a) confers a power or imposes a duty on a court-martial or a Standing Civilian Court; or

(b) amends any provision of the Army Act 1955, the Air Force Act 1955 or the Naval Discipline Act 1957.

SCHEDULES

SCHEDULE 1

TRANSFER OF PRISONERS WITHIN THE BRITISH ISLES

PART I
POWERS OF TRANSFER

Transfer of prisoners: general

1 (1) The Secretary of State may, on the application of—

(a) a person remanded in custody in any part of the United Kingdom in connection with an offence; or

(b) a person serving a sentence of imprisonment in any part of the United Kingdom,

make an order for his transfer to another part of the United Kingdom or to any of the Channel Islands, there to be remanded in custody pending his trial for the offence or, as the case may be, to serve the whole or any part of the remainder of his sentence, and for his removal to an appropriate institution there.

(2) Where—

(a) a person is remanded in custody in any of the Channel Islands in connection with an offence; or

(b) a person has been sentenced to imprisonment in any of the Channel Islands,

the Secretary of State may, without application in that behalf, make an order for his transfer to any part of the United Kingdom, there to be remanded in custody pending his trial for the offence or, as the case may be, to serve the whole or any part of his sentence or the remainder of his sentence, and for his removal to an appropriate institution there.

(3) In this paragraph 'appropriate institution'—

(a) in relation to a person remanded in custody, means any prison or other institution;

(b) in relation to a person sentenced to imprisonment, means, subject to sub-paragraph (4) below, any institution which would be appropriate for the detention of an offender of the same age serving an equivalent sentence passed by a court in the country or island to which he is transferred.

(4) Sub-paragraph (3)(b) above shall have effect in relation to a person serving a sentence of a length which could not have been passed on an offender of his age by a court in the place to which he has been transferred as if it defined 'appropriate institution' as meaning such place as the Secretary of State may direct.

Transfer of prisoners for trial

2 (1) If it appears to the Secretary of State that—

(a) a person remanded in custody in any part of the United Kingdom in connection with an offence; or

(b) a person serving a sentence of imprisonment in any part of the United Kingdom, should be transferred to another part of the United Kingdom or to any of the Channel Islands for the purpose of attending criminal proceedings against him there, the Secretary of State may make an order for his transfer to that other part or that island and for his removal to a prison or other institution there.

(2) If it appears to the Secretary of State that—

    (a) a person remanded in custody in any of the Channel Islands in connection with an offence; or

    (b) a person serving a sentence of imprisonment in any of the Channel Islands,

should be transferred to a part of the United Kingdom for the purpose of attending criminal proceedings against him there, the Secretary of State may make an order for his transfer to that part and for his removal to a prison or other institution there.

(3) Where a person has been transferred under sub-paragraph (1)(a) or (2)(a) above for the purpose of any proceedings, the Secretary of State may, if that person is not sentenced to imprisonment in those proceedings, make an order for his return to the country or island from which he was transferred under that sub-paragraph.

(4) Where a person has been transferred under sub-paragraph (1)(b) or (2)(b) above for the purpose of any proceedings, the Secretary of State may—

    (a) if that person is sentenced to imprisonment in those proceedings, make an order under paragraph 1(1)(b) or (2)(b) above (but without application in that behalf) transferring him back to the country or island from which he was transferred under that sub-paragraph;

    (b) if he is not so sentenced, make an order for his return to the said country or island, there to serve the remainder of the sentence referred to in that sub-paragraph.

Transfer of prisoners for other judicial purposes

3 (1) If the Secretary of State is satisfied, in the case of—

    (a) a person remanded in custody in any part of the United Kingdom in connection with an offence;

    (b) a person serving a sentence of imprisonment in any part of the United Kingdom; or

    (c) a person not falling within paragraph (a) or (b) above who is detained in a prison in any part of the United Kingdom,

that the attendance of that person at any place in that or any other part of the United Kingdom or in any of the Channel Islands is desirable in the interests of justice or for the purposes of any public inquiry, the Secretary of State may direct that person to be taken to that place.

(2) If the Secretary of State is satisfied, in the case of—

    (a) a person remanded in custody in any of the Channel Islands in connection with an offence;

    (b) a person serving a sentence of imprisonment in any of the Islands; or

    (c) a person not falling within paragraph (a) or (b) above who is detained in a prison in any of the Channel Islands,

that the attendance of that person at any place in the United Kingdom is desirable in the interests of justice or for the purposes of any public inquiry, the Secretary of State may direct that person to be taken to that place.

(3) Where any person is directed under this paragraph to be taken to any place he shall, unless the Secretary of State otherwise directs, be kept in custody while being so taken, while at that place, and while being taken back to the prison or other institution or place in which he is required in accordance with law to be detained.

Transfer of supervision of released prisoners

4 (1) The Secretary of State may, on the application of a person undergoing or about to undergo supervision in any part of the United Kingdom, make an order for the transfer of his supervision to another part of the United Kingdom or to any of the Channel Islands, that is to say, an order—

    (a) for his supervision or, as the case may be, the remainder of his supervision to be undergone in that country or island; and

    (b) for responsibility for his supervision to be transferred to an appropriate person there.

(2) The Secretary of State may, on the application of a person undergoing or about to undergo supervision in any of the Channel Islands, make an order for the transfer of his supervision to any part of the United Kingdom, that is to say, an order—

    (a) for his supervision or, as the case may be, the remainder of his supervision to be undergone in that country; and

    (b) for responsibility for his supervision to be transferred to an appropriate person there.

Conditions of transfers

5 (1) A transfer under this Part shall have effect subject to such conditions (if any) as the Secretary of State may think fit to impose.

(2) Subject to sub-paragraph (3) below, a condition imposed under this paragraph may be varied or removed at any time.

(3) Such a condition as is mentioned in paragraph 6(1)(a) below shall not be varied or removed except with the consent of the person to whom the transfer relates.

PART II
EFFECT OF TRANSFERS

Preliminary

6 (1) For the purposes of this Part of this Schedule, a transfer under Part I of this Schedule—

    (a) is a restricted transfer if it is subject to a condition that the person to whom it relates is to be treated for the relevant purposes as if he were still subject to the provisions applicable for those purposes under the law of the place from which the transfer is made; and

    (b) is an unrestricted transfer if it is not so subject.

(2) In this Part of this Schedule 'the relevant purposes' means—

    (a) in relation to the transfer of a person under paragraph 1(1)(a) or (2)(a), 2(1)(a) or (2)(a) or 3(1)(a) or (2)(a) above, the purposes of his remand in custody and, where applicable, the purposes of his detention under and release from any sentence of imprisonment that may be imposed;

(b) in relation to the transfer of a person under paragraph 1(1)(b) or (2)(b), 2(1)(b) or (2)(b) or 3(1)(b) or (2)(b) above, the purposes of his detention under and release from his sentence and, where applicable, the purposes of his supervision and possible recall following his release; and

(c) in relation to the transfer of a person's supervision under paragraph 4(1) or (2) above, the purposes of his supervision and possible recall.

(3) In this paragraph 'recall' means—

(a) in relation to a person who is supervised in pursuance of an order made for the purpose, being sentenced to imprisonment, or being recalled to prison, for a breach of any condition of the order;

(b) in relation to a person who is supervised in pursuance of a condition contained in a licence, being recalled to prison under the licence, whether for a breach of any condition of the licence or otherwise.

Restricted transfers: general

7 (1) Where—

(a) a person's transfer under paragraph 1, 2 or 3 above; or

(b) a transfer under paragraph 4 above of a person's supervision,

is a restricted transfer, that person or, as the case may be, his supervision may by order be transferred back to the country or island from which he or it was transferred.

(2) Where a person's transfer under paragraph 1 or 2 above is a restricted transfer, that person shall while in the country or territory to which he is transferred be kept in custody except in so far as the Secretary of State may in any case or class of case otherwise direct.

Restricted transfers from England and Wales to Scotland

8 (1) Where a person's transfer under paragraph 1(1)(a), 2(1)(a) or 3(1)(a) above from England and Wales to Scotland is a restricted transfer—

(a) regulations made under section 22 of the Prosecution of Offences Act 1985 (time limits in relation to preliminary stages of proceedings) shall apply to him in place of the corresponding provisions of the law of Scotland; but

(b) subject to that and to any conditions to which the transfer is subject, he shall be treated for the relevant purposes as if he had been remanded for an offence committed in Scotland.

(2) Where a person's transfer under paragraph 1(1)(b), 2(1)(b) or 3(1)(b) above from England and Wales to Scotland is a restricted transfer—

(a) sections 10, 12, 16, 17(1) to (4) and (6), 18(1) and (2), 19(1), (2), (6)(a) and (8) to (10), 20(1) and (2), 21(1) and (2), 23 and 27 of this Act or, as the case may require, sections 28 to 32 and 34 of this Act shall apply to him in place of the corresponding provisions of the law of Scotland; but

(b) subject to that, to sub-paragraph (3) below and to any conditions to which the transfer is subject, he shall be treated for the relevant purposes as if his sentence had been an equivalent sentence passed by a court in Scotland.

(3) A person who has been sentenced to a sentence of a length which could not have been passed on an offender of his age in the place to which he has been transferred shall be treated for the purposes mentioned in sub-paragraph (2) above as the Secretary of State may direct.

(4) Where a transfer under paragraph 4(1) above of a person's supervision from England and Wales to Scotland is a restricted transfer—

    (a) sections 16, 17(1) to (4) and (6), 18(1) and (2), 19(1), (2), (6)(a) and (8) to (10), 20(1) and (2), 21(1) and (2) and 27 of this Act or, as the case may require, sections 31, 32 and 34 of this Act shall apply to him in place of the corresponding provisions of the law of Scotland; but

    (b) subject to that and to any conditions to which the transfer is subject, he shall be treated for the relevant purposes as if his period of supervision had been an equivalent period of supervision directed to be undergone in Scotland.

(5) Any provision of Part II of this Act which is applied by sub-paragraph (2) or (4) above shall have effect (as so applied) as if any reference to an expression specified in the first column of the following Table were a reference to the expression set out opposite it in the second column of that Table.

TABLE

Expression	Substituted expression
Crown Court	High Court of Justiciary
Information on oath	Evidence on oath
Magistrates' court	Sheriff
Probation officer	Relevant officer within the meaning given by section 27(1) of the Prisoners and Criminal Proceedings (Scotland) Act 1993

Restricted transfers from England and Wales to Northern Ireland

9 (1) Where a person's transfer under paragraph 1(1)(a), 2(1)(a) or 3(1)(a) above from England and Wales to Northern Ireland is a restricted transfer—

    (a) sections 13 and 15 of this Act shall apply to him as if they were part of the law of Northern Ireland; but

    (b) subject to that and to any conditions to which the transfer is subject, he shall be treated for the relevant purposes as if he had been remanded for an offence committed in Northern Ireland.

(2) Where a person's transfer under paragraph 1(1)(b), 2(1)(b) or 3(1)(b) above from England and Wales to Northern Ireland is a restricted transfer—

    (a) sections 10 to 12, 14, 16, 17(1), (2), (4) and (6), 18, 19(1), (2), (4), (6) and (8) to (10), 20(1) and (2), 21(1) and (2), 23 and 27 of this Act or, as the case may require, sections 28 to 32 and 34 of this Act shall apply to him in place of the corresponding provisions of the law of Northern Ireland; but

    (b) subject to that, to sub-paragraph (3) below and to any conditions to which the transfer is subject, he shall be treated for the relevant purposes as if that sentence had been an equivalent sentence passed by a court in Northern Ireland.

(3) A person who has been sentenced to a sentence of a length which could not have been passed on an offender of his age in the place to which he has been transferred shall be treated for the purposes mentioned in sub-paragraph (2) above as the Secretary of State may direct.

(4) Where a transfer under paragraph 4(1) above of a person's supervision from England and Wales to Northern Ireland is a restricted transfer—

   (a) sections 16, 17(1), (2), (4) and (6), 18, 19(1), (2), (6) and (8) to (10), 20(1) and (2), 21(1) and (2) and 27 of this Act or, as the case may require, sections 31, 32 and 34 of this Act shall apply to him in place of the corresponding provisions of the law of Northern Ireland; but

   (b) subject to that and to any conditions to which the transfer is subject, he shall be treated for the relevant purposes as if his period of supervision had been an equivalent period of supervision directed to be undergone in Northern Ireland.

(5) In sub-paragraph (2) above, the reference to section 11 of this Act includes a reference to any rules under section 47 of the Prison Act 1952 which prescribe a minimum standard of behaviour for the purposes of the said section 11.

(6) Any provision of Part II of this Act which is applied by sub-paragraph (1), (2) or (4) above shall have effect (as so applied) as if any reference to an expression specified in the first column of the following Table were a reference to the expression set out opposite it in the second column of that Table.

TABLE

Expression	*Substituted expression*
Community home	Training School
Information on oath	Complaint on oath
Prison rules	Rules made under section 13 of the Prison Act (Northern Ireland) 1953
Section 8 of the Police and Criminal Evidence Act 1984	Article 10 of the Police and Criminal Evidence (Northern Ireland) Order 1989
Social worker of a local authority social services department	Officer of a Board or an authorised Health and Social Services (HSS) Trust

Restricted transfers from Scotland to England and Wales

10 (1) Where a person's transfer under paragraph 1(1)(a), 2(1)(a) or 3(1)(a) above from Scotland to England and Wales is a restricted transfer—

   (a) sections 65 and 147 of the Criminal Procedure (Scotland) Act 1995 (time limits for solemn and summary prosecutions where prisoner remanded in custody) shall apply to him in the place of the corresponding provisions of the law of England and Wales; but

   (b) subject to that and to any conditions to which the transfer is subject, he shall be treated for the relevant purposes as if he had been remanded for an offence committed in England and Wales.

(2) Where a person's transfer under paragraph 1(1)(b), 2(1)(b) or 3(1)(b) from Scotland to England and Wales is a restricted transfer—

   (a) sections 15, 18 and 19 of the Prisoners and Criminal Proceedings (Scotland) Act 1993 ('the 1993 Act') and sections 33(5), 34, 37 and 39 of the Crime and Punishment (Scotland) Act 1997 ('the 1997 Act') or, as the case may require, sections 1(4), 2, 3, 11 to 13 and 17 of the 1993 Act shall apply to him in place of the corresponding provisions of the law of England and Wales; but

(b) subject to that, to sub-paragraphs (3) and (4) below and to any conditions to which the transfer is subject, he shall be treated for the relevant purposes as if his sentence had been an equivalent sentence passed by a court in England and Wales.

(3) A person who has been sentenced to a sentence of a length which could not have been passed on an offender of his age in the place to which he is transferred shall be treated for the purposes mentioned in sub-paragraph (2) above as the Secretary of State may direct.

(4) Notwithstanding anything contained in sub-paragraph (2)(b) above, sections 16 to 18 of this Act shall not apply to a person whose transfer from Scotland to England and Wales is a restricted transfer.

(5) Where a transfer under paragraph 4(1) above of a person's supervision from Scotland to England and Wales is a restricted transfer—

(a) sections 15, 18 and 19 of the 1993 Act and sections 33(5) and 37 of the 1997 Act or, as the case may require, sections 2(4), 11 to 13 and 17 of the 1993 Act shall apply to him in place of the corresponding provisions of the law of England and Wales; but

(b) subject to that and to any conditions to which the transfer is subject, he shall be treated for the relevant purposes as if his period of supervision had been an equivalent period of supervision directed to be undergone in England and Wales.

(6) Any reference in—

(a) sub-paragraphs (2) and (5) above to sections 15, 18 and 19 of the 1993 Act is a reference to those sections so far as relating to supervised release orders;

(b) in the said sub-paragraph (2)—

    (i) to section 34 of the 1997 Act includes a reference to any rules under section 39 of the Prisons (Scotland) Act 1989 made by virtue of subsections (13) to (16) of that section; and

    (ii) to section 39 of the 1997 Act is a reference to that section so far as it relates to section 37 of that Act.

(7) Any provision of Part I of the 1993 Act or Part III of the 1997 Act which is applied by sub-paragraph (2) or (5) above shall have effect (as so applied) as if any reference to an expression specified in the first column of the following Table were a reference to the expression set out opposite it in the second column of that Table.

TABLE

Expression	*Substituted expression*
Chief social work officer	Chief social worker of a local authority social services department
Young offenders institution	Young offender institution

Restricted transfers from Scotland to Northern Ireland

11 (1) Where a person's transfer under paragraph 1(1)(a), 2(1)(a) or 3(1)(a) above from Scotland to Northern Ireland is a restricted transfer—

(a) sections 65 and 147 of the Criminal Procedure (Scotland) Act 1995 (time limits for solemn and summary prosecutions where prisoner remanded in custody) shall apply to him as if they were part of the law of Northern Ireland; but

(b) subject to that and to any conditions to which the transfer is subject, he shall be treated for the relevant purposes as if he had been remanded for an offence committed in Northern Ireland.

(2) Where a person's transfer under paragraph 1(1)(b), 2(1)(b) or 3(1)(b) from Scotland or Northern Ireland is a restricted transfer—

(a) sections 15, 18 and 19 of the Prisoners and Criminal Proceedings (Scotland) Act 1993 ('the 1993 Act') and sections 33(5), 34, 37 and 39 of the Crime and Punishment (Scotland) Act 1997 ('the 1997 Act') or, as the case may require, sections 1(4), 2, 3, 11 to 13 and 17 of the 1993 Act shall apply to him in place of the corresponding provisions of the law of Northern Ireland; but

(b) subject to that, to sub-paragraph (3) below and to any conditions to which the transfer is subject, he shall be treated for the relevant purposes as if his sentence had been an equivalent sentence passed by a court in Northern Ireland.

(3) A person who has been sentenced to a sentence of a length which could not have been passed on an offender of his age in the place to which he is transferred shall be treated for the purposes mentioned in sub-paragraph (2) above as the Secretary of State may direct.

(4) Where a transfer under paragraph 4(1) above of a person's supervision from Scotland to Northern Ireland is a restricted transfer—

(a) sections 15, 18 and 19 of the 1993 Act and sections 33(5) and 37 of the 1997 Act or, as the case may require, sections 2(4), 11 to 13 and 17 of the 1993 Act shall apply to him in place of the corresponding provisions of the law of Northern Ireland; but

(b) subject to that and to any conditions to which the transfer is subject, he shall be treated for the relevant purposes as if his period of supervision had been an equivalent period of supervision directed to be undergone in Northern Ireland.

(5) Sub-paragraph (5) of paragraph 10 above shall apply for the purposes of this paragraph as it applies for the purposes of that paragraph.

(6) Any provision of Part I of the 1993 Act or Part III of the 1997 Act which is applied by sub-paragraph (2) or (4) above shall have effect (as so applied) as if any reference to an expression specified in the first column of the following Table were a reference to the expression set out opposite it in the second column of that Table.

TABLE

Expression	*Substituted expression*
Chief social work officer	Chief Officer of a Board or an authorised Health and Social Services (HSS) Trust
Justices for a petty sessions area	Probation Board for Northern Ireland
Young offenders institution	Young offenders centre

Restricted transfers from Northern Ireland to England and Wales

12 (1) Where a person's transfer under paragraph 1(1)(a), 2(1)(a) or 3(1)(a) above from Northern Ireland to England and Wales is a restricted transfer, subject to any conditions to which the transfer is subject, he shall be treated for the relevant purposes as if he had been remanded for an offence committed in England and Wales.

(2) Where a person's transfer under paragraph 1(1)(b), 2(1)(b) or 3(1)(b) above from Northern Ireland to England and Wales is a restricted transfer—

  (a) sections 13(7), 23 and 24 of the Prison Act (Northern Ireland) 1953, Articles 3 to 6 of the Treatment of Offenders (Northern Ireland) Order 1976 and Articles 26 to 28 of the Criminal Justice (Northern Ireland) Order 1996 or, as the case may require, section 1 of the Northern Ireland (Remission of Sentences) Act 1995 shall apply to him in place of the corresponding provisions of the law of England and Wales; but

  (b) subject to that, to sub-paragraph (3) below and to any conditions to which the transfer is subject, he shall be treated for the relevant purposes as if that sentence had been an equivalent sentence passed by a court in England and Wales.

(3) A person who has been sentenced to a sentence of a length which could not have been passed on an offender of his age in the place to which he has been transferred shall be treated for the purposes mentioned in sub-paragraph (2) above as the Secretary of State may direct.

(4) Where a transfer under paragraph 4(1) of a person's supervision from Northern Ireland to England and Wales is a restricted transfer, subject to any conditions to which the transfer is subject, he shall be treated for the relevant purposes as if his period of supervision had been an equivalent period of supervision directed to be undergone in England and Wales.

(5) Any provision of the Prison Act (Northern Ireland) 1953, the Treatment of Offenders (Northern Ireland) Order 1976, the Criminal Justice (Northern Ireland) Order 1996 or the Northern Ireland (Remission of Sentences) Act 1995 which is applied by sub-paragraph (2) above shall have effect (as so applied) as if any reference to an expression specified in the first column of the following Table were a reference to the expression set out opposite it in the second column of that Table.

TABLE

Expression	*Substituted Expression*
Complaint on oath	Information on oath
Court of summary jurisdiction	Magistrates' court
Prison rules	Rules made under section 47 of the Prison Act 1952

Restricted transfers from Northern Ireland to Scotland

13 (1) Where a person's transfer under paragraph 1(1)(a), 2(1)(a) or 3(1)(a) above from Northern Ireland to Scotland is a restricted transfer, subject to any conditions to which the transfer is subject, he shall be treated for the relevant purposes as if he had been remanded for an offence committed in Scotland.

(2) Where a person's transfer under paragraph 1(1)(b), 2(1)(b) or 3(1)(b) above from Northern Ireland to Scotland is a restricted transfer—

  (a) sections 13(7), 23 and 24 of the Prison Act (Northern Ireland) 1953, Articles 3 to 6 of the Treatment of Offenders (Northern Ireland) Order 1976 and Articles 26 to 28 of the Criminal Justice (Northern Ireland) Order 1996 or, as the case may require, section 1 of the Northern Ireland (Remission of Sentences) Act 1995 shall apply to him in place of the corresponding provisions of the law of Scotland; but

(b) subject to that, to sub-paragraph (3) below and to any conditions to which the transfer is subject, he shall be treated for the relevant purposes as if that sentence had been an equivalent sentence passed by a court in Scotland.

(3) A person who has been sentenced to a sentence of a length which could not have been passed on an offender of his age in the place to which he has been transferred shall be treated for the purposes mentioned in sub-paragraph (2) above as the Secretary of State may direct.

(4) Where a transfer under paragraph 4(1) above of a person's supervision from Northern Ireland to Scotland is a restricted transfer, subject to any conditions to which the transfer is subject, he shall be treated for the relevant purposes as if his period of supervision had been an equivalent period of supervision directed to be undergone in Scotland.

(5) Any provision of the Prison Act (Northern Ireland) 1953, the Treatment of Offenders (Northern Ireland) Order 1976, the Criminal Justice (Northern Ireland) Order 1996 or the Northern Ireland (Remission of Sentences) Act 1995 which is applied by sub-paragraph (2) above shall have effect (as so applied) as if any reference to an expression specified in the first column of the following Table were a reference to the expression set out opposite it in the second column of that Table.

TABLE

Expression	Substituted Expression
Complaint on oath	Evidence on oath
Court of summary jurisdiction	Sheriff
Crown Court	High Court of Justiciary
Prison rules	Rules made under section 39 of the Prisons (Scotland) Act 1989
Probation officer	Relevant officer within the meaning of section 27(1) of the Prisoners and Criminal Proceedings (Scotland) Act 1993

Restricted transfers between the United Kingdom and the Channel Islands

14 (1) Her Majesty may by Order in Council make, in relation to restricted transfers under Part I of this Schedule between any part of the United Kingdom and any of the Channel Islands, provision broadly corresponding to that made by any of paragraphs 8 to 13 above.

(2) An Order in Council under this paragraph may make such consequential, incidental, transitional and supplementary provision as Her Majesty considers appropriate.

(3) An Order in Council under this paragraph shall be subject to annulment in pursuance of a resolution of either House of Parliament.

Unrestricted transfers: general

15 (1) Where a person's transfer under paragraph 1(1)(a) or (2)(a), 2(1)(a) or (2)(a) or 3(1)(a) or (2)(a) above to any part of the United Kingdom or to any of the Channel

Islands is an unrestricted transfer, he shall be treated for the relevant purposes as if he had been remanded for an offence committed in the place to which he is transferred.

(2) Subject to sub-paragraph (3) below, where a person's transfer under paragraph 1(1)(b) or (2)(b), 2(1)(b) or (2)(b) or 3(1)(b) or (2)(b) above to any part of the United Kingdom or to any of the Channel Islands is an unrestricted transfer, he shall be treated for the relevant purposes as if his sentence had been an equivalent sentence passed by a court in the place to which he is transferred.

(3) A person who has been sentenced to a sentence of a length which could not have been passed on an offender of his age in the place to which he has been transferred shall be treated for the purposes mentioned in sub-paragraph (2) above as the Secretary of State may direct.

(4) Where a transfer under paragraph 4(1) or (2) above of a person's supervision to any part of the United Kingdom or to any of the Channel Islands is an unrestricted transfer—

    (a) that person shall be treated for the relevant purposes as if his period of supervision had been an equivalent period of supervision directed to be undergone in the place to which he is transferred; and

    (b) any functions of the Secretary of State under any provision of the law of that place which applies for those purposes shall be exercisable in relation to that person by any person appointed by the Secretary of State for the purpose.

(5) Where the relevant purposes in relation to a transfer to Scotland which is an unrestricted transfer include supervision, the person to whom the transfer relates shall be treated as if a supervised release order had been made in respect of him by such court as the Secretary of State may specify.

Transfers ceasing to be restricted

16 Where a transfer under Part I of this Schedule ceases to be a restricted transfer at any time by reason of the removal of such a condition as is mentioned in paragraph 6(1)(a) above, paragraph 15 above shall apply as if the transfer were an unrestricted transfer and had been effected at that time.

PART III
SUPPLEMENTAL

Prisoners unlawfully at large

17 (1) The following enactments (relating to the arrest and return of prisoners and other persons unlawfully at large), namely—

    (a) section 49(1) of the Prison Act 1952;

    (b) section 40(1) of the Prisons (Scotland) Act 1989; and

    (c) section 38(1) of the Prison Act (Northern Ireland) 1953,

shall extend throughout the United Kingdom and the Channel Islands.

(2) Any reference in those enactments to a constable shall include a reference—

    (a) to a person being a constable under the law of any part of the United Kingdom;

    (b) to a police officer within the meaning of the Police Force (Jersey) Law 1974 or any corresponding law for the time being in force; and

    (c) to an officer of police within the meaning of section 31(4) of the Theft (Bailiwick of Guernsey) Law 1983 or any corresponding law for the time being in force.

(3) Those enactments shall also apply to persons who, being unlawfully at large under the law of any of the Channel Islands, are for the time being within the United Kingdom as they apply to persons unlawfully at large under the law of any part of the United Kingdom.

(4) Any person arrested in the United Kingdom under those enactments as applied by sub-paragraph (3) above may be taken to the place in the Channel Islands in which he is required in accordance with the law in force there to be detained.

(5) Where a person who, having been sentenced to imprisonment, is unlawfully at large during any period during which he is liable to be detained in a prison in any part of the United Kingdom is sentenced to imprisonment by a court in another part of the United Kingdom—

(a) the provisions of Part II of this Schedule relating to the treatment of persons transferred under sub-paragraph (1)(b) of paragraph 1 above shall apply to him, while he remains in that other part of the United Kingdom, as if he had been transferred there under that sub-paragraph immediately before he was so sentenced; and

(b) the Secretary of State may, if he thinks fit, make an order under that sub-paragraph (but without application in that behalf) transferring him back to the part of the United Kingdom from which he was unlawfully at large.

(6) In the following provisions, namely—

(a) paragraph (a) of the proviso to section 49(2) of the Prison Act 1952 (which in effect enables a person who is unlawfully at large during the currency of his original sentence to count towards that sentence any period during which he is detained in pursuance of a sentence of any court);

(b) the proviso to section 40(2) of the Prisons (Scotland) Act 1989 (which contains corresponding provisions for Scotland); and

(c) section 38(3) of the Prison Act (Northern Ireland) 1953 (which contains corresponding provisions for Northern Ireland),

references to a court shall include references to any court in the United Kingdom.

Subsequent sentence in case of transferred prisoners

18 (1) The power of a court in any part of the United Kingdom to order that the term of any sentence of imprisonment passed by the court shall commence at or before the expiration of another term of imprisonment shall include power to make such an order where that other term was imposed by sentence of a court elsewhere in the United Kingdom or in any of the Channel Islands if the offender—

(a) is serving that other sentence in that part of the United Kingdom; or

(b) is for the time being present in that part of the United Kingdom,

by virtue of an order under this Schedule, or is unlawfully at large under the law of the country or island in which that other sentence was passed.

(2) The provisions of this paragraph shall be without prejudice to the powers exercisable by any court apart from those provisions.

Application to the Isle of Man

19 (1) Her Majesty may by Order in Council direct that any of the foregoing provisions of this Schedule which extend to, or apply in relation to, the Channel Islands shall extend to, or apply in relation to, the Isle of Man with such modifications (if any) as Her Majesty considers appropriate.

(2) An Order in Council under this paragraph may make such consequential, incidental, transitional and supplementary provision as Her Majesty considers appropriate.

(3) An Order in Council under this paragraph shall be subject to annulment in pursuance of a resolution of either House of Parliament.

Interpretation

20 (1) In this Schedule—

'prison', unless the context otherwise requires, includes a young offender institution, a young offenders institution, a young offenders centre and a remand centre;

'sentence of imprisonment' includes any sentence of detention and a sentence of custody for life under section 8 of the 1982 Act, and cognate expressions shall be construed accordingly;

'supervision' means supervision in pursuance of an order made for the purpose or, in the case of a person released from prison on licence, in pursuance of a condition contained in his licence.

(2) References in this Schedule to a person being remanded in custody are references to his being remanded in or committed to custody by an order of a court.

(3) In determining, in relation to any person serving a sentence of imprisonment, the time which is to be served in respect of an equivalent sentence treated as passed in another country or island, regard shall be had, not only to any time already served by him, but also to—

(a) any periods for which he has been remanded in custody, being either—
    (i) periods by which his sentence falls to be reduced; or
    (ii) periods which have been directed to count as time served as part of his sentence; and
(b) any early release or additional days awarded to him.

SCHEDULE 2
REPATRIATION OF PRISONERS TO THE BRITISH ISLANDS

Preliminary

1 Any reference in this Schedule to prisoners repatriated to any part of the United Kingdom is a reference to prisoners transferred there in pursuance of a warrant issued under the Repatriation of Prisoners Act 1984 ('the 1984 Act').

Prisoners repatriated to England and Wales

2 (1) This paragraph applies in relation to—

(a) prisoners repatriated to England and Wales before 25th October 1996 who were still serving their sentences on that date; and

(b) prisoners repatriated to England and Wales on or after that date and before the commencement of this Schedule.

(2) Paragraph 2 of the Schedule to the 1984 Act shall have effect, and shall be deemed always to have had effect, with the omission of sub-paragraph (1A) and the insertion after sub-paragraph (2) of the following sub-paragraphs—

'(3) The following questions, namely—

(a) whether the prisoner is a short-term or long-term prisoner for the purposes of the enactments relating to release on licence; and

(b) whether or not he is an existing prisoner for the purposes of paragraph 8 of Schedule 12 to the 1991 Act,

shall be determined by reference to the length or, as the case may require, commencement of the sentence imposed in the country or territory from which he is transferred.

(4) In this paragraph—

'the enactments relating to release on licence' means sections 33(1)(b) and (2), 34(3) and (5), 35(1) and 37(1) and (2) of the Criminal Justice Act 1991;

'sentence', except in sub-paragraph (3) above, means the provision included in the warrant which is equivalent to a sentence.'

3 (1) This paragraph applies in relation to prisoners repatriated to England and Wales after the commencement of this Schedule whose sentences in the country or territory from which they are transferred were imposed for offences committed before the commencement of Chapter I of Part II of this Act.

(2) In paragraph 2 of the Schedule to the 1984 Act, for sub-paragraphs (1A) and (2) there shall be substituted the following sub-paragraphs—

'(2) If the warrant specifies a period to be taken into account for the purposes of sections 34(3) and (5) and 35(1) of the Criminal Justice Act 1991—

(a) the amount of time the prisoner has served; and

(b) where his sentence is a determinate one, his sentence,

shall, so far only as the question whether he has served any particular proportion or part of his sentence is concerned, be deemed to be increased by that period.

(3) The following questions, namely—

(a) whether the prisoner is a long-term prisoner for the purposes of the enactments relating to release on licence; and

(b) whether or not he is an existing prisoner for the purposes of paragraph 8 of Schedule 12 to the 1991 Act,

shall be determined by reference to the length or, as the case may require, commencement of the sentence imposed in the country or territory from which he is transferred.

(4) In this paragraph—

"the enactments relating to release on licence" means sections 33(1)(b) and (2), 34(3) and (5), 35(1) and 37(1) and (2) of the Criminal Justice Act 1991;

"sentence", except in sub-paragraph (3) above, means the provision included in the warrant which is equivalent to a sentence.'

4 (1) This paragraph applies in relation to prisoners repatriated to England and Wales after the commencement of this Schedule whose sentences in the country or territory from which they are transferred were imposed for offences committed after the commencement of Chapter I of Part II of this Act.

(2) In section 2 of the 1984 Act (transfer of prisoners out of United Kingdom), in subsection (4)(b), for sub-paragraph (i) there shall be substituted the following sub-paragraph—

> '(i) subject to a release supervision order under section 16 of the Crime (Sentences) Act 1997, or released on licence under section 28(5) or 29(1) of that Act;'.

(3) In section 3 of the 1984 Act (transfer of prisoners into United Kingdom), in subsection (9)—

- (a) for the words 'section 48 of the Criminal Justice Act 1991 (discretionary life prisoners transferred to England and Wales)' there shall be substituted the words 'section 33 of the Crime (Sentences) Act 1997 (life prisoner transferred to England and Wales)'; and
- (b) for the words 'section 34 of that Act (duty of Secretary of State to release discretionary life prisoners)' there shall be substituted the words 'section 28 of that Act (duty to release certain life prisoners)'.

(4) For paragraph 2 of the Schedule to the 1984 Act there shall be substituted the following paragraph—

'Early release

2 (1) Subject to sub-paragraph (2) below, the prisoner's sentence, that is to say, the provision included in the warrant which is equivalent to a sentence, shall be deemed—

- (a) for the purposes of Chapter I of Part II of the Crime (Sentences) Act 1997, to have been imposed on the day on which the relevant provisions take effect;
- (b) for the purposes of Chapter II of that Part, to have been imposed on the same day as the sentence imposed in the country or territory from which he is transferred.

(2) The question whether—

- (a) section 11 of the Crime (Sentences) Act 1997 (award of early release days for good behaviour); or
- (b) section 12 of that Act (release on Parole Board recommendation),

applies in the case of the prisoner shall be determined by reference to the length of the sentence imposed in the country or territory from which he is transferred.'

(5) For paragraph 3 of that Schedule there shall be substituted the following paragraph—

'Life imprisonment

3. Where the relevant provisions include provision equivalent to a sentence in relation to which subsection (1) of section 29 of the Crime (Sentences) Act 1997 (power to release certain life prisoners etc.) applies, that subsection shall have effect as if the reference to consultation with the trial judge if available were omitted.'

Prisoners repatriated to Scotland

5 (1) This paragraph applies in relation to—

(a) prisoners repatriated to Scotland before 25th October 1996 (the 'relevant date') who were still serving sentences, which were imposed before 1st October 1993 in the country or territory from which they were transferred, on the relevant date; and

(b) prisoners repatriated to Scotland in respect of such sentences on or after the relevant date.

(2) Paragraph 2 of the Schedule to the 1984 Act, as originally enacted, shall have effect, and shall be deemed to have had effect since 16th February 1990, as if—

(a) in sub-paragraph (1), for the words 'section 60 of the Criminal Justice Act 1967' there were substituted the words 'section 22 of the Prisons (Scotland) Act 1989'; and

(b) at the end there were added the following sub-paragraph—

'(3) In this paragraph "sentence" means the provision included in a warrant which is equivalent to a sentence.'

6 (1) This paragraph applies in relation to—

(a) prisoners repatriated to Scotland before 25th October 1996 (the 'relevant date') who were still serving sentences, which were imposed on or after 1st October 1993 in the country or territory from which they were transferred, on the relevant date; and

(b) prisoners repatriated to Scotland in respect of such sentences on or after the relevant date and before the commencement of this Schedule.

(2) Paragraph 2 of the Schedule to the 1984 Act shall have effect, and shall be deemed always to have had effect, with the omission of sub-paragraph (1A) and the insertion after sub-paragraph (2) of the following sub-paragraphs—

'(3) The question whether the prisoner is a short-term or long-term prisoner for the purposes of the enactments relating to release on licence shall be determined by reference to the length of the sentence imposed in the country or territory from which he is transferred.

(4) For the purposes of Schedule 6 to the Prisoners and Criminal Proceedings (Scotland) Act 1993 a prisoner's sentence shall be deemed to have been imposed on the day on which the relevant provisions take effect.

(5) In this paragraph—

"the enactments relating to release on licence" means sections 1(2) and (3), 2(2) and (7) and 7(1) of the Prisoners and Criminal Proceedings (Scotland) Act 1993;

"sentence", except in sub-paragraph (3) above, means the provision included in the warrant which is equivalent to a sentence.'

7 (1) This paragraph applies in relation to prisoners repatriated to Scotland after the commencement of this Schedule whose sentences in the country or territory from which they are transferred were imposed on or after 1st October 1993 for offences committed before the commencement of section 33 of the Crime and Punishment (Scotland) Act 1997.

(2) In paragraph 2 of the Schedule to the 1984 Act, for sub-paragraphs (1A) and (2) there shall be substituted the following sub-paragraphs—

'(2) If the warrant specifies a period to be taken into account for the purposes of sections 1(3) and 2(2) and (7) of the Prisoners and Criminal Proceedings (Scotland) Act 1993—

(a) the amount of time the prisoner has served; and
(b) where his sentence is a determinate one, his sentence,

shall, so far only as the question whether he has served any particular proportion or part of his sentence is concerned, be deemed to be increased by that period.

(3) The question whether the prisoner is a long-term prisoner for the purposes of the enactments relating to release on licence shall be determined by reference to the length of the sentence imposed in the country or territory from which he is transferred.

(4) For the purposes of Schedule 6 to the Prisoners and Criminal Proceedings (Scotland) Act 1993 a prisoner's sentence shall be deemed to have been imposed on the day on which the relevant provisions take effect.

(5) In this paragraph—

"the enactments relating to release on licence" means sections 1(2) and (3), 2(2) and (7) and 7(1) of the Prisoners and Criminal Proceedings (Scotland) Act 1993;

"sentence", except in sub-paragraph (3) above, means the provision included in the warrant which is equivalent to a sentence.'

8 (1) This paragraph applies in relation to prisoners repatriated to Scotland after the commencement of this Schedule whose sentences in the country or territory from which they are transferred were imposed for offences committed after the commencement of section 33 of the Crime and Punishment (Scotland) Act 1997.

(2) For paragraph 2 of the Schedule to the 1984 Act there shall be substituted the following paragraph—

'Early release

2 The prisoner's sentence, that is to say, the provision included in the warrant which is equivalent to a sentence, shall be deemed—

(a) for the purposes of Chapter I of Part III of the Crime and Punishment (Scotland) Act 1997, to have been imposed on the day on which the relevant provisions take effect;
(b) for the purposes of section 2(2) and (7) of the Prisoners and Criminal Proceedings (Scotland) Act 1993, to have been imposed on the same day as the sentence imposed in the country or territory from which he is transferred.'

(3) For paragraph 3 of that Schedule there shall be substituted the following paragraph—

'Life imprisonment

3 Where the relevant provisions include provision equivalent to a sentence in relation to which subsection (4) of section 1 of the Prisoners and Criminal Proceedings (Scotland) Act 1993 (power to release certain life prisoners etc.)

applies, that subsection shall have effect as if the reference to consultation with the trial judge if available were omitted.'

Prisoners repatriated to Northern Ireland

9 (1) This paragraph applies in relation to—

(a) prisoners repatriated to Northern Ireland before 25th October 1996 who were still serving their sentences on that date; and

(b) prisoners repatriated to Northern Ireland on or after that date.

(2) Paragraph 2 of the Schedule to the 1984 Act shall have effect, and shall be deemed always to have had effect, with the insertion after sub-paragraph (2) of the following sub-paragraph—

'(3) In this paragraph "sentence" means the provision included in the warrant which is equivalent to a sentence.'

10 (1) This paragraph applies in relation to prisoners repatriated to Northern Ireland after the commencement of this Schedule.

(2) For paragraph 3 of the Schedule to the 1984 Act there shall be substituted the following paragraph—

'Life imprisonment

3 Where the relevant provisions include provision equivalent to a sentence in relation to which subsection (3) of section 1 of the Northern Ireland (Emergency Provisions) Act 1973 (power to release certain life prisoners etc.) applies, that subsection shall have effect as if the reference to consultation with the trial judge if available were omitted.'

Prisoners repatriated to the Islands

11 (1) This paragraph applies where any Order in Council under section 9(4) of the 1984 Act extends the provisions of that Act to any of the Channel Islands or the Isle of Man.

(2) The modifications of that Act made by the Order may include modifications broadly corresponding to those made by any of paragraphs 1 to 10 above.

SCHEDULE 3
TRANSFERS WITHIN THE BRITISH ISLANDS OF RESPONSIBILITY
FOR OFFENDERS CONDITIONALLY DISCHARGED FROM HOSPITAL

PART I
AMENDMENTS OF THE 1983 ACT

Transfers from England and Wales to Scotland

1 After section 80 of the 1983 Act there shall be inserted the following section—

'80A   Transfer of responsibility for patients to Scotland

(1) If it appears to the Secretary of State, in the case of a patient who—

(a) is subject to a restriction order under section 41 above; and

(b) has been conditionally discharged under section 42 or 73 above,

that a transfer under this section would be in the interests of the patient, the Secretary of State may, with the consent of the Minister exercising corresponding functions in Scotland, transfer responsibility for the patient to that Minister.

(2) Where responsibility for such a patient is transferred under this section, the patient shall be treated—

(a) as if on the date of the transfer he had been conditionally discharged under the corresponding enactment in force in Scotland; and

(b) as if he were subject to a restriction order under the corresponding enactment in force in Scotland.

(3) Where a patient responsibility for whom is transferred under this section was immediately before the transfer subject to a restriction order of limited duration, the restriction order to which he is subject by virtue of subsection (2) above shall expire on the date on which the first-mentioned order would have expired if the transfer had not been made.'

Transfers from England and Wales to Northern Ireland

2 After section 81 of the 1983 Act there shall be inserted the following section—

'81A Transfer of responsibility for patients to Northern Ireland

(1) If it appears to the Secretary of State, in the case of a patient who—

(a) is subject to a restriction order or restriction direction under section 41 or 49 above; and

(b) has been conditionally discharged under section 42 or 73 above,

that a transfer under this section would be in the interests of the patient, the Secretary of State may, with the consent of the Minister exercising corresponding functions in Northern Ireland, transfer responsibility for the patient to that Minister.

(2) Where responsibility for such a patient is transferred under this section, the patient shall be treated—

(a) as if on the date of the transfer he had been conditionally discharged under the corresponding enactment in force in Northern Ireland; and

(b) as if he were subject to a restriction order or restriction direction under the corresponding enactment in force in Northern Ireland.

(3) Where a patient responsibility for whom is transferred under this section was immediately before the transfer subject to a restriction order or restriction direction of limited duration, the restriction order or restriction direction to which he is subject by virtue of subsection (2) above shall expire on the date on which the first-mentioned order or direction would have expired if the transfer had not been made.'

Transfers from Northern Ireland to England and Wales

3 After section 82 of the 1983 Act there shall be inserted the following section—

'82A Transfer of responsibility for patients to England and Wales from Northern Ireland

(1) If it appears to the relevant Minister, in the case of a patient who—

(a) is subject to a restriction order or restriction direction under Article 47(1) or 55(1) of the Mental Health (Northern Ireland) Order 1986; and

(b) has been conditionally discharged under Article 48(2) or 78(2) of that Order,

that a transfer under this section would be in the interests of the patient, that Minister may, with the consent of the Secretary of State, transfer responsibility for the patient to the Secretary of State.

(2) Where responsibility for such a patient is transferred under this section, the patient shall be treated—

(a) as if on the date of the transfer he had been conditionally discharged under section 42 or 73 above; and

(b) as if he were subject to a restriction order or restriction direction under section 41 or 49 above.

(3) Where a patient responsibility for whom is transferred under this section was immediately before the transfer subject to a restriction order or restriction direction of limited duration, the restriction order or restriction direction to which he is subject by virtue of subsection (2) above shall expire on the date on which the first-mentioned order or direction would have expired if the transfer had not been made.

(4) In this section "the relevant Minister" means the Minister exercising in Northern Ireland functions corresponding to those of the Secretary of State.'

Transfers from England and Wales to the Islands

4 After section 83 of the 1983 Act there shall be inserted the following section—

'83A Transfer of responsibility for patients to Channel Islands or Isle of Man

If it appears to the Secretary of State, in the case of a patient who—

(a) is subject to a restriction order or restriction direction under section 41 or 49 above; and

(b) has been conditionally discharged under section 42 or 73 above,

that a transfer under this section would be in the interests of the patient, the Secretary of State may, with the consent of the authority exercising corresponding functions in any of the Channel Islands or in the Isle of Man, transfer responsibility for the patient to that authority.'

Transfers from the Islands to England and Wales

5 After section 85 of the 1983 Act there shall be inserted the following section—

'85A Responsibility for patients transferred from Channel Islands or Isle of Man

(1) This section applies to any patient responsibility for whom is transferred to the Secretary of State by the authority exercising corresponding functions in any of the

Channel Islands or the Isle of Man under a provision corresponding to section 83A above.

(2) The patient shall be treated—

- (a) as if on the date of the transfer he had been conditionally discharged under section 42 or 73 above; and
- (b) as if he were subject to a restriction order or restriction direction under section 41 or 49 above.

(3) Where the patient was immediately before the transfer subject to an order or direction restricting his discharge, being an order or direction of limited duration, the restriction order or restriction direction to which he is subject by virtue of subsection (2) above shall expire on the date on which the first-mentioned order or direction would have expired if the transfer had not been made.'

PART II
AMENDMENTS OF THE 1984 ACT

Transfers from Scotland to England and Wales

6 After section 77 of the 1984 Act there shall be inserted the following section—

'77A Transfer of responsibility for patients to England and Wales

(1) If it appears to the Secretary of State, in the case of a patient who—

- (a) is subject to a restriction order under section 59 of the Criminal Procedure (Scotland) Act 1995; and
- (b) has been conditionally discharged under section 64 or 68 of this Act,

that a transfer under this section would be in the interests of the patient, the Secretary of State may, with the consent of the Minister exercising corresponding functions in England and Wales, transfer responsibility for the patient to that Minister.

(2) Where responsibility for such a patient is transferred under this section, the patient shall be treated—

- (a) as if on the date of the transfer he had been conditionally discharged under the corresponding enactment in force in England and Wales; and
- (b) as if he were subject to a restriction order under the corresponding enactment in force in England and Wales.'

Transfers from Scotland to Northern Ireland

7 After section 80 of the 1984 Act there shall be inserted the following section—

'80A Transfer of responsibility for patients to Northern Ireland

(1) If it appears to the Secretary of State, in the case of a patient who—

- (a) is subject to a restriction order under section 59 of the Criminal Procedure (Scotland) Act 1995; and

(b) has been conditionally discharged under section 64 or 68 of this Act,

that a transfer under this section would be in the interests of the patient, the Secretary of State may, with the consent of the Minister exercising corresponding functions in Northern Ireland, transfer responsibility for the patient to that Minister.

(2) Where responsibility for such a patient is transferred under this section, the patient shall be treated—

(a) as if on the date of the transfer he had been conditionally discharged under the corresponding enactment in force in Northern Ireland; and

(b) as if he were subject to a restriction order under the corresponding enactment in force in Northern Ireland.'

Transfers from Northern Ireland to Scotland

8 After section 81 of the 1984 Act there shall be inserted the following section—

'81A Transfer of responsibility for patients to Scotland from Northern Ireland

(1) If it appears to the relevant Minister, in the case of a patient who—

(a) is subject to a restriction order under Article 47(1) of the Mental Health (Northern Ireland) Order 1986; and

(b) has been conditionally discharged under Article 48(2) or 78(2) of that Order,

that a transfer under this section would be in the interests of the patient, that Minister may, with the consent of the Secretary of State, transfer responsibility for the patient to the Secretary of State.

(2) Where responsibility for such a patient is transferred under this section, the patient shall be treated—

(a) as if on the date of the transfer he had been conditionally discharged under section 64 or 68 of this Act; and

(b) as if he were subject to a restriction order within the meaning of this Act.

(3) Where a patient responsibility for whom is transferred under this section was immediately before the transfer subject to a restriction order of limited duration, the restriction order to which he is subject by virtue of subsection (2) above shall expire on the date on which the first-mentioned order would have expired if the transfer had not been made.

(4) In this section "the relevant Minister" means the Minister exercising in Northern Ireland functions corresponding to those of the Secretary of State.'

Transfers from the Islands to Scotland

9 After section 82 of the 1984 Act there shall be inserted the following section—

'82A Responsibility for patients transferred from Channel Islands or Isle of Man to Scotland

(1) This section applies to any patient responsibility for whom is transferred to the Secretary of State by the authority exercising corresponding functions in any of the Channel Islands or the Isle of Man under a provision corresponding to section 82B of this Act.

(2) The patient shall be treated—

(a) as if on the date of the transfer he had been conditionally discharged under section 64 or 68 of this Act; and

(b) as if he were subject to a restriction order within the meaning of this Act.

(3) Where the patient was immediately before the transfer subject to an order restricting his discharge, being an order of limited duration, the restriction order to which he is subject by virtue of subsection (2) above shall expire on the date on which the first-mentioned order would have expired if the transfer had not been made.'

Transfers from Scotland to the Islands

10 After section 82A of the 1984 Act there shall be inserted the following section—

'82B Transfer of responsibility for patients to Channel Islands or Isle of Man

If it appears to the Secretary of State, in the case of a patient who—

(a) is subject to a restriction order under section 59 of the Criminal Procedure (Scotland) Act 1995; and

(b) has been conditionally discharged under section 64 or 68 of this Act,

that a transfer under this section would be in the interests of the patient, the Secretary of State may, with the consent of the authority exercising corresponding functions in any of the Channel Islands or in the Isle of Man, transfer responsibility for the patient to that authority.'

SCHEDULE 4
MINOR AND CONSEQUENTIAL AMENDMENTS

Army Act 1955 (c.18)

1 (1) After subsection (3) of section 70 of the Army Act 1955 (civil offences) there shall be inserted the following subsection—

'(3A) Where the corresponding civil offence is one to which section 2, 3 or 4 of the Crime (Sentences) Act 1997 would apply, the court-martial shall impose the sentence required by subsection (2) of that section unless it is of the opinion that there are exceptional circumstances which justify its not doing so.'

(2) For subsection (1A) of section 71A of that Act (juveniles) there shall be substituted the following subsection—

'(1A) Where—

(a) a person under 21 years of age is convicted of murder or any other civil offence the sentence for which is fixed by law as imprisonment for life; or

(b) a person under that age is convicted of any civil offence to which section 2 of the Crime (Sentences) Act 1997 would apply and the court is not of the opinion mentioned in subsection (2) of that section,

the court shall sentence him to custody for life unless he is liable to be detained under subsection (3) below.'

(3) In subsection (6A) of section 71AA of that Act (young service offenders: custodial orders), for the words 'Section 65 of the Criminal Justice Act 1991' there shall be

substituted the words 'Sections 16 and 17 of the Crime (Sentences) Act 1997 (as modified by section 19 of that Act)'.

(4) In paragraph 3(1) of Schedule 5A to that Act (powers of court on trial of civilian), after the words 'fixed by law' there shall be inserted the words 'or falls to be imposed under section 70(3A) above'.

(5) In paragraph 10(6A) of that Schedule, for the words 'Section 65 of the Criminal Justice Act 1991' there shall be substituted the words 'Sections 16 and 17 of the Crime (Sentences) Act 1997 (as modified by section 19 of that Act)'.

Air Force Act 1955 (c.19)

2 (1) After subsection (3) of section 70 of the Air Force Act 1955 (civil offences) there shall be inserted the following subsection—

'(3A) Where the corresponding civil offence is one to which section 2, 3 or 4 of the Crime (Sentences) Act 1997 would apply, the court-martial shall impose the sentence required by subsection (2) of that section unless it is of the opinion that there are exceptional circumstances which justify its not doing so.'

(2) For subsection (1A) of section 71A of that Act (juveniles) there shall be substituted the following subsection—

'(1A) Where—

(a) a person under 21 years of age is convicted of murder or any other civil offence the sentence for which is fixed by law as imprisonment for life; or

(b) a person under that age is convicted of any civil offence to which section 2 of the Crime (Sentences) Act 1997 would apply and the court is not of the opinion mentioned in subsection (2) of that section,

the court shall sentence him to custody for life unless he is liable to be detained under subsection (3) below.'

(3) In subsection (6A) of section 71AA of that Act (young service offenders: custodial orders), for the words 'Section 65 of the Criminal Justice Act 1991' there shall be substituted the words 'Sections 16 and 17 of the Crime (Sentences) Act 1997 (as modified by section 19 of that Act)'.

(4) In paragraph 3(1) of Schedule 5A to that Act (powers of court on trial of civilian), after the words 'fixed by law' there shall be inserted the words 'or falls to be imposed under section 70(3A) above'.

(5) In paragraph 10(6A) of that Schedule, for the words 'Section 65 of the Criminal Justice Act 1991' there shall be substituted the words 'Sections 16 and 17 of the Crime (Sentences) Act 1997 (as modified by section 19 of that Act)'.

Naval Discipline Act 1957 (c.53)

3 (1) After subsection (1) of section 42 of the Naval Discipline Act 1957 (civil offences) there shall be inserted the following subsection—

'(1A) Where the corresponding civil offence is one to which section 2, 3 or 4 of the Crime (Sentences) Act 1997 would apply, the court-martial shall impose the sentence required by subsection (2) of that section unless it is of the opinion that there are exceptional circumstances which justify its not doing so.'

(2) For subsection (1A) of section 43A of that Act (juveniles) there shall be substituted the following subsection—

'(1A) Where—

(a) a person under 21 years of age is convicted of murder or any other civil offence the sentence for which is fixed by law as imprisonment for life; or

(b) a person under that age is convicted of any civil offence to which section 2 of the Crime (Sentences) Act 1997 would apply and the court is not of the opinion mentioned in subsection (2) of that section,

the court shall sentence him to custody for life unless he is liable to be detained under subsection (3) below.'

(3) In subsection (6A) of section 43AA of that Act (young service offenders: custodial orders), for the words 'Section 65 of the Criminal Justice Act 1991' there shall be substituted the words 'Sections 16 and 17 of the Crime (Sentences) Act 1997 (as modified by section 19 of that Act)'.

(4) In paragraph 3(1) of Schedule 4A to that Act (powers of court on trial of civilian), after the words 'fixed by law' there shall be inserted the words 'or falls to be imposed under section 42(1A) above'.

(5) In paragraph 10(6A) of that Schedule, for the words 'Section 65 of the Criminal Justice Act 1991' there shall be substituted the words 'Sections 16 and 17 of the Crime (Sentences) Act 1997 (as modified by section 19 of that Act)'.

Children and Young Persons Act 1963 (c.37)

4 After subsection (2) of section 16 of the Children and Young Persons Act 1963 (offences committed by children under 14 to be disregarded for purposes of evidence relating to previous convictions) there shall be inserted the following subsection—

'(3) Nothing in subsection (2) of this section shall be taken to prevent the adduction of evidence of previous convictions for the purpose of establishing the application of any provision of Part I of the Crime (Sentences) Act 1997 (mandatory and minimum custodial sentences).'

Criminal Justice Act 1967 (c.80)

5 (1) In subsection (2) of section 56 of the Criminal Justice Act 1967 (committal for sentence for offences tried summarily)—

(a) for the words 'sections 37 and 38' there shall be substituted the words 'sections 37, 38 and 38A'; and

(b) for the words 'and section 62(6) of this Act' there shall be substituted the words ', section 17(3) of the Crime (Sentences) Act 1997 (committal for breach of conditions of release supervision order),'.

(2) In subsection (4) of section 72 of that Act (power of magistrates to issue warrants for escaped prisoners and mental patients), after the words 'restricting his discharge' there shall be inserted the words 'or in pursuance of a hospital direction and a limitation direction'.

Criminal Appeal Act 1968 (c.19)

6 (1) In subsection (1) of section 50 of the Criminal Appeal Act 1968 (meaning of sentence)—

(a) after paragraph (b) there shall be inserted the following paragraph—

'(bb) a hospital direction and a limitation direction under that Part;'; and

(b) after paragraph (c) there shall be inserted the following paragraph—

'(cc) a direction under section 20(3) or 21(3) of the Crime (Sentences) Act 1997 (extended supervision for sexual or violent offenders);'.

(2) In sub-paragraph (4) of paragraph 2 of Schedule 2 to that Act (procedural and other provisions applicable on order for retrial), for the words 'Section 67 of the Criminal Justice Act 1967 (deduction from certain sentences of time spent in custody before sentence)' there shall be substituted the words 'Section 9 of the Crime (Sentences) Act 1997 (crediting of periods of remand in custody)'.

Immigration Act 1971 (c.77)

7. In subsection (4) of section 7 of the Immigration Act 1971 (exemption from deportation for certain existing residents), for the words 'section 67 of the Criminal Justice Act 1967' there shall be substituted the words 'section 9 of the Crime (Sentences) Act 1997'.

Powers of Criminal Courts Act 1973 (c.62)

8 (1) In section 1A(1) of the 1973 Act (absolute and conditional discharge), after the words 'is fixed by law' there shall be inserted the words 'or falls to be imposed under section 2(2), 3(2) or 4(2) of the Crime (Sentences) Act 1997'.

(2) In section 2(1) of that Act (probation orders), after the words 'is fixed by law' there shall be inserted the words 'or falls to be imposed under section 2(2), 3(2) or 4(2) of the Crime (Sentences) Act 1997'.

(3) In section 30(1) of that Act (general power to fine offender), after the words 'is fixed by law' there shall be inserted the words 'or falls to be imposed under section 2(2), 3(2) or 4(2) of the Crime (Sentences) Act 1997'.

(4) In subsection (1) of section 42 of that Act (power of Crown Court on committal for sentence), after the words 'section 38' there shall be inserted the words 'or 38A'.

Rehabilitation of Offenders Act 1974 (c.53)

9 (1) In subsection (2) of section 1 of the Rehabilitation of Offenders Act 1974 (rehabilitated persons and spent convictions), after paragraph (c) there shall be inserted the following paragraph—

'(d) breach of any condition of a release supervision order made under section 16 of the Crime (Sentences) Act 1997.'

(2) In subsection (6) of section 6 of that Act (the rehabilitation period applicable to a conviction), at the end of paragraph (a) there shall be inserted the words 'or of an offence under section 17 of the Crime (Sentences) Act 1997 (breach of conditions of release supervision order)'.

Magistrates' Courts Act 1980 (c.43)

10 (1) In subsection (4A) of section 82 of the 1980 Act (restriction on power to impose imprisonment for default), in paragraph (e) for the words 'under the age of 21' there shall be substituted the words 'under the age of 25'.

(2) For subsection (3) of section 85 of that Act (power to remit fine) there shall be substituted the following subsections—

'(2A) Where the court remits the whole or part of the fine after an order has been made under section 35(2)(a) or (b) of the Crime (Sentences) Act 1997, it shall also reduce the total number of hours or days to which the order relates by a number which bears the same proportion as the amount remitted bears to the whole sum or, as the case may be, shall revoke the order.

(3) In calculating any reduction required by subsection (2) or (2A) above any fraction of a day or hour shall be left out of account.'

Criminal Justice Act 1982 (c.48)

11. In subsection (4) of section 1A of the 1982 Act (detention in a young offender institution), for the words 'section 65(6) of the Criminal Justice Act 1991' there shall be substituted the words 'section 17(1) of the Crime (Sentences) Act 1997 as it has effect by virtue of section 19 of that Act'.

Mental Health Act 1983 (c.20)

12 (1) In subsection (1) of section 37 of the 1983 Act (powers of courts to order hospital admission or guardianship), after the words 'is fixed by law' there shall be inserted the words 'or falls to be imposed under section 2(2) of the Crime (Sentences) Act 1997'.

(2) After that subsection there shall be inserted the following subsection—

'(1A) In the case of an offence the sentence for which would otherwise fall to be imposed under subsection (2) of section 3 or 4 of the Crime (Sentences) Act 1997, nothing in that subsection shall prevent a court from making an order under subsection (1) above for the admission of the offender to a hospital.'

(3) In subsection (4) of that section, the words 'in the event of such an order being made by the court' shall cease to have effect.

(4) After subsection (3) of section 50 of that Act (further provisions as to prisoners under sentence) there shall be inserted the following subsection—

'(3A) In applying subsection (3) above account shall be taken of any early release days awarded to the person under section 11 of the Crime (Sentences) Act 1997 (read with section 22 of that Act).'

(5) After subsection (4) of that section there shall be inserted the following subsection—

'(5) The preceding provisions of this section shall have effect as if—

(a) the reference in subsection (1) to a transfer direction and a restriction direction having been given in respect of a person serving a sentence of imprisonment included a reference to a hospital direction and a limitation direction having been given in respect of a person sentenced to imprisonment;

(b) the reference in subsection (2) to a restriction direction included a reference to a limitation direction; and

(c) references in subsections (3) and (4) to a transfer direction included references to a hospital direction.'

(6) In section 54 of that Act (requirements as to medical evidence), after the words '38(1)' there shall be inserted the words '45A(2)'.

(7) In subsection (2) of section 61 of that Act (review of treatment)—

(a) after the words 'restriction order' there shall be inserted the words ', limitation direction'; and

(b) in paragraph (b), after the words 'section 41(6)' there shall be inserted the words ', 45B(3)'.

(8) In subsection (2)(b) of section 69 of that Act (applications to tribunals concerning patients subject to hospital and guardianship orders), after the word 'section' there shall be inserted '45B(2),'.

(9) In section 70(a) of that Act (applications to tribunals concerning restricted patients), after the words 'hospital order' there shall be inserted the words ', hospital direction'.

(10) In subsection (1) of section 74 of that Act (restricted patients), after the words 'who is subject to' there shall be inserted the words 'a limitation direction or'.

(11) In subsection (5) of that section, after the word 'above' there shall be inserted the words 'the relevant hospital direction and the limitation direction or, as the case may be,'.

(12) In subsection (6) of that section, after the words 'references to', in the second place where they occur, there shall be inserted the words 'the hospital direction and the limitation direction or, as the case may be, to'.

(13) In section 75(1)(b) of that Act (applications and references concerning conditionally discharged restricted patients), after the words 'hospital order' there shall be inserted the words ', hospital direction'.

(14) In subsection (1) of section 79 of that Act (interpretation of Part V), after the words 'restriction order' there shall be inserted the words ', limitation direction'.

(15) In subsection (2) of that section—

(a) after the words 'the relevant hospital order' there shall be inserted the words ', "the relevant hospital direction"'; and

(b) after the words 'the hospital order' there shall be inserted the words ', the hospital direction'.

(16) After subsection (3) of section 92 of that Act (interpretation of Part VI) there shall be inserted the following subsections—

'(4) Sections 80 to 85A above shall have effect as if—

(a) any hospital direction under section 45A above were a transfer direction under section 47 above; and

(b) any limitation direction under section 45A above were a restriction direction under section 49 above.

(5) Sections 80(5), 81(6) and 85(4) above shall have effect as if any reference to a transfer direction given while a patient was serving a sentence of imprisonment imposed by a court included a reference to a hospital direction given by a court after imposing a sentence of imprisonment on a patient.'

(17) In subsection (1) of section 117 of that Act (after-care), after the words 'transferred to a hospital in pursuance of' there shall be inserted the words 'a hospital direction made under section 45A above or'.

(18) In subsection (3) of section 143 of that Act (general provisions as to regulations, orders and rules), after the word 'section' there shall be inserted the word '45A(10),'.

(19) In subsection (1) of section 145 of that Act (interpretation)—

(a) after the definition of 'hospital' there shall be inserted the following definition—

"hospital direction" has the meaning given in section 45A(3)(a) above;';

(b) after the definition of 'interim hospital order' there shall be inserted the following definition—

"limitation direction" has the meaning given in section 45A(3)(b) above;'.

Criminal Justice Act 1988 (c.33)

13 At the end of subsection (2) of section 36 of the Criminal Justice Act 1988 (review of sentencing) there shall be inserted the words 'or failed to impose a sentence required by section 2(2), 3(2) or 4(2) of the Crime (Sentences) Act 1997'.

Prevention of Terrorism (Temporary Provisions) Act 1989 (c.4)

14 In sub-paragraph (5) of paragraph 9 of Schedule 2 to the Prevention of Terrorism (Temporary Provisions) Act 1989 (exemption from exclusion orders), for the words 'section 67 of the Criminal Justice Act 1967' there shall be substituted the words 'section 9 of the Crime (Sentences) Act 1997'.

Criminal Justice Act 1991 (c.53)

15 (1) In subsection (1) of section 1 of the 1991 Act (restrictions on imposing custodial sentences), after the words 'fixed by law' there shall be inserted the words 'or falling to be imposed under section 2(2), 3(2) or 4(2) of the Crime (Sentences) Act 1997'.

(2) For subsection (3) of that section there shall be substituted the following subsection—

'(3) Nothing in subsection (2) above shall prevent the court from passing a custodial sentence on the offender if he fails to express his willingness to comply with a requirement which is proposed by the court to be included in a probation order or supervision order and which requires an expression of such willingness.'

(3) In subsection (1) of section 2 of that Act (length of custodial sentences), after the words 'fixed by law' there shall be inserted the words 'or falling to be imposed under section 2(2) of the Crime (Sentences) Act 1997'.

(4) At the beginning of subsection (2) of that section there shall be inserted the words 'Subject to sections 3(2) and 4(2) of that Act,'.

(5) After subsection (4) of that section there shall be inserted the following subsection—

'(5) Subsection (3) above shall not apply in any case where the court passes a custodial sentence falling to be imposed under subsection (2) of section 3 or 4 of the Crime (Sentences) Act 1997 which is for the minimum term specified in that subsection.'

(6) In subsection (1) of section 4 of that Act (additional requirements in the case of mentally disordered offenders)—

(a) the words 'section 3(1) above applies and' shall cease to have effect; and
(b) after the words 'fixed by law' there shall be inserted the words 'or falling to be imposed under section 2(2) of the Crime (Sentences) Act 1997'.

(7) In subsection (3) of that section, after the words 'fixed by law' there shall be inserted the words 'or falling to be imposed under section 2(2) of the Crime (Sentences) Act 1997'.

(8) In subsection (1) of section 11 of that Act (orders combining probation and community service), after the words 'is fixed by law' there shall be inserted the words 'or falls to be imposed under section 2(2), 3(2) or 4(2) of the Crime (Sentences) Act 1997'.

(9) In subsection (1) of section 12 of that Act (curfew orders), after the words 'is fixed by law' there shall be inserted the words 'or falls to be imposed under section 2(2), 3(2) or 4(2) of the Crime (Sentences) Act 1997'.

(10) In section 32 of that Act (the Parole Board)—

    (a) in subsection (1), for the words from 'be constituted' to the end there shall be substituted the following paragraphs—

        '(a) be constituted in accordance with this Part; and
        (b) have the functions conferred by Part II of the Crime (Sentences) Act 1997 ("Part II").'; and

    (b) in subsections (3), (4) and (6), for the words 'this Part' there shall be substituted the words 'Part II'.

(11) In sub-paragraph (2) of each of paragraphs 3 and 4 of Schedule 2 to that Act (powers of magistrates' court and Crown Court), for paragraph (b) there shall be substituted the following paragraph—

        '(b) in the case of an offender who has wilfully and persistently failed to comply with those requirements, may impose a custodial sentence notwithstanding anything in section 1(2) of this Act.'

(12) In sub-paragraph (2)(a)(ii) of paragraph 13 of that Schedule (amendment of requirements of probation or curfew order), after the word 'unless' there shall be inserted the words 'the offender has expressed his willingness to comply with such a requirement and'.

(13) In sub-paragraph (2)(b) of paragraph 14 of that Schedule (amendment of certain requirements of probation order), the words from 'being treatment' to the end shall cease to have effect.

Prisoners and Criminal Proceedings (Scotland) Act 1993 (c.9)

16 (1) In section 10(4) of the Prisoners and Criminal Proceedings (Scotland) Act 1993 (meaning of transferred life prisoner), for the words 'section 26 of the Criminal Justice Act 1961' there shall be substituted the words 'paragraph 1 of Schedule 1 to the Crime (Sentences) Act 1997'.

(2) In Schedule 6 to that Act, in paragraph 1, in the definition of 'new provisions', after the word 'Act' where it last occurs, there shall be inserted the words 'and the Repatriation of Prisoners Act 1984 as it has effect by virtue of paragraphs 6 and 7 of Schedule 2 to the Crime (Sentences) Act 1997'.

Criminal Justice and Public Order Act 1994 (c.33)

17 After subsection (2) of section 48 of the Criminal Justice and Public Order Act 1994 (reduction in sentences for guilty pleas) there shall be inserted the following subsection—

'(3) In the case of an offence the sentence for which falls to be imposed under subsection (2) of section 3 or 4 of the Crime (Sentences) Act 1997, nothing in that subsection shall prevent the court, after taking into account any matter referred to in subsection (1) above, from imposing any sentence which is not less than 80 per cent of that specified in that subsection.'

SCHEDULE 5
TRANSITIONAL PROVISIONS AND SAVINGS

Sentences for offences committed before the commencement of Chapter I of Part II

1 Notwithstanding their repeal by this Act, sections 33, 35 to 47, 49 to 51 and 65 of the 1991 Act shall, so far as applicable and subject to the following provisions of this Schedule, continue to have effect in relation to persons sentenced to determinate sentences of imprisonment for offences committed before the commencement of Chapter I of Part II of this Act.

Consecutive sentences for offences committed before and after that commencement

2 (1) This paragraph applies where consecutive terms of imprisonment include—

(a) the term of a sentence imposed on an offender for an offence committed after the commencement of Chapter I of Part II of this Act; and
(b) the term of a sentence imposed on him for an offence committed before that commencement.

(2) Subject to sub-paragraphs (3) and (4) below, the time to be served by the offender shall be determined separately in respect of each sentence under whichever of Chapter I of Part II of this Act and Part II of the 1991 Act is applicable to that sentence.

(3) Where the offender was remanded in custody in connection with—

(a) an offence falling within sub-paragraph (1)(a) above; and
(b) an offence falling within sub-paragraph (1)(b) above,

any additional days which have been both conditionally and provisionally awarded to him shall be taken into account for the purposes of Chapter I of Part II of this Act and not for the purposes of Part II of the 1991 Act.

(4) The time to be served by the offender in respect of a sentence falling within sub-paragraph (1)(b) above which—

(a) is for a term of four years or more; and
(b) is not the final sentence,

shall be determined as if section 35(1) of the 1991 Act were omitted.

(5) The offender shall be released when he has served the time required to be served in respect of the final sentence.

(6) Subject to sub-paragraph (7) below, whichever of Chapter I of Part II of this Act and Part II of the 1991 Act is applicable to the final sentence shall apply in relation to the offender after his release.

(7) Notwithstanding anything in Part II of the 1991 Act, the offender's supervision shall be for the period which would be applicable if each of his terms of imprisonment had been imposed in respect of offences committed after the commencement of Chapter I of Part II of this Act.

(8) In this paragraph 'the final sentence', in relation to any time, means the sentence which at that time falls to be served after the other or others.

(9) In this paragraph and paragraph 3 below—

'conditionally awarded' means conditionally awarded under prison rules made by virtue of section 42(1) of the 1991 Act;

'provisionally awarded' means provisionally awarded under prison rules having effect by virtue of section 15(2) of this Act;

and any reference to Part II of the 1991 Act includes, unless the context otherwise requires, a reference to section 65 of that Act.

Concurrent sentences for offences committed before and after that commencement

3 (1) This paragraph applies where terms of imprisonment which are wholly or partly concurrent include—

(a) the term of a sentence imposed on an offender for an offence committed after the commencement of Chapter I of Part II of this Act; and
(b) the term of a sentence imposed on him for an offence committed before that commencement.

(2) Subject to sub-paragraph (3) below, the time to be served by the offender in respect of the final sentence shall be determined under whichever of Chapter I of Part II of this Act and Part II of the 1991 Act is applicable to that sentence.

(3) Where the offender was remanded in custody in connection with—

(a) an offence falling within sub-paragraph (1)(a) above; and
(b) an offence falling within sub-paragraph (1)(b) above,

any additional days which have been both conditionally and provisionally awarded to him shall be taken into account only for the purposes of whichever of Chapter I of Part II of this Act and Part II of the 1991 Act is applicable to the final sentence.

(4) The offender shall be released when he has served the time required to be served in respect of the final sentence.

(5) Subject to sub-paragraph (6) below, whichever of Chapter I of Part II of this Act and Part II of the 1991 Act is applicable to the final sentence shall apply in relation to the offender after his release.

(6) Notwithstanding anything in Part II of the 1991 Act, the offender's supervision shall be for the period which would be applicable if each of his terms of imprisonment had been imposed in respect of offences committed after the commencement of Chapter I of Part II of this Act.

(7) Where at any time a sentence falling within sub-paragraph (1)(a) above ('sentence A') becomes the final sentence in place of a sentence falling within sub-paragraph (1)(b) above ('sentence B') either—

(a) because the term of sentence A is increased on appeal; or
(b) because sentence B is set aside, or its term is reduced, on appeal,

then, for each assessment period for the purposes of section 11 of this Act beginning before that time, the prescribed person or, as the case may be, the Secretary of State shall assume, for the purposes of subsection (2) or (3) of that section, that the prisoner's behaviour was such as to entitle him to the maximum number of early release days available under that subsection.

(8) In this paragraph 'the final sentence', in relation to any time, means the sentence which at that time will have the later or latest release date on the following assumptions, namely—

(a) that the time to be served in respect of a sentence falling within sub-paragraph (1)(a) above is equal to the term imposed by the court less the number of days (if any) directed by the court to count as time served as part of the sentence; and

(b) that the time to be served in respect of a sentence falling within sub-paragraph (1)(b) above is equal to the appropriate proportion of the term imposed by the court less any period by which the sentence falls to be reduced under section 67 of the Criminal Justice Act 1967.

(9) In sub-paragraph (8) above 'the appropriate proportion' means one-half in the case of a term of less than four years and two thirds in the case of a term of four years or more.

Crediting of periods of remand in custody

4 In relation to any time between the commencement of section 9 of this Act and the commencement of Chapter I of Part II of this Act, sections 34, 41 and 47 of the 1991 Act shall have effect as if any reference (however expressed) to a relevant period by which a sentence falls to be reduced under section 67 of the 1967 Act were a reference to a number of days directed under section 9 of this Act to count as time served as part of a sentence.

Duty to release certain life prisoners

5 (1) In relation to any time before the commencement of section 9 of this Act, section 28 of this Act shall have effect as if, in paragraph (b) of subsection (3), for the words 'of any direction it would have given under section 9 above' there were substituted the words 'which section 67 of the Criminal Justice Act 1967 would have had'.

(2) In relation to any time before the commencement of Chapter I of Part II of this Act, section 28 of this Act shall have effect as if—

(a) after paragraph (b) of subsection (3), there were inserted the words 'and

(c) the provisions of this section as compared with those of sections 33(2) and 35(1) of the 1991 Act'; and

(b) in paragraph (c) of subsection (7), for the words from 'the time when' to the end there were substituted the words 'he has served one-half of that sentence'.

(3) Section 28(7) of this Act shall have effect as if—

(a) any reference of a prisoner's case made to the Parole Board under section 32(2) or 34(4) of the 1991 Act had been made under section 28(6) of this Act; and

(b) any such reference made under section 39(4) of that Act had been made under section 32(4) of this Act.

Life prisoners transferred to England and Wales

6 In relation to any time before the commencement of Schedule 1 to this Act, section 33 of this Act shall have effect as if, in paragraph (b)(i) of subsection (4), for the words 'paragraph 1 of Schedule 1 to this Act' there were substituted the words 'section 26 of the Criminal Justice Act 1961'.

Recall of life prisoners while on licence

7 (1) Section 32(3) and (4) of this Act shall have effect as if any life prisoner recalled to prison under subsection (1) or (2) of section 39 of the 1991 Act had been recalled to prison under the corresponding subsection of section 32 of this Act.

(2) Section 32(4) of this Act shall have effect as if any representations made by a life prisoner under section 39(3) of the 1991 Act had been made under section 32(3) of this Act.

Transfers of prisoners: general

8 In relation to any person serving a determinate custodial sentence in respect of an offence committed before the commencement of Chapter I of Part II of this Act, paragraph 6 of Schedule 1 to this Act shall have effect as if, in sub-paragraph (3)(b) of that paragraph, for the words 'recalled to prison under the licence' there were substituted the words 'recalled or returned to prison'.

Transfers of prisoners from England and Wales to Scotland

9 (1) In relation to any person serving a determinate custodial sentence imposed in respect of an offence committed before the commencement of Chapter I of Part II of this Act, paragraph 8 of Schedule 1 to this Act shall have effect as if—

  (a) references in sub-paragraph (2) to provisions of that Chapter were references to sections 33, 35 to 39, 41 to 46 and 65 of the 1991 Act and paragraphs 8, 10 to 13 and 19 of Schedule 12 to that Act, so far as relating to short-term or long-term prisoners;
  (b) references in sub-paragraph (4) to provisions of that Chapter were references to sections 37 to 39, 43 to 46 and 65 of the 1991 Act and paragraphs 8, 10 to 13 and 19 of Schedule 12 to that Act, so far as so relating;
  (c) the reference in sub-paragraph (5) to any provision of Part II of this Act were a reference to any provision of Part II of that Act; and
  (d) section 67 of the Criminal Justice Act 1967 (computation of sentences of imprisonment passed in England and Wales) or, as the case may require, section 9 of this Act extended to Scotland.

(2) In relation to any time before the commencement of Chapter II of Part II of this Act, paragraph 8 of Schedule 1 to this Act shall have effect as if—

  (a) references in sub-paragraph (2) to provisions of that Chapter were references to sections 34 to 37, 39, 43 and 46 of the 1991 Act and paragraphs 8 and 9 of Schedule 12 to that Act, so far as relating to life prisoners;
  (b) references in sub-paragraph (4) to provisions of that Chapter were references to sections 37, 39, 43 and 46 of the 1991 Act and paragraphs 8 and 9 of Schedule 12 to that Act, so far as so relating; and
  (c) the reference in sub-paragraph (5) to any provision of Part II of this Act were a reference to any provision of Part II of that Act.

Transfers of prisoners from England and Wales to Northern Ireland

10 (1) In relation to any person serving a determinate custodial sentence imposed in respect of an offence committed before the commencement of Chapter I of Part II of this Act, paragraph 9 of Schedule 1 to this Act shall have effect as if—

  (a) in sub-paragraph (1), paragraph (a) and, in paragraph (b), the words 'to that and' were omitted;

(b) references in sub-paragraph (2) to provisions of that Chapter were references to sections 33, 35 to 46 and 65 of the 1991 Act and paragraphs 8, 10 to 13 and 19 of Schedule 12 to that Act, so far as relating to short-term or long-term prisoners;

(c) references in sub-paragraph (4) to provisions of that Chapter were references to sections 37 to 40, 43 to 46 and 65 of the 1991 Act and paragraphs 8, 10 to 13 and 19 of Schedule 12 to that Act, so far as so relating;

(d) the reference in sub-paragraph (6) to any provision of Part II of this Act were a reference to any provision of Part II of that Act; and

(e) section 67 of the Criminal Justice Act 1967 or, as the case may require, section 9 of this Act extended to Northern Ireland.

(2) In relation to any time before the commencement of Chapter II of Part II of this Act, paragraph 9 of Schedule 1 to this Act shall have effect as if—

(a) references in sub-paragraph (2) to provisions of that Chapter were references to sections 34 to 37, 39, 43 and 46 of the 1991 Act and paragraphs 8 and 9 of Schedule 12 to that Act, so far as relating to life prisoners;

(b) references in sub-paragraph (4) to provisions of that Chapter were references to sections 37, 39, 43 and 46 of the 1991 Act and paragraphs 8 and 9 of Schedule 12 to that Act, so far as so relating; and

(c) the reference in sub-paragraph (5) to any provision of Part II of this Act were a reference to any provision of Part II of that Act.

Transfers of prisoners from Scotland to England and Wales

11 (1) In relation to any prisoner sentenced on or after 1st October 1993 in respect of an offence committed before the commencement of section 33 of the Crime and Punishment (Scotland) Act 1997 ('the 1997 Act'), paragraph 10 of Schedule 1 to this Act shall have effect as if—

(a) references in sub-paragraph (2) to sections 15, 18 and 19 of the Prisoners and Criminal Proceedings (Scotland) Act 1993 ('the 1993 Act') and to sections 33(5), 34, 37 and 39 of the 1997 Act were references to sections 1 to 3, 5, 6(1)(a) and (b)(i) and (iii), 9, 11 to 13, 15 to 21 and 27 of, and Schedules 2 and 6 to, the 1993 Act;

(b) references in sub-paragraph (5) to sections 15, 18 and 19 of the 1993 Act and to sections 33(5) and 37 of the 1997 Act were references to sections 11 to 13, 15 to 21 and 27 of, and Schedules 2 and 6 to, the 1993 Act;

(c) references in that sub-paragraph to sections 2(4), 11 to 13 and 17 of the 1993 Act were references to sections 26 and 28 of the Prisons (Scotland) Act 1989 ('the 1989 Act'); and

(d) the reference in sub-paragraph (7) to any provision of Part I of the 1993 Act or Part III of the 1997 Act were a reference to any provision of the 1993 Act.

(2) In relation to any prisoner to whom the existing provisions apply, paragraph 10 of Schedule 1 to this Act shall have effect as if—

(a) references in sub-paragraph (2) to sections 15, 18 and 19 of the 1993 Act and to sections 33(5), 34, 37 and 39 of the 1997 Act were references to Schedule 6 to the 1993 Act and to the following existing provisions, namely, sections 18, 19(4), 22, 24, 26, 28 to 30, 32 and 43 of, and Schedule 1 to, the 1989 Act and any rules made under section 18 or 39 of that Act;

(b) references in sub-paragraph (5) to sections 15, 18 and 19 of the 1993 Act and to sections 33(5) and 37 of the 1997 Act were references to the said Schedule 6 and to the following existing provisions, namely, sections 30, 32 and 43 of the 1989 Act; and

(c) the reference in sub-paragraph (7) to any provision of Part I of the 1993 Act or Part III of the 1997 Act were a reference to any provision of the said Schedule 6 or the 1989 Act.

(3) In sub-paragraph (1) above the reference to section 6(1)(b)(i) of the 1993 Act is a reference to that provision so far as it relates to a person sentenced under section 205(3) of the Criminal Procedure (Scotland) Act 1995; and in sub-paragraph (2) above—

(a) the reference to section 19(4) of the 1989 Act is a reference to that provision so far as it applies section 24 of that Act in relation to persons detained in young offenders institutions; and

(b) any reference to the existing provisions is a reference to the existing provisions within the meaning of Schedule 6 to the 1993 Act.

Transfers of prisoners from Scotland to Northern Ireland

12 (1) In relation to any prisoner sentenced on or after 1st October 1993 for an offence committed before the commencement of section 33 of the Crime and Punishment (Scotland) Act 1997 ('the 1997 Act'), paragraph 11 of Schedule 1 to this Act shall have effect as if—

(a) references in sub-paragraph (2) to sections 15, 18 and 19 of the Prisoners and Criminal Proceedings (Scotland) Act 1993 ('the 1993 Act') and sections 33(5), 34, 37 and 39 of the 1997 Act were references to sections 1, 2, 3, 5, 6(1)(a) and (b)(i) and (iii), 9, 11 to 13, 15 to 21 and 27 of, and Schedules 2 and 6 to, the 1993 Act;

(b) references in sub-paragraph (4) to sections 15, 18 and 19 of the 1993 Act and to sections 33(5) and 37 of the 1997 Act were references to sections 11 to 13, 15 to 21 and 27 of, and Schedules 2 and 6 to, the 1993 Act;

(c) references in that sub-paragraph to sections 2(4), 11 to 13 and 17 of the 1993 Act were references to sections 26 and 28 of the Prisons (Scotland) Act 1989 ('the 1989 Act'); and

(d) the reference in sub-paragraph (5) to any provision of Part I of the 1993 Act or Part III of the 1997 Act were a reference to any provision of the 1993 Act, and the Table set out in that sub-paragraph contained the following entry—

'Probation officer appointed for or assigned to such petty sessions area	Probation Officer appointed by the Probation Board for Northern Ireland'

(2) In relation to any prisoner to whom the existing provisions apply, paragraph 11 of Schedule 1 to this Act shall have effect as if—

(a) references in sub-paragraph (2) to sections 15, 18 and 19 of the 1993 Act and to sections 33(5), 34, 37 and 39 of the 1997 Act were references to Schedule 6 to the 1993 Act and to the following existing provisions, namely, sections 18, 19(4), 22, 24, 26, 28 to 30, 32 and 43, and Schedule 1 to, the 1989 Act and any rules made under section 18 or 39 of that Act;

(b) references in sub-paragraph (4) to sections 15, 18 and 19 of the 1993 Act and sections 33(5) and 37 of the 1997 Act were references to the said Schedule 6 and to the following existing provisions, namely, sections 30, 32 and 43 of the 1989 Act; and

(c) the reference in sub-paragraph (6) to any provision of Part I of the 1993 Act or Part III of the 1997 Act were a reference to any provision of the said Schedule 6 or the 1989 Act.

(3) Sub-paragraph (3) of paragraph 11 above shall apply for the purposes of this paragraph as it applies for the purposes of that paragraph.

Interpretation

13 In this Schedule—

'life prisoner' has the same meaning as in Chapter II of Part II of this Act;

'term of imprisonment' includes a sentence of detention in a young offender institution or under section 53 of the 1933 Act.

SCHEDULE 6
REPEALS

Chapter	Short title	Extent of repeal
9 & 10 Eliz. 2 c. 39	Criminal Justice Act 1961	Part III.
		In section 36(1), the words 'or under Part III'.
		In section 38, in subsection (3), the words 'of Part III and' and, in subsection (6), the words 'and of any enactment referred to in Part III of this Act'.
		In section 39, in subsection (1), the definitions of 'appropriate institution' and 'responsible Minister', and subsection (1A).
		In section 42, in subsection (1), the words 'Part III except section thirty-three' and, in subsection (2), the words 'Part III'.
1967 c. 80	Criminal Justice Act 1967	Section 67.
1973 c. 62	Powers of Criminal Courts Act 1973	In section 2(3), the words from 'and the court' to the end.
		In section 14(2), the words 'the offender consents and'.
		In section 42(1), the words 'or section 62 of the Criminal Justice Act 1967'.
1983 c. 20	Mental Health Act 1983	In section 37(4), the words 'in the event of such an order being made by the court'.
		In section 47(1), the words '(not being a mental nursing home)'.
		In Schedule 1, in Part II, in paragraph 5, the word 'and' immediately following sub-paragraph (a).

Chapter	*Short title*	*Extent of repeal*
1991 c. 53	Criminal Justice Act 1991	In section 4(1), the words 'section 3(1) above applies and'.
		In section 12, in subsection (1), the words 'of or over the age of sixteen years' and, in subsection (5), the words from 'and the court' to the end.
		Sections 33 to 51.
		Section 65.
		In Schedule 2, in paragraph 14, in sub-paragraph (2)(b), the words from 'being treatment' to the end.

INDEX

References are to paragraph numbers except where they are in *italics* which are references to page numbers.